Mapping Your Retirement

A Personal Guide to Maintaining Your Health,
Managing Your Money, and Living Well

Edited by
Mark Skeie
Janet Skeie
Julie Roles

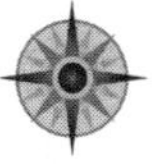

MYR
Publications
www.mappingyourretirement.org

Mapping Your Retirement is a workbook designed to help you plan emotionally, physically, and financially for this stage of life. It is not intended as a substitute for personal advice from doctors, health care professionals, or legal or financial advisors. For expert assistance tailored to your specific needs, please consult an appropriate professional.

Published by
MYR Publications
www.mappingyourretirement.org

Published in the United States of America
Printed in Canada on acid-free paper

ISBN-13: 978-0-9794688-0-3

LCCN: 2007905183

Copyediting by Kathleen Cleberg and Erin Peterson
Cover and interior design by Julie Roles
Exercise illustrations by John Molstad
Layout production by Mavis Wheeler

To order additional copies of this book please go to www.itascabooks.com.

Contents

Contents *continued*

Worksheets

INTRODUCTION

LIVING YOUR LIFE

MAINTAINING YOUR HEALTH

Worksheets *continued*

MANAGING YOUR MONEY

Thank You

We want to acknowledge and thank the many people who contributed to publishing this book. The book was a collaborative effort from the inception to the printing.

First, thank you to the contributors, without your excellent material there would be no book. You shared our vision for a book to help people through the retirement transition. A special thanks to our copyeditors, Kathleen Cleberg and Erin Peterson, who provided the skills to combine material from 15 contributors into a user-friendly, unique workbook. Thanks to the volunteer readers who provided valuable feedback as we developed the final version of the book. Thank you to the people who shared their stories with us; they are an inspiration and provided an added dimension to the book. To everyone who talked with us, shared their time and expertise, we appreciate your support and encouragement. Finally, a big thank you to our families and friends who listened and supported us during this journey.

Contributors

Editors

Mark Skeie worked for 3M Company for more than 34 years, where he held a variety of management positions. He left 3M with a broad range of skills and the desire to contribute to the community. Since completing the Advocacy Leadership for Vital Aging certificate sponsored by the Vital Aging Network (VAN) in 2004, he has focused his energy on developing tools to help people enjoy fulfilling and purposeful lives in retirement. Skeie is currently chair of VAN's leadership group. He also is on the board of the Metropolitan Area Agency on Aging. He and Janet Skeie founded MYR, Inc., a nonprofit organization with the mission of helping individuals and organizations prepare for active, healthy, and productive retirement. Skeie earned a BA from the University of Minnesota in industrial psychology.

Janet Skeie retired from General Reinsurance in 2003 after a long career with several different companies. She became interested in the subject of retirement planning after experiencing the transition herself. She encourages others to think about meaning and purpose during the retirement phase of life, as well as the legacy they want to leave for their children and community. She completed the Advocacy Leadership for Vital Aging certificate sponsored by the Vital Aging Network (VAN) in 2006. Skeie is cofounder of MYR, Inc. She earned a BA from the University of Minnesota in psychology.

Julie Roles is the principal of J Roles & Associates. She is co-author of *Civic Organizing 101* with Peg Michels, and has written and designed publications for the University of Minnesota, Wells Fargo Home Mortgage, 3M, Trane, and others. She serves on the board of MYR, Inc. and Civic Organizing Foundation. Roles operates a full-service communications company and provides services to a broad range of businesses and nonprofit organizations. Roles has a BS in business administration and an MA in visual communications/applied design from the University of Minnesota.

Contributors

LIVING YOUR LIFE

Carol Daly was state director for Minnesota Elderhostel at the University of Minnesota's College of Continuing Education for 23 years. During her tenure, Daly served on the International Elderhostel Board of Directors and on the National Steering Committee of Elderhostel State Directors. She has spoken at numerous national and local conferences and has written dozens of articles for Minnesota publications. She serves on the board of the Osher Lifelong Learning Institute and was a member of the first leadership group of the Vital Aging Network, both at the University of Minnesota. Daly received a BA in English from Cornell University and an MA in adult education from the University of Minnesota.

Trish Herbert, a retired psychologist, is the author of *The Vintage Journey: A Guide to Artful Aging*. During her career, she created and led a program for community elderly that specialized in issues of aging, caregiving, self-care, grief, and adult children's concerns about their aging parents. She also cofounded a small company, Journeywell, and presently works as a counselor, volunteer, support group leader, and workshop facilitator. Herbert has a PhD in psychology and gerontology.

Jan Hively is a senior fellow in the College of Continuing Education at the University of Minnesota. She is the founder of and senior advisor for the Vital Aging Network (VAN), a statewide network shaping a multigenerational, strengths-based vision of aging. Hively teaches courses at the University of Minnesota on lifework after retirement and education for midlife and beyond. She earned a BA from Harvard University and an MA and a PhD from the University of Minnesota.

Helen Kivnick is a professor of social work at the University of Minnesota. She was trained as a clinical psychologist and has focused on healthy life cycle development and intercultural relations. In *Vital Involvement in Old Age*, Kivnick collaborated with developmentalist Erik Erikson to adapt his theory of psychosocial development to be more useful in promoting psychosocial health and strength for people at each stage of the life cycle. Kivnick has spearheaded the development of Vital Involvement Practice (VIP) as a way to improve elders' personal vitality and community engagement, despite physical frailties and needs for assistance. She is the founder and executive director of CitySongs, an after-school program for urban youth that combines strength-based social work and music participation activities to promote children's health and community vitality. Kivnick has an MA and a PhD from the University of Michigan.

Sue Meyers spent more than 30 years as a family sociologist with the University of Minnesota Extension Service. She is an active member of the Minnesota Council of Family Relations and the National Council of Family Relations. She is past president of the Minnesota Council. Meyers has an MS from Iowa State University. She has been a member of the Minnesota Gerontological Society from its inception and a longtime member of the Gerontological Society of America and the American Society on Aging.

MAINTAINING YOUR HEALTH

Susan Bradley is a freelance writer with a research background in health care delivery. She directed a two-year study for InterStudy on rural health care delivery in Minnesota and Oregon and participated in research on HMOs and outcomes management. She worked for Health Partners, a start-up HMO serving rural Minnesota through local providers and the University of Minnesota. Her publications include journal articles and several book chapters on the topic of rural health care. Bradley has a BS and an MS from Cornell University.

Luke Carlson is an American College of Sports Medicine–certified health and fitness instructor and the CEO of Discover Strength Personal Fitness Center, Inc. He coauthored *The Female Athlete: Train for Success* and is the founder and director of the National Strength and Science Seminar. Carlson received a BS in kinesiology from the University of Minnesota, where he is currently a graduate student in exercise physiology. He has served as the strength and conditioning assistant with the Minnesota Vikings.

Catherine Johnson is a licensed psychologist who provides services to older-adult health care providers through the Associated Clinic of Psychology and the Dementia Identification Project, a grant project administered by the Metropolitan Area Agency on Aging. Johnson has more than 30 years of health care experience, serving in administrative positions in private and public health care centers. She has served on state and national committees to create and improve health care delivery systems. Johnson received a PsyD from St. Thomas University specializing in older-adult development and completed a long-term care administration licensure program at the University of Minnesota.

Mary Jo Kreitzer is the founder and director of the Center for Spirituality and Healing at the University of Minnesota, where she conducts NIH-funded research and teaches graduate courses in complementary therapies and healing practices. She is an associate professor in the University's School of Nursing and the author of numerous publications for health professionals and consumers. She speaks nationally and internationally on topics related to health and well-being. Kreitzer earned a BA and an MA in nursing and a PhD in health services research. She is vice-chair of the Consortium of Academic Health Centers for Integrative Medicine, an association of 36 medical schools in North America.

Arthur Leon is the Henry L. Taylor Professor of Exercise Science, director of the Laboratory of Physiological Hygiene and Exercise Science, and director of graduate studies in the University of Minnesota's School of Kinesiology. He teaches graduate courses on nutrition and exercise and holds joint academic appointments in the School of Public Health, the Medical School, and in Food Science and Nutrition. For 40 years, Leon's research has focused on the effects of physical activity, diet, prescription drugs, and heredity on cardiovascular health. He earned a BS in chemistry from the University of Florida, and MS and MD degrees from the University of Wisconsin. He is a Fellow of the American College of Sports Medicine, the American College of Cardiology, and the American Society for Nutritional Sciences. Leon is a retired colonel in the Medical Corps of the United States Army Reserve.

MANAGING YOUR MONEY

Mark Fischer, a Certified Financial Planner, is president of Fischer on Finance, a fee-based financial planning firm. He has taught at universities in Minnesota, Massachusetts, and California, and has presented seminars with numerous organizations and associations. Fischer has an MBA and a PhD in chemistry. He is a registered principal of Multi-Financial Securities Corporation (MFSC) and a member of NASD/SIPC. MFSC is not affiliated with Fischer on Finance.

Karen Hansen is an attorney with Felhaber Larson Fenlon & Vogt, in St. Paul, Minnesota. For more than 20 years, she has focused her legal career in the areas of estate planning and probate and trust administration. She is chair of the firm's estate planning and probate section. Hansen has worked with thousands of individuals, families, and businesses in planning their estates and implementing the estate plan after the death of a client, and she teaches advanced estate planning to financial professionals. Hansen earned a BA and a JD from the University of Illinois at Urbana-Champaign.

Other Contributors

Sharon Roe Anderson is a consultant and serves as a strategist and coach in the areas of leadership, strategic change, facilitation, and community and organizational development. Anderson has 29 years of experience developing programs for people at all levels in the educational, political, community, and business arenas. Her background includes extensive public affairs work in executive and professional development, international and intercultural relationships, and leadership education. She is coauthor of *Leadership for the Common Good Fieldbook: Tools for Working in a Shared-Power World* (2003) and *Facilitation Resources* (1999). Anderson developed and taught in the Advocacy Leadership for Vital Aging Certificate Program at the University of Minnesota. She has served as principal and cofounder of Aurora Consulting; director of Professional Development Programs, the Reflective Leadership Center, and the International Fellows Programs at the Humphrey Institute, University of Minnesota. Anderson earned a BA from St. Olaf College and an MA from the University of Minnesota.

Karen Bowen worked with the Minnesota Department of Natural Resources for 20 years, eight as assistant commissioner. Bowen retired in 2000 after nine years as director of operations with the Suburban Hennepin Regional Park District. She is past president of the Osher Lifelong Learning Institute of the University of Minnesota.

Karen Greer has over 20 years of experience engaging individuals and groups as they create a compelling lifestyle for their future and view their "retirement as opportunity." She has been featured on cable television and in a *Women's Business MN* magazine article about meaningful retirement issues. She teaches retirement-related coursework through community education programs and the University of Minnesota College of Continuing Education. Greer's credentials include certifications in Empowerment Life Coaching and the *Too Young to Retire* concept, training by the Purpose Project, as well as an MA in adult education.

Judy Schuck is the retired Dean of Students at Minneapolis Community and Technical College. Since retiring, she has worked part time as an educational consultant most recently for the General College at the University of Minnesota. Schuck earned her PhD in educational psychology from the University of Minnesota. She currently serves as the chair of the curriculum committee for the Osher Lifelong Learning Institute at the University of Minnesota.

N

Introduction

Retirement for the 21st Century

THE INDISPENSABLE FIRST STEP TO GETTING THE THINGS YOU WANT OUT OF LIFE IS THIS: DECIDE WHAT YOU WANT.

—Ben Stein, writer and actor

W

Over the next three decades, some 78 million baby boomers will retire. For many, it's been the prize they've been eyeing for decades—a life of leisure, free of deadlines and stress. But retirement isn't just a destination: after all, once you get there, where will you go?

This question weighed heavily on our minds as we planned our own retirement in 2003. How could we shape our retirement so that we would feel we had spent these years purposefully, and have the resources to achieve these goals?

We explored a range of different programs and read countless books and articles to help us find the right path in retirement. We looked not only for ways to spend our time but also for ways to find meaning.

This topic became increasingly important to us, and we began to do more investigation. We both earned Advocacy Leadership for Vital Aging certificates from the Vital Aging Network. Mark joined the board of directors at the Metropolitan Area Agency on Aging and got involved with RSVP, a nationwide volunteer program for those 55 and older. During our work with these organizations, we met with experts who shared their insights on the challenges and opportunities that come with retirement.

We realized that these experts could do more than help us as individuals—they could help the many other people like us who were asking the same questions: How do I know if I'm financially ready to retire? What am I going to do? How will I get started? How do I find meaning in these years of my life?

These questions seem both basic and important. Yet while there are dozens—if not hundreds—of books on planning the financial aspect of retirement, few make more than a token effort to address equally important aspects of these years of your life: how to spend your time and how to manage your health.

Our goal for this book was to address retirement holistically: to focus on the financial, emotional, and physical considerations we all face in retirement. We wanted to combine the best information and research with hands-on, practical worksheets to help you determine your goals and help you achieve them.

We have learned some things along the way that we think are worth passing on:

- **Define what retirement means to you.** Retirement is just another word for living. It can take almost any form, and you have to decide for yourself what it means for you. The division between full-time work and retirement life is no longer as clear as it once was. Many people will move from one career to another, from working full-time to gradually working less, from a paid job to an unpaid job. You might not work at all for a period of time and then go back to work. Even people who are on a traditional retirement path may find this part of life has little resemblance to their parents' retirement. It could last 20 to 30 years, and for many, it will be as (if not more) productive and meaningful as any other part of their lives.

- **Know yourself.** You may be tired of bosses and deadlines, but a dream that consists of what you *don't* want is not enough to build a life on. Spend the time to understand what matters to you and what will give you purpose and meaning. Then make choices that support what you say is important.

- **Recognize opportunities.** Use your skills, talents, and experience to build on what's important to you. As millions of boomers retire, a talent shortage may provide opportunities for those who want to do meaningful work. Many will choose to use their retirement years to create better communities and a better world. Consider taking classes, teaching classes, and joining groups. Find what has meaning in your life and go for it. Studies show it will make you healthier and happier. Don't set your sights too low.

- **Prepare for challenges.** Financial issues, health problems, and changes in relationships can pose difficulties in retirement. Managing your health is particularly important as you age. Skyrocketing health care costs and increased longevity mean that you may need more money than you think, so it's important to pinpoint your target—and know how to hit it.

Retirement can mean a shift in the amount and quality of time you spend with your spouse and other significant people in your life, and may require learning new ways to relate. A lot of people take their work-related social network for granted. Taking the time to understand what you valued in those relationships will help you know how to fill those needs in other ways.

- **Have a plan.** Retirement planning is often reduced to numbers: How much have you saved? Is it enough? Finances are important, but only one part of an overall plan.

  A retirement plan can help you:

  - Set realistic financial and personal expectations
  - Make choices that reflect your values
  - Reduce stress
  - Maintain a healthy and active lifestyle
  - Create your legacy

  Remember to leave some white space in your life. As J. R. R. Tolkien, author of *Lord of the Rings*, said, "Not all those who wander are lost." Sometimes, unstructured wandering will take you exactly where you want to go.

- **Share your plan.** Research shows that good relationships are the foundation of a fulfilling life. Work, achievement, and contribution are important. But the bottom line is this: people make our lives meaningful. For that reason, it's important to include others in your planning.

  Spouses may want to make their own plans first and then create an integrated plan that they can share. Friends, family, and professional help may also play a role in your retirement planning. Sharing your goals with someone else improves your chances of achieving them. When you get stuck, ask for help.

- **Be flexible.** Retirement involves change, and change—whether good or bad—is stressful. Learning to recognize and manage stress will help you make smooth transitions. A positive attitude and sense of humor will also serve you well.

We do not just prescribe this advice to others. In fact, we've taken it to heart. Developing the *Mapping Your Retirement* workbook and website (*www.mappingyourretirement.org*) has allowed us to fulfill some of our own goals in retirement. Much of what we have learned along the way is in this book, and we hope that it will help you achieve your own dreams.

One final thought: A friend on the brink of retirement recently asked us if this book would help take away the butterflies in his stomach. Unfortunately, there's probably nothing that can take away the anxiety that accompanies any big transition. But this book will help make sure that you're as prepared as possible for this new stage of life.

With good health, good luck, and good planning, retirement can be a wonderful new adventure. It takes commitment and some assembly is required. The reward can be a life well lived.

How to Use the Workbook

About *Mapping Your Retirement*

Mapping Your Retirement provides tools to help you prepare emotionally, physically, and financially for this stage of life. There are three parts to the workbook:

- **Living Your Life** helps you examine what is important to you. Knowing what matters to you will help you shape your goals, your relationships, and even your day-to-day activities.
- **Maintaining Your Health** provides information and worksheets to help you get—and stay—in shape. Good health makes it possible to do what you want to do and live an independent, productive life.
- **Managing Your Money** helps you evaluate your financial situation before and during retirement. Financial security will give you a foundation from which to achieve your larger goals.

Each chapter includes up-to-date information and research from experts in the field. Chapters also include worksheets and additional resources. The latest updates and copies of worksheets are available at *www.mappingyourretirement.org*.

We are very proud of the collaboration of excellent contributors that has made this book possible. You will benefit from their broad scope of knowledge and expertise. But the most important factor in successful retirement planning is what you bring to the process. Use these tools to transform your thinking and to make a plan that will help you in your journey.

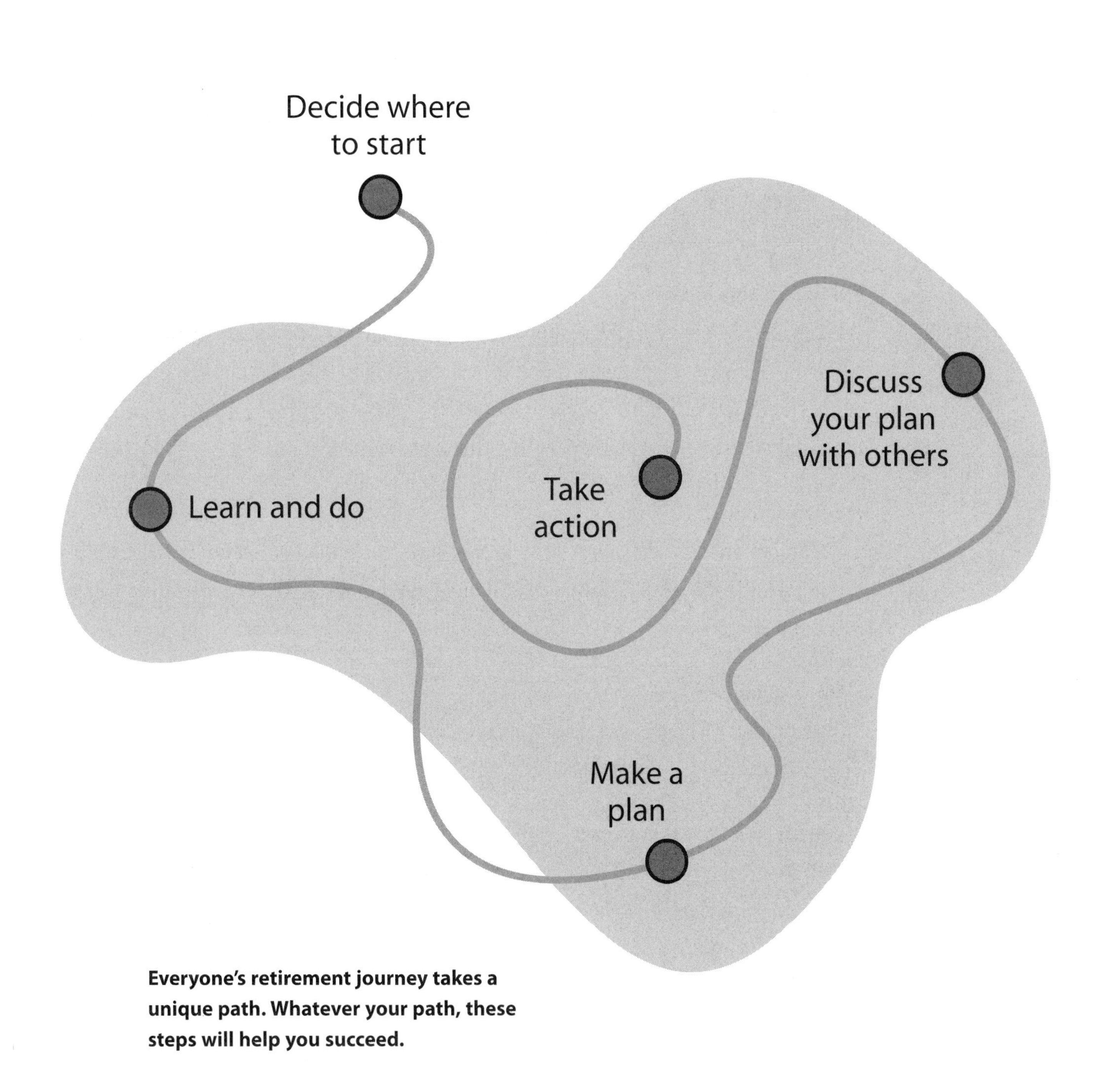

Everyone's retirement journey takes a unique path. Whatever your path, these steps will help you succeed.

Using the Workbook

Research backs up the idea that writing something down, taking an action, and telling someone else what you are going to do increase your chances of reaching a goal. That's what this workbook is all about.

Here are some steps that will help you succeed.

Decide Where to Start

If you already know the dreams you want to pursue, write them into the map on pages 10 and 11, and let them guide your journey. If getting in shape is your highest priority, start there. If you're not sure where to start, the "What Are My Priorities?" worksheet on pages 12–14 will help you set priorities that make sense for you.

Learn and Do

The information in *Mapping Your Retirement* gives you a foundation for making choices that are right for you. Read the material, then use the worksheets to write down what you think.

Make a Plan

At the end of each part, there is an action planning worksheet. Use it to start to make your plan. Bring it all together in the "My Retirement Map" worksheet on pages 10 and 11.

Discuss Your Plan with Others

Talk about your plan with people who are important in your life. You will be more motivated to work on goals if you have shared them with someone.

Take Action

Hold yourself accountable. A plan is of no use if you don't take action to achieve what you say is important. But be flexible. When your circumstances change, review and revise your plan.

A Note about Using the Internet as a Source of Information

We hope that this book and accompanying website, *www.mappingyourretirement.org*, provide a solid foundation for your retirement plans. As you progress in your journey you may want to use additional sources of information, including books, magazines, journals, and websites.

The Internet has become a valuable source of information and there are advantages to using the web: information is accessible, often free, may be up to date, and can be both comprehensive and factual. On the other hand, there is a lot of information that is false, inaccurate, and misleading. To be sure you're getting good information, ask yourself these questions:

- Who runs the site? Is it a government agency, educational institution, nonprofit group, or commercial enterprise?
- What is the purpose of the site? Is the purpose to provide information or sell a product?
- What is the original source of information on the website?
- How is information on the website documented? Medical facts and figures should have references.
- How current is the information on the website? Websites should be reviewed and updated on a regular basis.
- What information about users does the website collect and why? You should be cautious about giving personal information. (The National Cancer Institute)

My Retirement Map

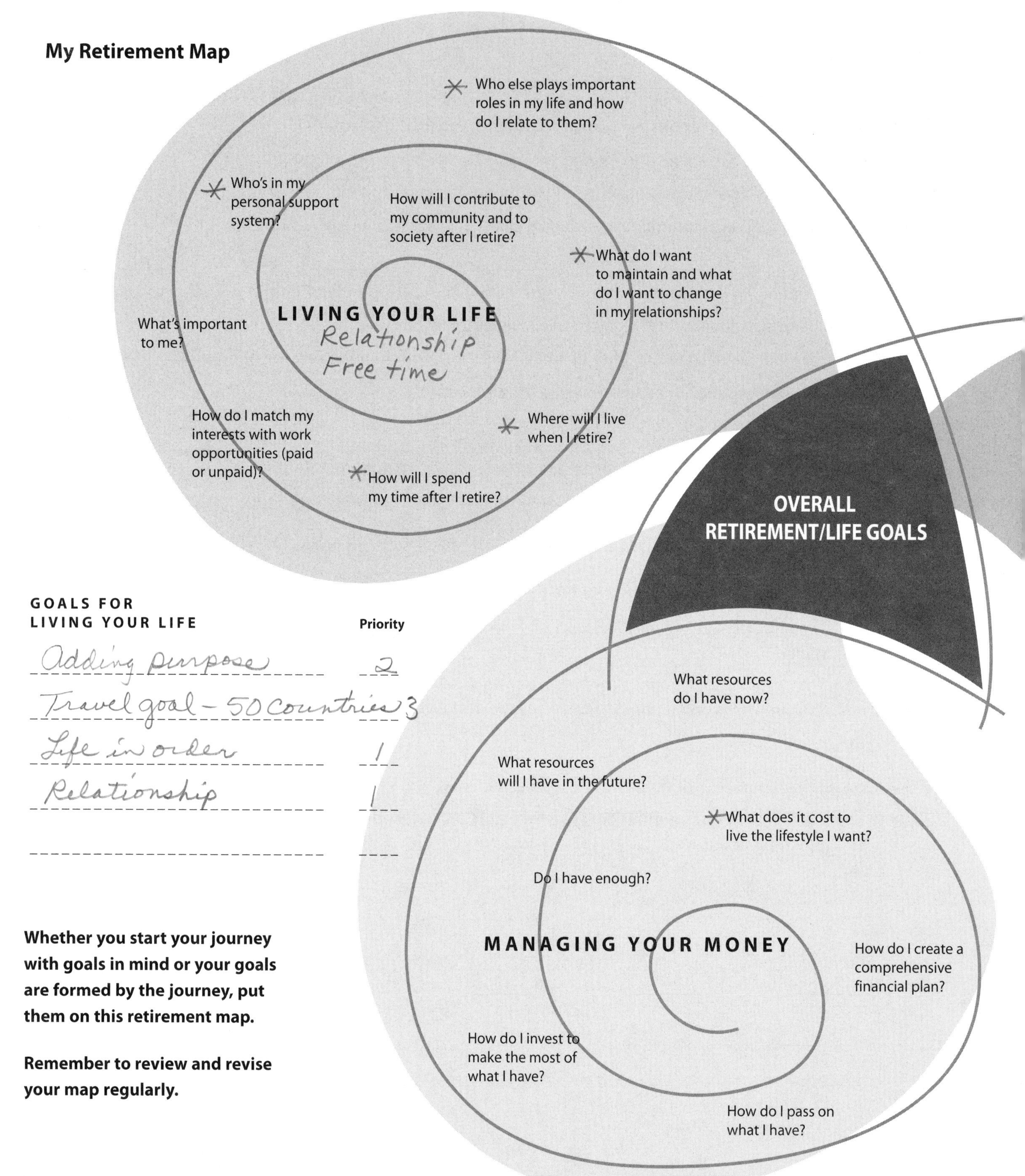

GOALS FOR LIVING YOUR LIFE	Priority
Adding purpose	2
Travel goal – 50 countries	3
Life in order	1
Relationship	1

Whether you start your journey with goals in mind or your goals are formed by the journey, put them on this retirement map.

Remember to review and revise your map regularly.

GOALS FOR
MAINTAINING YOUR HEALTH — Priority

Health + Relationship are the top goals.
- Singles events - Meeting people.

MAINTAINING YOUR HEALTH

What practices do I want to change to enhance my health?

What do I want to do to enhance my health?

What changes do I want to make in my diet?

How do I maintain my mental health?

Are there nontraditional approaches to maintaining my health?

What level of physical activity do I need?

How can I create a health care team to safeguard my health?

GOALS FOR
MANAGING YOUR MONEY — Priority

SUMMARY OF OVERALL RETIREMENT/LIFE GOALS

WORKSHEET

What Are My Priorities?

Not sure where to start in your retirement planning? Use these questions to help you set priorities. Mark each item with an *X*. Then begin with the chapters that cover the topics most important to you.

LIVING YOUR LIFE	No Change Needed		Needs Immediate Attention
Chapter 1 – Embracing What Matters			
Knowing what matters to me	●	···········	●
Having purpose in my life	●	···········	●
Leaving a legacy	●	···········	●
Chapter 2 – Building Strong Relationships			
Building my social network	●	···········	●
Strengthening relationships with family and friends	●	···········	●
Being part of a community	●	···········	●
Relocating to another city or state	●	···········	●
Chapter 3 – Using Your Time			
Exploring new options for spending my time	●	···········	●
Using my skills, talents, and experience	●	···········	●
Learning something new	●	···········	●
Spending more time in activities I enjoy	●	···········	●
Managing my time	●	···········	●
Doing meaningful work after I retire	●	···········	●
Finding opportunities that match my interests	●	···········	●
Chapter 4 – Making a Difference			
Developing my civic capacity	●	···········	●
Making a difference in my community and the world	●	···········	●

MAINTAINING YOUR HEALTH	No Change Needed	Needs Immediate Attention
Chapter 5 – Staying Healthy		
Losing excess weight	●	●
Getting enough sleep	●	●
Reducing stress in my life	●	●
Quitting smoking	●	●
Reducing my alcohol consumption	●	●
Addressing drug abuse / addictive behavior	●	●
Getting up to date on screening and testing	●	●
Getting immunizations	●	●
Preventing injuries	●	●
Chapter 6 – Eating for Life		
Eating a healthy diet	●	●
Getting the right vitamins and minerals	●	●
Chapter 7 – Keeping Strong, Fit, and Active		
Learning about physical activity	●	●
Exercising regularly	●	●
Chapter 8 – Maintaining Mental Fitness		
Doing activities to keep my mind sharp	●	●
Following keys to mental fitness	●	●
Making positive changes	●	●
Chapter 9 – Creating Your Health Care Team		
Finding a health care provider	●	●
Communicating with my health care provider	●	●
Making informed health care decisions	●	●
Preparing an advance directive	●	●
Chapter 10 – Finding Nontraditional Paths to Health		
Exploring complementary, alternative, or integrative therapies	●	●

What Are My Priorities? *continued*

MANAGING YOUR MONEY	No Change Needed		Needs Immediate Attention
Chapter 11 – Knowing How You Want to Live			
Knowing my life goals	●	························	●
Chapter 12 – Taking Inventory of Your Resources			
Calculating my current income and expenses	●	························	●
Estimating my future income and expenses	●	························	●
Increasing my savings contributions	●	························	●
Understanding my nonfinancial resources	●	························	●
Chapter 13 – Investing Basics			
Understanding investment options	●	························	●
Chapter 14 – Making the Most of Your Investments			
Developing my investment strategy	●	························	●
Rebalancing my investment portfolio	●	························	●
Finding a financial planner	●	························	●
Chapter 15 – Managing Tax Obligations			
Developing a tax management strategy	●	························	●
Chapter 16 – Making Your Money Last a Lifetime			
Determining if I will have enough	●	························	●
Chapter 17 – Passing On What You Have			
Creating an estate plan	●	························	●
Preparing a living will/advance directive	●	························	●
Chapter 18 – Pulling Together Your Financial Plan			
Creating a comprehensive financial plan	●	························	●

Part 1

Living Your Life

Frank headed into retirement without a plan and he found himself struggling to fill his time. Most mornings, he'd head to a popular breakfast restaurant just to have a place to go. The rush of activity was comforting at first but ultimately unsatisfying. Everyone else had somewhere else to go; for Frank, this was the final destination. He ultimately found projects and volunteer work that gave him purpose, but his journey could have been eased with some thoughtful planning.

Whether you are beginning a transition into retirement or just anticipating this next life chapter, you will want to map your way thoughtfully. How do you want to spend your time? Where do you feel you belong? Will you find satisfaction in service to others?

The choices you make, the level of your involvement, and the relationships you nurture may determine the course of your life.

In this section we will look at:

- **Embracing What Matters.** To determine where you want to go in retirement, you must first have a good sense of who you are and what your values are. Thinking about the work, the people, and the periods of time that have been most meaningful to you can help you chart a course for future years.

- **Building Strong Relationships.** Many of your closest relationships will change in retirement. Knowing the challenges that may follow will help you maintain strong connections with your friends and family while helping you build new relationships.
- **Using Your Time.** Your decisions about how to split your days between leisure, learning, and work will influence your satisfaction in retirement.
- **Making a Difference.** Many people feel a strong pull to contribute their energy and resources to organizations and causes that help make a better world. Matching your skills with the principles you support will increase the impact of your work.

IN THIS CHAPTER

Chapter 1

Embracing What Matters

Finding meaning, purpose, and a path that's right for you

NOBODY GROWS OLD BY MERELY LIVING A NUMBER OF YEARS; PEOPLE GROW OLD BY DESERTING THEIR IDEALS. YEARS MAY WRINKLE THE SKIN, BUT TO GIVE UP ENTHUSIASM WRINKLES THE SOUL.

—*Samuel Ullman, American businessman, poet, humanitarian*

One of the most common questions you'll be asked as you near retirement is, "What will you do next?" Like graduation from high school or college, retirement marks a significant transition in your life, and people will be curious about your plans. But just like recent high school and college graduates, you might not know exactly what your plans are.

To understand where you want to go in retirement, you must first understand who you are. On the surface, this may seem like a strange statement—you've had a lifetime to get to know who you are; your soul searching happened decades ago. However, as you've gone about your life, you probably haven't had to spend much time trying to articulate what motivates you and what is meaningful to you. Your day-to-day actions might not have always aligned with your most deeply held values.

Trish Herbert
Retired psychologist and author of *The Vintage Journey*

As you make the transition to retirement, you have a new opportunity to think about what's most important to you —and to make changes that will allow you to focus on these things. By analyzing your past decisions and reflecting on your beliefs, you'll be able to make choices that will make the coming years happy, productive, and meaningful.

What's Important in Your Life?

Knowing what's important to you will help you find meaning in your life, which will in turn help you feel purposeful and happy. Use the worksheet on pages 19–21 to help you know what is important to you. These choices will be different for everyone.

Whose Path Do I Admire?

Whose path in retirement do you most admire? Why?

WORKSHEET

What Matters to Me?

Reflect on these questions and write your answers. Use additional sheets of paper, if needed.

If you were asked by a child to tell about the most important thing you have learned in your life, what would you say?

What was the best period of your life? Why?

What was the worst period of your life? Why? Did you know it at the time? What did you learn?

How do you want to be remembered?

What Matters to Me? *continued*

What do you think was the best thing you ever did for someone else?

If you could have anything in the world, what would it be?

If you could give anything in the world to someone else, what would you give? To whom?

What projects have given you the most pleasure?

What have you worked hardest at (work, social causes, friendships, marriage, parenting)?

What Matters to Me? *continued*

What role does spirituality have in your life?

What makes you feel most alive?

What common threads do you find in your answers?

Write a sentence or two that summarizes what is most important to you.

Views from Middle Years and Later Life

You and your priorities change as you get older. Some things are better; some things are worse. Unfortunately, society often encourages us to continue to accept the standards of middle years instead of embracing the values of later life.

View from Middle Years	View from Later Life
Attitude of "more is better"	Enough is enough
External accomplishments valued	Inner work more important
Control/independence of major importance	Control/independence still important but balanced with freeing ability to "let go"
Do what you "have to"	Do what you want to
Focus on self and/or immediate world (work, children, family, friends)	See self as part of greater whole
Facade necessary to present best self, to "fit in"	Time to be real, free to be yourself
Important to look confident	Okay to feel humble, without answers
Society sets your agenda: need to produce, earn money, perform	Set your own agenda
Time to be serious, responsible	Time to reclaim sense of awe, lightheartedness
Look for "answers," assuredness	Tolerate ambiguity, uncertainty, affirm importance of questions
Worry about future	Focus on present
Feel immortal (even though you know you are not)	Feel mortal, have greater appreciation of living
Feel stressed, fatigued	Time to nap
Feel negative and fearful about old age	You are there: know that it can be anything
Problems are "making it," getting ahead	Problems are adjusting to losses such as loved ones who die and your own health problems
Parenting full time	Enjoy the good stuff about grandchildren; send them home
No safety net for health care or financial emergency	Medicare and Social Security

There is no clear dividing line between the middle years and later life. The distinctions are only generalizations leading to the following point: in order to find life meaningful, it is important to believe that your later years are as valuable as your earlier years.

Discovering Your Passions

Joseph was a sales manager at a media company when he retired. For most of his life, he'd focused on his career. He frequently worked 50 or 60 hours a week, even into his 60s. When he finally retired, he felt untethered and uneasy.

When a friend who had gone through a similar transition recommended that Joseph take some time each day to think about and write down what was important to him, he grudgingly agreed to give it a try. While at first he didn't see the point, he realized over time that there were many things that were important to him that he had let fall to the wayside as he focused on his job.

He wrote about the camping trips he had taken as a boy with his family, spending long weekends fishing with his father and hiking through forests. It made him realize how little time he now spent with his aging parents, as well as how long it had been since he had spent any serious amount of time outdoors, in the sorts of serene places where he'd found refuge as a boy.

Joseph also wrote about how much he missed the easy camaraderie of his colleagues, with whom he'd frequently shared lunches, dinners, and trips to conferences and sales meetings. While he didn't miss the accompanying sales reports, deadlines, and stressful clients that also came with his job, he became aware of his desire to find a group of people with whom he could share stories and jokes.

By writing down what he had once loved and what he now missed, Joseph realized that his image of himself in retirement differed from what he actually wanted. He began spending more time with his parents, going on camping trips, and meeting groups of friends in local cafés. He was able to focus on the things he valued, which made him feel happier, more purposeful, and fulfilled.

How Will Retirement Influence Your Sense of Self?

Your sense of self is often dictated by your career, so retirement often brings conflicting emotions about identity and self-worth. Time you once spent working is now your own. In retirement more than any other time in your life, you have freedom to make your own decisions. Along with freedom may come fear and loneliness. On the one hand, you may enjoy being finished with the problems and routine of the workplace. On the other, you may miss the satisfactions and stability of your work life.

Some of the issues you might face include:

- **Identity.** Who am I if I'm not my job title? When meeting new people, the first question often is, "What do you do?" How do you answer that question now?
- **Power and position.** You had a title and responsibilities. You made decisions and perhaps supervised others. You had a niche in your organization. If you were proud of what you did, you may miss the feeling of importance and significance that came with your job.
- **Community.** Your place of work and the people you worked with provided you with an important community. What will substitute?
- **Regular paychecks.** You may have to adjust your spending to accommodate reduced income. You may miss the act of receiving a regular paycheck.

What Legacy Will You Leave?

See chapter 17, "Passing On What You Have," page 251.

Have you thought about what you would like to pass on to your family, friends, or community? Traditionally we think of money and property when we think of legacy, but it can be much more. Some of the most precious things we can leave behind are the principles by which we live, the beliefs that give meaning to our lives, and the knowledge and wisdom we have gained through our experiences.

A venerated Jewish custom of bequeathing a spiritual legacy includes leaving an ethical will. Preparing an ethical will can help you clarify what is meaningful to you. Whenever you find yourself saying wise or meaningful words, write them down.

WORKSHEET

What Words Do I Want to Leave?

Spend some time completing the statements below. You may want to share some of your answers with people close to you so they understand who you are and what's important to you.

I write this to you, [their name], in order to . . .

These were the formative events of my life . . .

These are the people who most influenced me . . .

These are the values and principles that are most important to me . . .

These are some of my favorite possessions that I want you to have, and these are the stories that explain what makes these things so precious to me . . .

Some of the poems, essays, scriptural passages that have meant the most to me are . . .

These are the mistakes I most regret having made in my life that I hope you will not repeat . . .

What Words Do I Want to Leave? *continued*

I would like to ask your forgiveness for . . . , and I forgive you for . . .

I want you to know how much I love you and how grateful I am to you for . . .

These are some of the important lessons that I have learned in my life . . .

These are some of the memories of you I cherish . . .

The best advice I ever got was . . .

These are my hopes for the future . . .

These are my hopes for you . . .

These are some messages that I would like to leave my [friend, partner, spouse, child, grandchild, niece, nephew] . . .

Tools for a Meaningful Journey

John Lennon once joked that life is what happens when you're busy making other plans. Indeed, it's easy to get caught up in day-to-day activities. But turning your attention to the small acts of daily life can help you slow down and pay attention to life as it happens. These simple activities can help you be more purposeful in all that you do.

- **Savor peak moments.** Peak moments are those times when you know that life doesn't get any better: moments when you stand in awe of nature or a work of art, when you know that you've truly connected with another person, when you have achieved a personal victory, or when you have done a job well. Appreciate these moments fully before charging ahead to the next thing.
- **Notice what's going on around you.** Whenever you can, notice with your senses what you are seeing, hearing, touching, smelling, or tasting. Observe your thoughts. Name your feelings. You can learn to make even trivial-seeming acts luminous and vital. By observing every detail, you can return to these moments fully in your memory.
- **Visit places you enjoy.** It may sound obvious, but many of us don't spend much time in the places we find ourselves the happiest, whether it's at the local farmers' market, a nearby park, or the library.
- **Rediscover simplicity.** When you were a child, simple things probably delighted you. As you got older, you may have begun to value complexity and speed. In later life, many move back to an appreciation of simple things. This appreciation (or what the 20th-century American poet Theodore Roethke called "perpetual astonishment") is much more nuanced and hopeful. You have experienced much of what life has to offer, and now, with deeper perception of its enormous value, you might once again choose to attribute meaning to the simple things.

Do Nothing

Sit quietly by yourself for 20 minutes. Focus on breathing from your diaphragm. On your inhalation, say "this moment" and on your exhalation, say "only moment."

This is doing nothing in the finest sense of the word. When you are sitting quietly with yourself, thoughts inevitably appear. Observe them, and then return to thinking about your breath and this particular moment. Practice returning to your breath whenever your thoughts stray.

No matter how difficult your life may seem, you can deal with moments. You don't have to carry the worries and the planning about the future or the pains of the past into this very moment. The goal is to recognize that you can move from whatever difficult thoughts and feelings you have to peaceful moments. Being able to shift back to the moment anytime that you are feeling stressed is a transformative tool for finding meaning.

See "Relaxed Breathing," page 142.

WORKSHEET

Finding Meaning in My Journey

Pay attention to life as it happens and keep a journal of what you notice. Write, draw, or use other creative ways to capture your insights. These questions will help you get started.

What peak moments did I experience in the past week?

What have I seen, heard, touched, smelled, or tasted that I want to capture and observe?

What places make me happiest? Why?

What ordinary things give me extraordinary pleasure?

Questions & Answers

Q. Who am I without my job?

A. One obstacle to a positive transition at retirement is to equate self-worth with paid employment. This diminishes the value of worthy avocations such as reading, painting, traveling, learning, volunteering, and caregiving.

See "Views from Middle Years and Later Life," page 22.

Q. I don't want to retire because it feels like it would be admitting that I'm getting old. Is there another way of looking at it?

A. It is time to attribute new, positive meaning to getting older and ignore the societal adoration of youth. All stages of life have merit and problems. The stress of supporting yourself and your family during middle age is just as much of a problem as is adjusting to various losses in later life. This time of life is loaded with opportunities for meaning and satisfaction.

Resources

Aging Well: Surprising Guideposts to a Happier Life from the Landmark Harvard Study of Adult Development
George E. Vaillant, MD
Boston: Little, Brown. 2002.

Another Country: Navigating the Emotional Terrain of Our Elders
Mary Pipher
New York: Riverhead Books. 1999.

Claiming Your Place at the Fire: Living the Second Half of Your Life on Purpose
Richard Leider
San Francisco, CA: Berrett-Koehler Publishers. 2004.

The Creative Age: Awakening Human Potential in the Second Half of Life
Gene Cohen
New York: HarperCollins. 2001.

From Age-ing to Sage-ing: A Profound New Vision of Growing Older
Rabbi Zalman Schachter-Shalomi and Ronald S. Miller
New York: Warner Books. 1995.

Gerotranscendance from Young to Old to Old Old Age
Lars Tornstam
Uppsala, Sweden: University of Uppsala, Social Gerontology Group. 2003.

Guideposts to Meaning: Discovering What Really Matters
Joseph Fabry
Oakland, CA: New Harbinger. 1988.

Man's Search for Meaning
Viktor E. Frankl
Mass market paperback. 1984.

Older and Wiser: Wit, Wisdom, and Spirited Advice from the Older Generation
Eric W. Johnson
New York: Walker. 1986.

Secrets of Becoming a Late Bloomer: Extraordinary Ordinary People on the Art of Staying Creative, Alive, and Aware in Midlife and Beyond
Connie Goldman and Richard Mahler
Center City, MN: Hazelden. 2000.

Still Here: Embracing Aging, Changing, and Dying
Ram Dass
New York: Riverhead Books. 2000.

Too Young to Retire: 101 Ways to Start the Rest of Your Life
Marika Stone and Howard Stone
New York: Plume. 2004.

The Vintage Journey: A Guide to Artful Aging
Trish Herbert
Cleveland, OH: United Church Press. 1995.

What Are Old People For? How Elders Will Save the World
Bill Thomas
Acton, MA: VanderWyk and Burnham. 2004.

IN THIS CHAPTER

N

Chapter 2

Building Strong Relationships

Mutually beneficial relationships provide social, intellectual, and emotional support

LET US BE GRATEFUL TO PEOPLE WHO MAKE US HAPPY; THEY ARE THE CHARMING GARDENERS WHO MAKE OUR SOULS BLOSSOM.

—Marcel Proust, French novelist

W

Helen Kivnick
Professor of social work

Sue Meyers
Retired family sociologist

You don't have to be a rocket scientist—or a television talk show host—to know that your relationships have an enormous influence on your happiness, satisfaction, and well-being. As a major change in your life, retirement will present new opportunities and challenges in the way you relate to other people. Understanding your past and current relationships will help you build on your strengths as you maintain, modify, and create new connections with others.

Participating in Social Networks

We all share our lives with people who are important to us in different ways. A spouse, friends, relatives, and acquaintances provide social, intellectual, and emotional support. They promote and challenge our development throughout life (Lang 2001).

But good relationships do more than make us happy; they make us healthy. Scientists have demonstrated that being in close, positive relationships can improve physical health by countering stress and producing feelings of calm. These relationships can even prevent chronic health conditions in later life (Carmichael 2006; Taylor et al. 2000).

All Relationships Are Not Equal

Chances are you don't think too much about the way you interact differently with people who play different roles in your life—you probably do it unconsciously. From the brief pleasantries you exchange with the familiar convenience store clerk while picking up a gallon of milk, to the conversation you have with a neighbor about the new construction across the street, to the heart-to-heart discussion you have with your spouse about a friend's terminal disease, you adapt the length and depth of your interactions, your emotional involvement, and the topics of conversation. You feel differently about and interact differently with your closest friend than you do with your boss at work or your fellow nonprofit board member.

See "Community Connections," page 43.

These varied interactions help you feel supported, challenged, connected, and loved. And no matter what kind of relationship you have with someone else, most of us want the give-and-take in a relationship to be about equal. This sense of equality is highly subjective, and in long-term relationships it may be evaluated over an entire lifetime (Uehara 1995).

Social Networks Strengthen Connections

One-to-one relationships don't exist in isolation. They are the building blocks of complex social networks. These networks can be especially useful for you as you think about your retirement. They are a good place to start to forge new connections.

Your family is an example of a social network. It includes relationships with your spouse and daughter; it also includes relationships with other family members, such as grandchildren, nieces and nephews, and in-laws.

Social networks are more than the sum of their parts. Being a member of a network helps you establish relationships with people with whom you are indirectly connected through other network members. Some of the networks in your work life may include people from your place of employment, your field or discipline, and more.

As you anticipate retiring, you may find yourself listening with more interest to a colleague's description of her book group. Perhaps that's a group you'd like to attend. Or perhaps you would like to start your own book club with friends or neighbors. Access to social networks helps you connect with others in a way that retains what is best from your past and creates something new for the future.

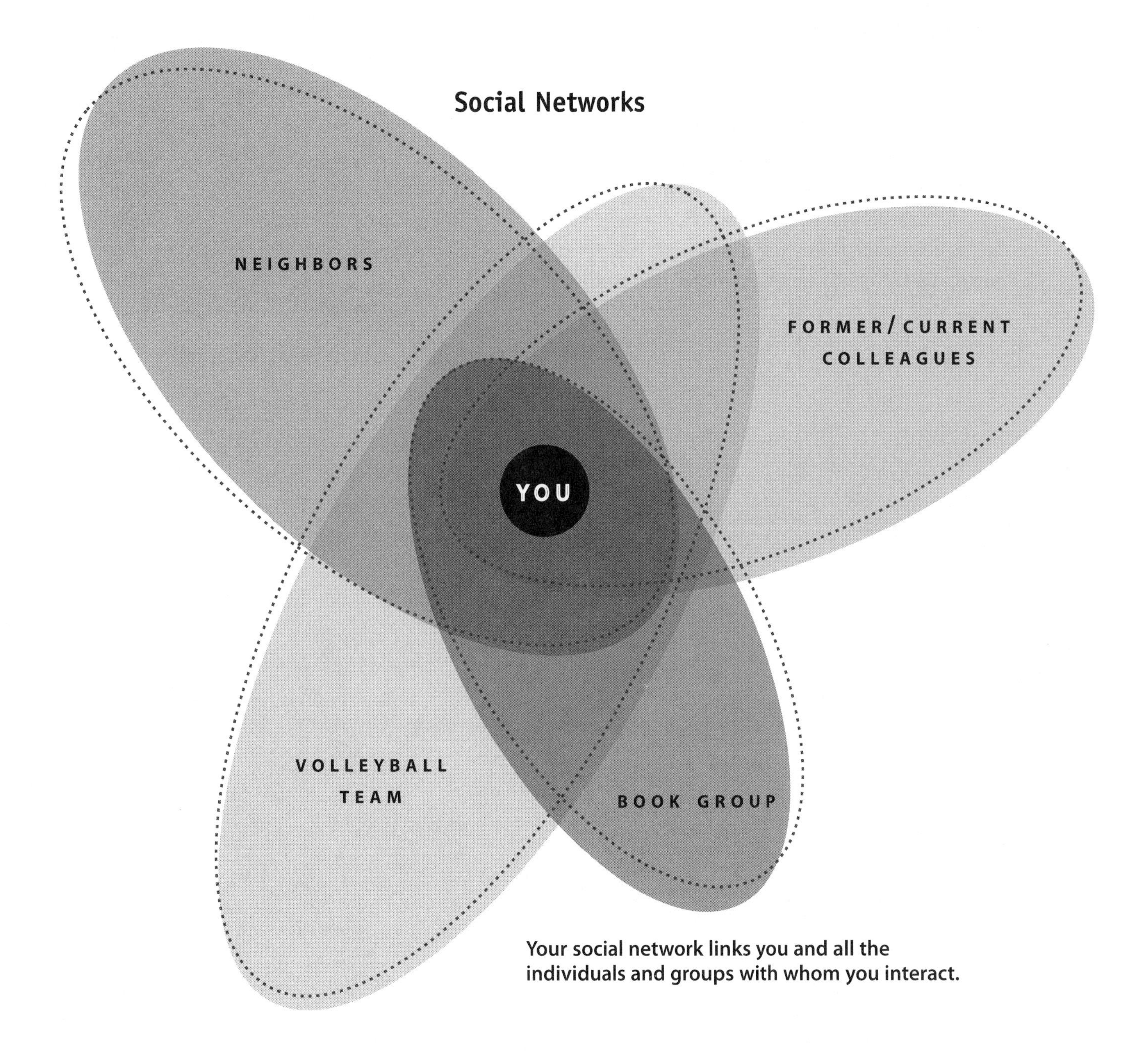

Your social network links you and all the individuals and groups with whom you interact.

Building Your Circles of Support

Think of your most important relationships—your close friends and family—forming concentric circles around you (Antonucci and Akiyama 1987, 1995; Kahn and Antonucci 1980). They are your circles of support (Toni Antonucci calls them your social convoy).

The people in these circles provide support *for* you, and, in return, they expect support *from* you. For most people, the circles of support include no more than eight or nine people. Together, these people hold the keys to much of your life satisfaction and success.

You are connected to each member on multiple levels, although members may or may not have much connection with each other. With most members of your circles of support, you have created a great deal of personal history together. For better or for worse, you have a powerful impact on each other's well-being.

Circles of Support: Where Do You Get and Give Support?

Your circles of support form supportive rings around you. You will want to recognize and appreciate the roles they play in your life. The following descriptions will help you identify the people in your life who make up your circles of support.

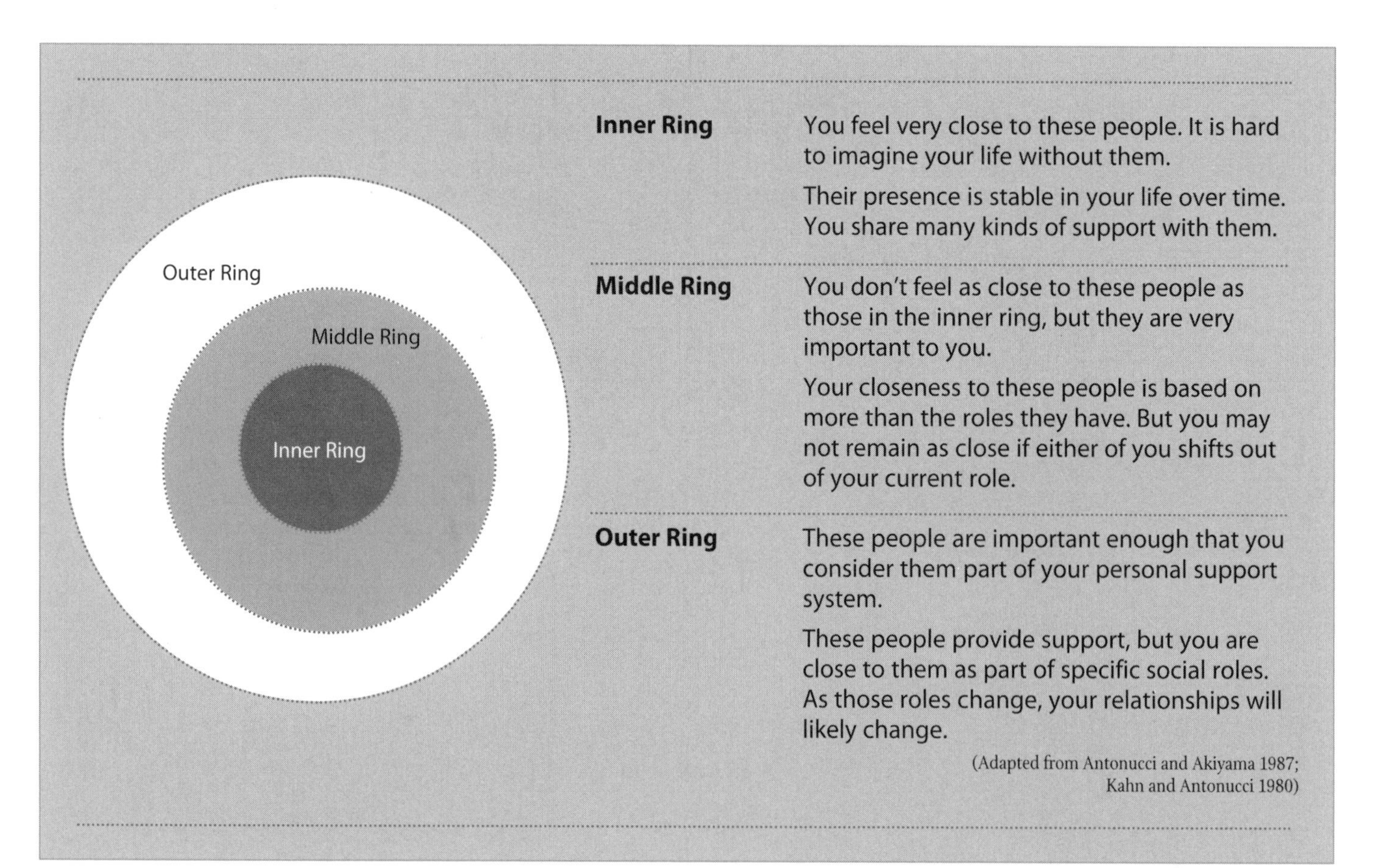

Inner Ring	You feel very close to these people. It is hard to imagine your life without them. Their presence is stable in your life over time. You share many kinds of support with them.
Middle Ring	You don't feel as close to these people as those in the inner ring, but they are very important to you. Your closeness to these people is based on more than the roles they have. But you may not remain as close if either of you shifts out of your current role.
Outer Ring	These people are important enough that you consider them part of your personal support system. These people provide support, but you are close to them as part of specific social roles. As those roles change, your relationships will likely change.

(Adapted from Antonucci and Akiyama 1987; Kahn and Antonucci 1980)

WORKSHEET

My Circles of Support

	Member	What Support Do I Give?	What Support Do I Get?
Inner Ring			
Middle Ring			
Outer Ring			

What changes do I want to make in my circles of support?

Keeping in Touch from a Distance

If you live far from a loved one, it may seem difficult to have the kind of relationship you'd have if you lived nearby, but distance is no obstacle for thoughtful gestures.

For example, daily conversations with staff at your mother's nursing home enable you to maintain working relationships, even from the opposite coast. If you were able to visit your mother daily, you might chat with the aide who helps change her clothes. From a distance, you can send the aide a thank-you card. In person, you might bring cookies for the night staff members who help your mother through difficult hours of sleeplessness. Delivery services can provide a variety of treats. Think about things you would do if you lived nearby and see if there are similar things you can do from a distance.

As you make the transition from work to retirement and out of your work-related network, you must prepare for changes in at least the outer ring of your circles of support. You may no longer be able to count, for example, on weekly lunches with a colleague. Some individuals in the outer ring may move to a closer ring. And as you have new experiences in new settings, you will find opportunities to create new relationships with individuals who become part of your circles of support.

You will probably rely on support from people in the inner two rings as you move through the transition to retirement. Wisely engaging these personal relationships can help you meet the challenges of this segment of life. Let's look more closely at these relationships.

Family

Most people's earliest relationships grow within the family: parent and child, brother and sister, grandparents, aunts, uncles, and cousins.

Your role within your family has likely changed greatly through your life. It will likely shift again in retirement. As a child, you expected protection and care from your parents. When you are an adult, you and your parents may provide protection and care for one another.

Your role in your children's lives is also changing as you and your children see that their lives are more their own responsibility than yours. As you age, you may count on their presence not only as an indication of their love for you but also as welcome support.

In retirement, you and your siblings may look to each other for more support than anticipated. After losing your partner, you may find yourself reinvesting in sibling relationships. You may also find yourself reverting to old habits from childhood as you address significant family changes. Fighting, cooperating, and competing may now play themselves out as you distribute the burdens of elder care and the blessings of inheritance (Connidis 2005).

Even if you are not close to the family you grew up in, you may have family-like friends and communities where similar dynamics play out.

Marriage(-like) Partners

Marriage or a marriage-like partnership provides a context for intimate relationships. This person is likely to be the one you will spend the most time with during your retirement, so it is essential to maintain a strong relationship with him or her.

Viewing your spouse (in this section "spouse" refers to a partner in a marriage or marriage-like relationship) as your best friend is an important factor in long-term marital happiness and personal well-being (Antonucci and Akiyama 1995). Passionate love tends to yield in importance to friendship over the course of a long-term relationship (Barnes and Sternberg 1997). This shift may help spouses meet the challenges in later life, such as mental deterioration, disease, and disability, all of which result in losses that may be as ambiguous as dementia or as clear and final as death.

Many spouses find themselves in a caregiving role. Caregiving tasks can be burdensome, but for people who manage to truly provide care (in contrast with simply

WORKSHEET

What Is Important to Me in My Relationships?

There is no single formula to find a good balance in relationships. Instead, you'll want to understand your own preferences and find relationships to match them.

In the following worksheet, look at the relationship characteristics listed and circle the number that best describes your preferences.

Relationship Characteristic	Strongly Agree				Neutral				Strongly Agree	Relationship Characteristic
I like to talk.	4	3	2	1	0	1	2	3	4	I prefer to listen.
I like to be in contact with my friends frequently.	4	3	2	1	0	1	2	3	4	It's okay if I don't hear from my friends for a week or two—or even longer.
I like to ask for help and advice from my friends when I deal with a challenging problem.	4	3	2	1	0	1	2	3	4	I prefer to do my own research and come to my own conclusions when I'm faced with an obstacle.
I like to share my feelings with others.	4	3	2	1	0	1	2	3	4	I prefer not to share my feelings with others.
It's important that my friends share most of my values.	4	3	2	1	0	1	2	3	4	It's okay if my friends share just a few of my values.
I prefer seeing friends face-to-face.	4	3	2	1	0	1	2	3	4	I'm happy to have friends where our primary communication is through phone calls, e-mails, and letters.
I like doing tried-and-true activities with my friends: favorite restaurants, coffee, movies.	4	3	2	1	0	1	2	3	4	I'll try anything once, whether it's a salsa dancing class or a weekend adventure kayaking trip.
Other										
Other										

What insights do I have from my answers?

"providing service"), new feelings of commitment and intimacy can emerge from the pain of this experience. Along with the burden, giving real care can be a source of satisfaction and growth.

Friends

Friendship is a relationship with loose, largely self-defined characteristics, in contrast to the more formal expectations of many other relationships. Knowing what you value in friendships will help you strengthen bonds with your current friends and make new ones.

Friendships range from acquaintanceships to vital relationships that enhance your well-being and help you feel safe in the world (Blieszner and Roberto 2004). Unlike blood relatives, our friendships are based on voluntary choices—we choose them, and they choose us.

Researchers have discovered that men and women often have different kinds of friendships. In general, women have more friendships than men, and these relationships tend to be more intimate and involve more contact than do men's. Men's friendships seem to be grounded more in shared activities and mutual assistance than do women's. This contrast may reflect gender-related differences in ways of experiencing intimacy rather than in need for intimacy.

Understanding how you experience intimacy will enable you to ensure that these needs are met as you move through retirement.

Old Friends, New Friends

Elizabeth and her younger friend, Jane, were avid bird watchers. Once a month, they'd spend a weekend morning in nearby parks and nature preserves identifying birds, and every year, they took a trip with a birding tour company to a new place where they could observe hundreds of species in a single weekend. When Elizabeth retired, she hoped that she and her friend would spend even more time birding. She frequently invited Jane to join her on her trips, but because of her family and work obligations, Jane often turned her down.

Elizabeth was disappointed until she read a newspaper article about a local birding group in her area. Although she was shy about attending the first meeting, she was welcomed into the group.

She now goes on birding field trips twice a month, and continues to meet Jane for their regular birding activities. She's met new friends who share her interest, and she's maintained the important bond with her friend.

How Retirement Affects Relationships

In some ways, retirement is like starting your life from scratch—but in others, it's a continuation of the things you've done in your past. As you have met life's challenges and adapted to new circumstances, you have made choices that led to the relationships you have today. Maintaining important relationships should be a top priority as you make decisions about your retirement.

When you retire, you will likely have more time and energy to devote to some of your relationships, and the balance of giving and receiving within them may shift. Thinking about obstacles you may face as you make this transition will help you prepare for surprises or disappointments—and adapt accordingly.

WORKSHEET

How Will Retirement Affect My Relationships?

Think about the characteristics of your relationships and identify specific elements that might change in retirement. If you foresee significant changes or potential problems, consider how you might address these issues.

Relationship	How Might the Relationship Change?	How Will I Address the Changes?

Trying New Things under Watchful Eyes

Martin is a retired engineer. He was excited about trying something new in his retirement, so he set up an easel and started experimenting with abstract watercolors. His spouse walked in on his early efforts and fondly recalled the precision of his professional draftsmanship. Martin's reaction was to pull back, feeling self-conscious and inadequate.

Was her comment intended to affirm or criticize? Was his reaction really expressing his own fear about learning a new skill? Should he have received this comment as an expression of companionship, admiration, interest, disdain, or intrusion?

Challenges in Relationships

Conflict

Although relationship tension, discord, and disappointment are likely to be familiar experiences, the changes that come with retirement may disrupt the effectiveness of long-used strategies for managing conflict. There are things you can do to manage conflict effectively—and to prevent it before it becomes an issue.

When familiar strategies no longer work, you may need to develop new ways of relating. If you develop good skills for managing conflict in your relationships, the transitions brought on by retirement can be more stimulating than stressful.

Disruption

As you move through retirement, changes can disrupt relationships and ripple throughout your social network.

For example, if your children put down roots on the other side of the country, you may be challenged to establish long-distance grandparent and parenting relationships that are different from those you knew when they were nearby. The easy routine of weekly visits and your immediate availability for emergency assistance are disrupted by distance. When spending time together requires planning and plane rides, visits are less frequent and more intense.

Similar relationship disruptions may result when you act on a longtime dream to make the cabin on the lake your full-time home, when your longtime confidant moves to be with a new partner, or when your business colleague relocates to be closer to family members. In all of these cases, established patterns are interrupted, and new ones must be created. Fortunately, technology like e-mail and cell phones provides good ways to keep in touch.

By the time we reach retirement, most of us have experienced temporary physical disability and the need for assistance, whether in ourselves, in our partner, or in other members of our social networks. Disability limits a person's capacity to provide emotional and physical support to others. As the people in your life age, there is an increased likelihood of competing claims on your time and emotional resources, and adjustments may be necessary.

Loss

The loss of a spouse, close family member, or intimate friend has long been recognized as among the most stressful of life's experiences (Holmes and Rahe 1967). Loss comes in many forms: death or divorce, dementia or natural catastrophe. Coping with loss requires the resolution of acute grief; in the long term, it also involves strengthening other ties in your social network and making new connections to replace some of what the lost relationship provided.

See "Learn to Resolve Conflict," page 143.

You can't replace shared memories, histories, worldviews, and mutual appreciations that have developed over decades. You can, however, treasure personal memories and appreciate shared experiences. You can also find new ways to meet your needs. To be sure, you can't make a new "old friend." But you can make a new friend, and you can strengthen your ongoing friendships.

Your circumstances will influence how successful you are in renewing and strengthening relationships as you deal with loss. Relocating to live with a child's family may provide needed physical support but may disrupt the bulk of your network ties. A nearby activity center may provide a great deal of superficial social contact, but if regular activities are dominated by golf and cards while you are looking for classical music or a book club, you may remain lonely and unconnected.

Choose your environment and cultivate your social network to improve the likelihood that you will be able to maintain social relationships in the face of loss. A vibrant, bustling 80-year-old widow explains, "You can't wait until you're all alone before starting to create a community. If you build community all along, it can support you when you need it." You can work to keep your long-term relationships active and reciprocal. You can participate in those group activities you have always enjoyed. If you decide to move, you can choose your new community based on things you like to do and the availability of people with whom you would like to spend time.

Finding New Ways to Communicate

After many years of marriage and after their daughter was established in her career, Henry acted on long-discussed plans for retirement. He contacted a real estate agent to put the family's home up for sale. He also priced a motor home for an anticipated retirement life of traveling. He was proud of the good shopping and went home to tell his wife of his efforts on their behalf. As Henry drove up, the agent was pounding the "for sale" sign into the front yard—and his wife, Rebecca, was on the porch, looking startled.

Although Henry had talked about the plan for more than 15 years, the discussion was primarily a monologue, with Rebecca providing only "uh-huh" in response. Rebecca was supportive of her husband and did not want to discourage his thinking, but she really thought they would have the opportunity to discuss the situation before taking action. She did not know that he was going to act on these plans, and do so without her signature or thoughtful discussion about the process and results.

Henry, meanwhile, had spent his career making important decisions for himself and others. As a manager in charge of many employees, he was used to making choices after careful research.

Fortunately, Henry and Rebecca were able to back out of the contract to sell the home with no penalty. They proceeded to discuss their plans and hopes for the future from both their points of view. They discussed their hopes, mapped out their plans, and compromised on a few of their destinations. In a year they had sold the house and were on the road. This time, they were both happy about it.

Commmunty Connections

Becoming part of new communities is another way to help fill your need for social connection and support. Your decision about where to live in retirement will, in large part, determine the kind of community connections that will be available to you.

In *Bowling Alone: The Collapse and Revival of American Community*, Harvard University professor of sociology Robert Putnam provides evidence that being integrated with your community has a direct connection to your physical health. He notes that the protective effect is true of family and friends, but it is also true for more distant social connections, such as participation in social events and affiliation with religious and civic associations.

Communities of Shared Interests

Although passions may change over time, the need for connection remains. As your interests change, you might need to find new people with whom to share them, whether it's members of a hiking club or a political group. If you're not sure where to start, try scanning your local newspaper for events you may be interested in attending, or see if there are classes at a local college or other educational opportunities that catch your eye. Check out the bulletin board at your local library—it can be a wonderful resource to help you find groups you'll enjoy.

Virtual Communities Connect You to the World

Finding a community of people who share your interests is easier than it once was. Online message boards, user forums, and chat groups are all places where people interact online. If you are interested in growing orchids, brewing your own beer, or mastering Spanish, you will find others who share your passion. Virtual communities do not provide all the social support of face-to-face connections, but they can offer satisfying relationships that meet a particular purpose. Here are a few places to get started:

Eons Groups
www.eons.com (click on "People")
Eons Groups focuses on groups with members 50 and older.

Meetup
www.meetup.com
Meetup helps people find others who share their interest or cause and then helps them form local community groups that regularly meet face-to-face.

Yahoo! Groups
groups.yahoo.com
Yahoo! Groups helps you get to know others with shared interests.

Communities of Residence

Deciding where to live in retirement can be a major decision. Often the decision is influenced by factors like closeness to family members, work and volunteer activities, friends, and contacts. Recognize that your postretirement stage may last 30 years or more and you may make more than one change in where you live during these years. You have many options. You can:

- Adapt your current home to meet your needs
- Sublet it and temporarily live in another part of the country
- Sell your home and buy another
- Move to a condominium, town house, loft, or apartment
- Move into a designed life care community with assisted living
- Buy a travel trailer and live on wheels
- Buy a houseboat and sail into your retirement

You can choose from a range of different living communities: older people only; a multigenerational living situation with your own family members; a group of friends of different ages; or an intentional community that builds on shared values (Brown 2006).

Think about housing options based on what matters to you. Although your children may urge you to move closer to them, consider what it would mean for your friendships, activities, and interests. If you make friends easily, the change may not be a problem. If you expect your children to meet all of your friendship and family needs, you may be disappointed. If you are thinking about moving to another part of the country or world, an extended visit may help you decide if the new location is right for you.

WORKSHEET

Where Will I Live?

Mark (✗) how important each of these factors are in choosing where to live.

	Not Important	Somewhat Important	Very Important	Notes
Proximity to family				
Ability to remain independent				
Cost of living				
Transportation availability				
Access to medical care				
Keeping active in areas of interest				
People similar to me				
People different from me				
Climate:				
Physical				
Social				
Political				
Age diversity				
Age similarity				
Size of community (urban, suburban, small town, country)				

What insights do I have from my answers?

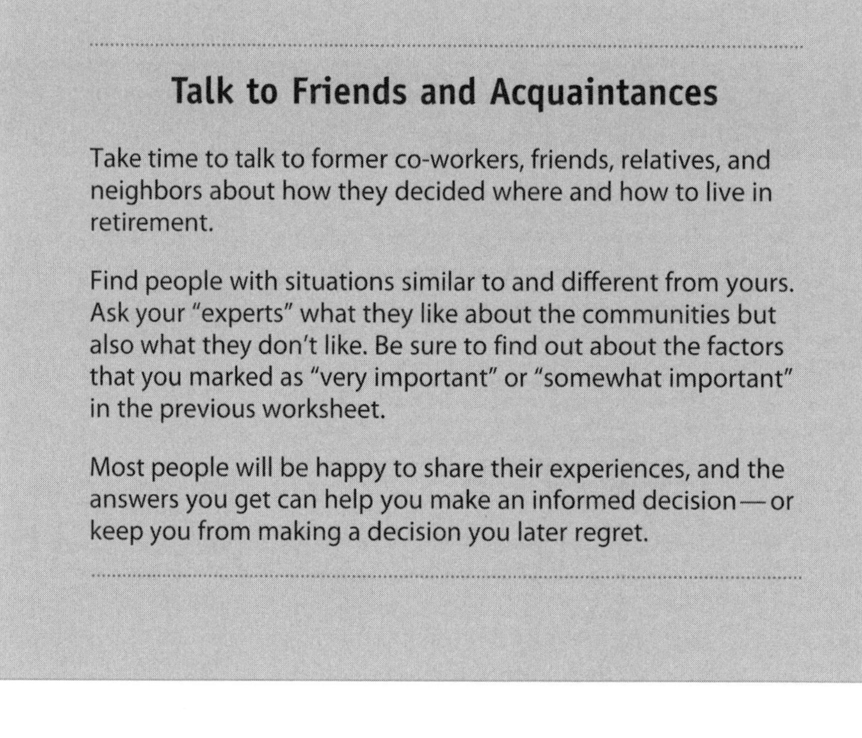

Talk to Friends and Acquaintances

Take time to talk to former co-workers, friends, relatives, and neighbors about how they decided where and how to live in retirement.

Find people with situations similar to and different from yours. Ask your "experts" what they like about the communities but also what they don't like. Be sure to find out about the factors that you marked as "very important" or "somewhat important" in the previous worksheet.

Most people will be happy to share their experiences, and the answers you get can help you make an informed decision—or keep you from making a decision you later regret.

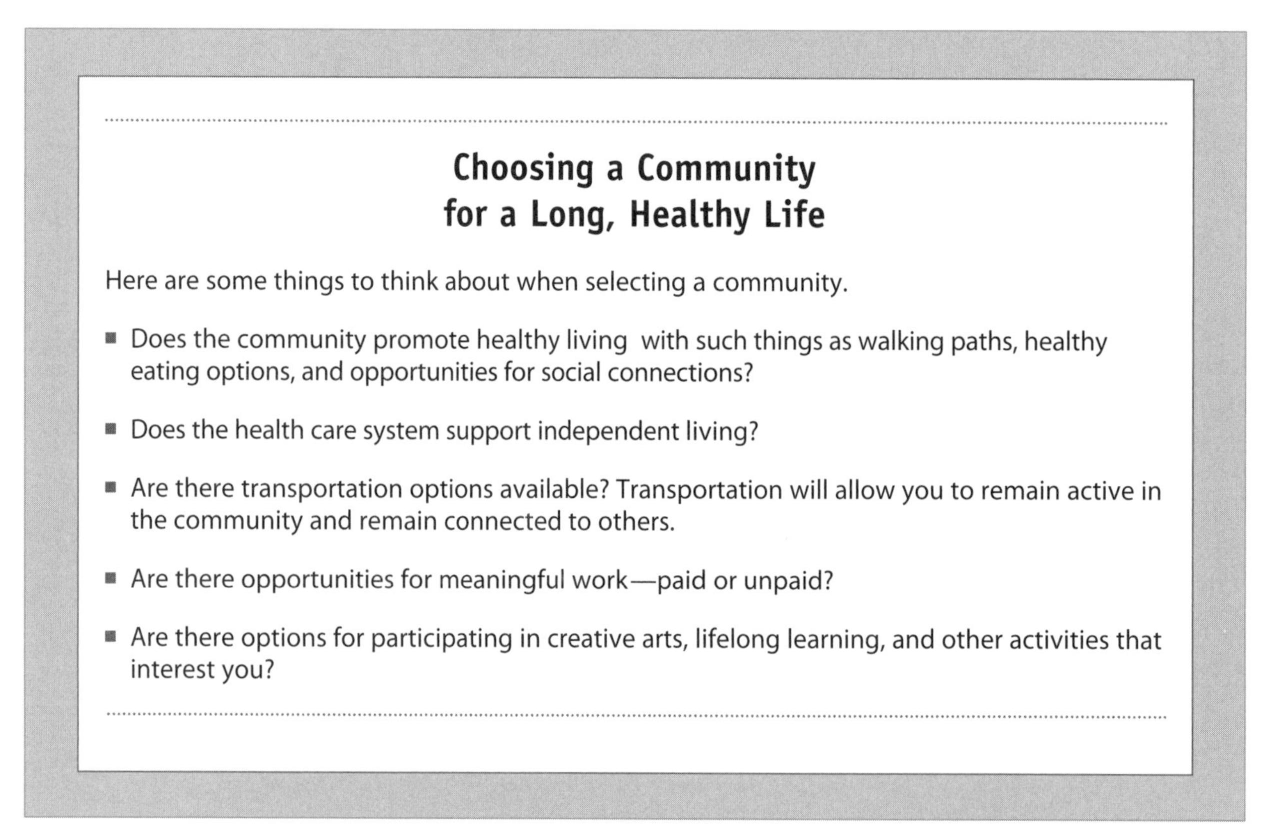

Choosing a Community for a Long, Healthy Life

Here are some things to think about when selecting a community.

- Does the community promote healthy living with such things as walking paths, healthy eating options, and opportunities for social connections?
- Does the health care system support independent living?
- Are there transportation options available? Transportation will allow you to remain active in the community and remain connected to others.
- Are there opportunities for meaningful work—paid or unpaid?
- Are there options for participating in creative arts, lifelong learning, and other activities that interest you?

Questions & Answers

Q. A longtime friend has suffered from health problems and increasingly relies on me for help. I'm willing to lend a hand, but I'm sometimes frustrated by his many requests. Why do I feel so resentful?

A. If a voluntary relationship remains out of balance for too long, one or both partners may decrease interest in the relationship. Think of the friend for whom you gladly do grocery shopping while he recovers from surgery. For a while, you are simply glad to help out when a loved one is in need, and you receive enough appreciation or self-validation in return. But what happens if he stops making progress in recovery or stops expressing appreciation? If you reach a point where you feel that you are being intolerably under-rewarded, you may need to withdraw support to maintain your own sense of balance.

Q. My sister has been widowed for more than 10 years, and has not been in a relationship since her husband died. I've asked her if she's ready to consider a new relationship, but she seems uninterested. Is this normal?

A. This may be the right choice for her. Widows and widowers who choose not to remarry usually do not actively mourn forever, but they reserve marital intimacy for memories of their lost partner, meeting their social needs through other relationships. On the other hand, some widows and widowers do find satisfying new marriages or marriage-like relationships. They do not renounce past love, but they are able to mourn through the pain of acute grief, come to terms with loss, and then move on, forever changed, to share life and love with a new partner.

Q. How can I prepare for unexpected changes?

A. Keep your plan flexible and change it if necessary. Circumstances will challenge you, whether it is the 40-year-old child moving in with you, your parent's need for care after surgery, a serious illness for you or your partner, or even the loss of your partner. Any crisis necessitates change and can throw us for a loop. If we expect that the unexpected will occur, we can more easily work through the issues that need to be handled. Don't be afraid to talk openly with people about your concerns. You can learn from others who have experienced similar changes. That's what your social network is for.

Q. What advice can I give a friend who just lost her spouse and is thinking about selling her house?

A. Tell her to take her time. At times of crises, we are vulnerable and may not be able to make the best decisions. Research supports the common wisdom that you should not make drastic changes quickly when a spouse dies. Some decisions cannot wait. If you can work through changes slowly, the outcomes can be much more to your benefit.

Resources

AARP
www.aarp.org/families/grief_loss
This section on the AARP website will help you address the challenges that come with the loss of a spouse, a partner, or a close friend.

Aging Well: Surprising Guideposts to a Happier Life from the Landmark Harvard Study of Adult Development
George E. Vaillant, MD
Boston: Little, Brown. 2002.

Ambiguous Loss: Learning to Live with Unresolved Grief
Pauline Boss
Cambridge, MA: Harvard University Press. 1999.

Find Your Spot
www.findyourspot.com
Find Your Spot uses criteria such as cost of living, access to cultural activities, medical system, climate, and crime rate to help you select where to live.

Friendshifts: The Power of Friendship and How It Shapes Our Lives
Jan Yager
Stamford, CT: Hannacroix Creek Books. 1999.

A Gift of Hope: How We Survive Our Tragedies
Robert L. Veninga
Boston: Little, Brown. 1985.

Guiding Lights: The People Who Lead Us Toward Our Purpose in Life
Eric Liu
New York: Random House. 2004.

Living a Connected Life: Creating and Maintaining Relationships That Last
Kathleen A. Brehony
New York: Henry Holt and Company. 2003.

Relationships in Old Age: Coping with the Challenge of Transition
Robert O. Hansson and Bruce N. Carpenter
New York: Guilford Press. 1994.

Social Intelligence: The Science of Human *Relationships*
Daniel Goleman
New York: Bantam. 2006.

Vital Involvement in Old Age: The Experience of Old Age in Our Time
Erik H. Erikson, Joan M. Erikson, and Helen Q. Kivnick
New York: W.W. Norton. 1986.

IN THIS CHAPTER

N

Chapter 3

Using Your Time

Spending your retirement years purposefully

TIME IS THE COIN OF YOUR LIFE. IT IS THE ONLY COIN YOU HAVE, AND ONLY YOU CAN DETERMINE HOW IT WILL BE SPENT. BE CAREFUL LEST YOU LET OTHER PEOPLE SPEND IT FOR YOU.

Carl Sandburg, American biographer and poet

W

Carol Daly
Retired director of
Minnesota Elderhostel

Jan Hively
Founder, Vital Aging Network

You probably know people who have thrived in retirement: men and women who have used their newfound freedom and time to volunteer for causes they believe in, to travel widely, to spend more time with their children and grandchildren. They seem vibrant, engaged, and accomplished.

You probably also know people who haven't fared so well in retirement. They may seem sullen and withdrawn, uninterested in many activities, and unsure about what the years ahead might hold for them.

The difference between these two types of people may be due to a variety of factors, but an important one is the ability to find purpose in the things they do over time.

What is meaningful for each person differs. It might be travel or a hobby. Paid work or volunteering. You may decide to take a class—or teach one. You may choose to buy season tickets for a favorite sports team or to direct a play at your community theater. The key is to enjoy what you're doing and spend time on the things that matter to you.

Studies show that retirees who are engaged in meaningful, productive work feel more satisfied and have better physical and mental health. A recent AARP study (Novelli 2001) found that 80% of baby boomers plan to continue to work at least part time after they retire (for pay or not). Their work may be paid employment or volunteering, teaching or learning, caring for children, or caregiving for older relatives.

You may choose to continue to work because you need additional income or supplemental benefits or because you are looking for something that's challenging and satisfying. Others are looking for opportunities for social interaction. The labor shortage that many predict as boomers retire will likely bring unprecedented opportunities for older workers.

Your Choices Matter

There are many things outside of your control in retirement that can affect your productivity and satisfaction, including unexpected illnesses, changes in your financial situation, or changes in your responsibilities. Still, there are things you can do that influence your overall happiness.

Stay Mentally Active

Research has proved what many have long suspected: the phrase "use it or lose it" applies to the mind as well as to the body. Both require exercise to do their best work. No matter what your age, keeping mentally active will cause your brain to produce new connections between nerve cells, allowing it to store and retrieve information more easily.

The Alzheimer's Association recommends staying mentally active by reading, writing, doing crossword puzzles, attending lectures, enrolling in courses at local colleges, and playing games.

See chapter 8, "Maintaining Mental Fitness," page 135.

Reduce Stress

Don't underestimate the benefit of reducing stress in your life. When you are engaged in activities that give you joy and satisfaction, when you are having fun, and when you laugh, your level of stress is reduced. Research has proved that lowering stress benefits your physical health. It often reduces blood pressure and heart rate; it decreases respiration rate and even improves your hearing and other senses. Stress reduction has also been shown to be beneficial in countering heart disease, chronic pain, asthma, and a number of other diseases. There are psychological benefits as well: decreased anxiety, improved sleep, less reliance on drugs, improved concentration and memory, and even increases in IQ (Serendip 2007).

Rediscover Yourself

Finding new challenges and a sense of your new self in retirement will give you confidence as you move through retirement. Authors Karen Bowen and Judy Schuck conducted focus groups with women who had retired within the past five years. They found that many who no longer worked for pay missed "the challenge of being challenged, the satisfaction [and] excitement of problem solving." Bowen and Schuck note that the past 10 years have seen the emergence of the first generation of women who had professional careers of 30 years or longer. Many are encountering challenges similar to those that men face after retiring from lifetime careers. For many men and women, retirement forces them to recreate their understanding of themselves—not only who they are, but how they can challenge themselves and live productive, rewarding lives after they leave their careers.

How Will You Spend Your Time?

Being free from deadlines set by others may be one of the greatest opportunities—and possibly one of the greatest challenges—you'll have during this time in your life. You get to determine the schedule. You get to decide how you might structure your days. Here are some ways you can spend your time.

Using Your Skills, Talents, and Experience

Research indicates that being productive and contributing are important during this period of your life (Civic Ventures 2007).

Most retirees find an exhilarating, newfound sense of freedom in retirement. After some time away from the workplace, however, retirees often feel that they are missing a sense of purposefulness or connectedness. They miss sharing their ideas, working with others, and feeling needed.

Keeping busy is different from being productive. When you notice the difference, it's time to think about meaningful work. This work can take many forms: a second career, a new entrepreneurial venture, a creative achievement, volunteer work. An examination of options for paid or unpaid work is in "Meaningful Work in Retirement" on page 60.

Learning

You don't have to be the kid who graduated at the top of the class to appreciate the knowledge you can gain from the classroom, from books, and from lectures. You may find that auditing a class at a local college or signing up for a community education course is an invigorating challenge. Classes you choose now are likely to be more appealing than the ones you sat through in high school or college. Because you choose them based on your interests, rather than to fulfill a requirement, you'll be engaged and interested. And learning isn't just a way to keep busy in retirement; it's a way to keep healthy. Using your brain sharpens mental agility and may delay or even ward off mental deterioration.

Ikigai

The Japanese use the term *ikigai*, "that which most makes one's life seem worth living" (the reason for getting up each day). *Ikigai* is what each of us most essentially lives for, day after day and year after year (Mathews 1996). If you don't know what that is for you, it's worth trying to find out.

The classroom is just one of the ways to keep your mind active. According to a 2007 study by Civic Ventures, a nonprofit organization that creates programs for older adults to use their experience for the greater good, 87% of pre-retirees say the primary reason they'd continue to work for pay is to keep mentally active. Travel, too, can have an educational component. Since its inception, Elderhostel, an international educational travel program for adults 55 and older, has used the tagline of "Come for the pleasure of learning." Elderhostel understands the richness and satisfaction that the combination of travel and education can provide.

Don't forget that exploring new hobbies is also a way to learn. If there are hobbies that you once pursued but gave up because there wasn't time to give to them, or if you've thought about new crafts or activities you'd like to try, now's the time to do it. Check out art and nature centers. Perhaps this is the time to hone your acting skills by joining a community theater, or to dust off your trumpet and try out for an amateur quartet. Reflect on what you wish you knew more about and then jump right in. You'll find there are many opportunities to learn—and homework and tests are optional.

Doing Things You Enjoy

- **Traveling and adventuring.** Travel organizations that cater to people 50 and older are proliferating, and they can fit almost any budget. Many of these organizations offer educational experiences along the way. Among the most popular and reasonably priced programs are Overseas Adventure Travel (OAT), Road Scholar, Elderhostel, and Grand Circle. The Smithsonian Institution and college alumni travel programs also offer a great variety of choices. Think about which destinations will be most physically demanding, and make plans for the most taxing adventures first.
- **Entertainment.** With a bit of sleuthing, you will likely unearth dozens of interesting local happenings, many of which won't cost you a cent. If you're looking for ideas, visit or check the website of your town's convention and visitors bureau. You might be surprised to find all that's available when you become a tourist in your own town.
- **Creative endeavors.** In *The Mature Mind: The Positive Power of the Aging Brain,* psychiatrist and gerontologist Gene Cohen describes the surge of creativity that occurs after age 55. Changes to your nerve cell receptors actually increase your capacity for creative expression, a state of mind that Cohen refers to as "all-wheel drive." Artistic endeavors let you take advantage of this increased creative ability.

  This artistic focus can be more than just a hobby. For some, it can be a springboard for a new career.
- **Playing and relaxing.** Perhaps you have been waiting for an opportunity to simply relax—an afternoon nap, walking the beach, playing with grandchildren, participating in a sport you love. Now is the time to work your favorite way to rejuvenate and refresh into your schedule.

  If you are looking for a group activity, you have many options from casual hiking groups to team sports to groups on almost any topic. Local community education programs or organizations like the YMCA and YWCA often provide classes and leagues, as do some school districts and city offices.

Above all, remember that you will probably have more flexibility during this phase of life than you've ever had. Don't limit yourself. You can add, reduce, or eliminate activities anytime. Be prepared for some disappointments and some surprises, but remember to always be on the lookout for the possibilities. Finances, health, and family responsibilities pose some constraints, but the opportunities for contribution, satisfaction, new learning, and new friendships are endless.

Scheduling for Success

Jack's and Nancy's lives were traditional in many ways. Jack provided most of the financial support as a manager at a corporation, while Nancy stayed home to take care of their children. As their children grew older, Nancy split her time between caring for the kids, substitute teaching, and volunteering for various organizations. When Jack retired at 62, they were both eager to see what retirement would hold for them. However, they quickly discovered that there were challenges to the new arrangement. Jack was disappointed when Nancy spent many hours during the day away at her volunteer jobs, and Nancy got frustrated when Jack complained of boredom. They spent much more time together than they had before, and they found themselves in trivial arguments. They needed to figure out new ways to live together. After months of floundering and arguing, they knew they had to do some serious talking. What did they want to do as a twosome? What did they want to do independently?

A weekly meeting, an additional calendar, and a willingness to compromise helped smooth rough waters. First, they agreed to sit down at the beginning of every week to share their individual plans and commitments for the week, which included time for exercise, time to read the newspaper, time for visits with friends, tennis games, community commitments, classes, and other engagements they foresaw. That way, they could discuss potential schedule problems before they happened. They also added another calendar, which they kept in the kitchen, to their own personal calendars. Each wrote down the commitments they had in their own calendar, as well as the appointments they had agreed to as a couple. They could check this calendar whenever a new appointment came up.

Of course, they periodically had to change their plans to accommodate unexpected opportunities and issues, but their calendars and system provided the structure they needed.

WORKSHEET

What Do I Do Now? What Do I Want to Do When I Retire?

Use the following list to think about how you spend your time now and how you want to spend your time when you retire. Actively making choices will help keep you satisfied throughout your retirement.

You may find many activities that you hope to spend more time on—which means you'll likely have to prioritize which things are most important. You may also find that there are some activities on which you are content spending the same amount of time before and during retirement.

	Now			When I Am Retired		
How much time do I spend	**Not Enough**	**Enough**	**Too Much**	**Want to Do More**	**About the Same**	**Want to Do Less**
Alone						
With family (face-to-face or by phone, e-mail)						
With friends						
On spiritual endeavors						
Helping others						
Coaching, mentoring, teaching						
Caregiving (spouse, parents, friends, babysitting)						
Working for pay						
Volunteering						
Reading						
Writing/painting/other creative work						
Taking classes; attending lectures						
Working out						
Walking/hiking/biking/golfing/rock climbing/ other physical activities						
Attending cultural events (theater, concerts, sports)						
Visiting museums, art galleries						
Listening to music/radio						
Shopping, errands						
Watching television						
Traveling						
Gardening						
Fishing/hunting						
Other						

What Do I Do Now? What Do I Want to Do When I Retire? *continued*

What can I do to change "not enough" to "enough" or "too much" to "enough"?

What changes do I need to make so that it's possible to do what I want when I retire?

WORKSHEET

Doing What I Want

Here's another way to explore how to use your time.

List 20 things I like to do.

What new things do I want to try?

What tried-and-true things that I know give me pleasure can I do more of now?

What priority do I put on each item listed?

What do I want to do right away?

For each of the things listed, what will I need to achieve my goals? Money? Information? Education?

Take Your Retirement for a Test Drive

Neal was past retirement age at age 68, but he had stayed at his job because he liked his boss and didn't know what he was going to do in retirement. Several weeks' worth of vacation days were sitting in his account, so he decided to use up his vacation and try out retirement. During the last few months of his work life, he took two days of vacation per week to explore. He attended a class on the culture of German-speaking countries, he volunteered to tutor an eight-year-old boy, he joined Toastmasters, and he took up biking. When he finally retired, he had a better plan to follow.

See "What's Important In Your Life?," page 18.

As You Explore Interests, Remember to:

- **Match your interests to what matters to you.** For instance, do you love being outdoors? You can volunteer to work in a community garden or to take children or friends on a nature hike. You might serve on a park board or a planning commission. Or, you can help a neighbor with yard work. You have a great deal of flexibility. Figure out how to use your talents in such a way that you're enjoying yourself and meeting your personal goals at the same time.
- **Share your ideas with important people in your life.** Talking with family and friends who share your interests will help you determine if your thinking is realistic, and may also remind you of interests you've forgotten to include. They may be able to provide contacts for other people who share your interest in softball or photography. Questions posed by others may also give you further insights into your own planning. You may even ask one or two others to read the worksheets you've done.
- **Consider all factors.** There are a number of other details that you'll likely want or need to consider as you make your plan. Besides the timing requirements you've already assessed, you'll have to take into account things like costs, potential risks, and your skill level.

Managing Time

Many retirees report that their lives have been taken over by "busyness." Your eagerness to keep active, and your familiarity with working long hours, can easily cut into the assets of retirement and push your life out of balance. It's important to evaluate your schedule frequently, and to lighten up as needed. It may take a while to determine the right balance.

Connie Goldman, author of *The Ageless Spirit*, suggests that you continue to use a daily planner. List exercise times, classes for which you've registered, luncheon dates with friends, community work, time with grandchildren, arts and sporting events you plan to attend, bridge games, even time to read the newspaper. Do this just as you would have scheduled a meeting with your boss or a conference with colleagues. The activities may be different, but the planning technique isn't.

Challenges to Managing Time

Busyness

Some retirees feel guilty having time on their hands. You hear this echoed by people who announce proudly, "I'm busier than ever." Many of the newly retired rapidly fill every hour without reflection or prioritizing. Others roar out of the gate, play golf, bridge, exercise like mad, and work on all the projects that they haven't had time to do. After doing this for a while they find that they need to do something that makes them feel like they are contributing. Others are startled by all their spare time and get into the existential "Who am I now?" questions right away. It takes a while to find out what works for you.

Lack of Focus

Some people flounder when they do not have the focus of a career. They may wonder about their identity, asking, "Who am I now? Why should I get up on Monday?" As your roles change and your life is no longer organized with work or children you may find that having too many choices is one of your greatest problems.

Idleness

Having time stretching out in front of you like a blank canvas can be intimidating—but it doesn't have to be. Sometimes it is helpful to think of this stage of life as you would look at vacations. What will you do today? What activities would make you feel good about yourself? It is time to do some of those things you regret not having done earlier. If you regret not being there enough as a parent, perhaps you can spend more time with your grandchildren. Perhaps you can attend to friendships that you have let slide. Now there is the time to make intentional choices.

WORKSHEET

Finding the Right Balance

As you move from full-time work to retirement, the balance in how you spend your time will probably change. It may help to visually represent how you divide the pie. Use the circles below to show how you use your time now and how you plan to use your time later. Use whatever categories make sense for you (for example, paid work, unpaid work, daily living, leisure).

Example:

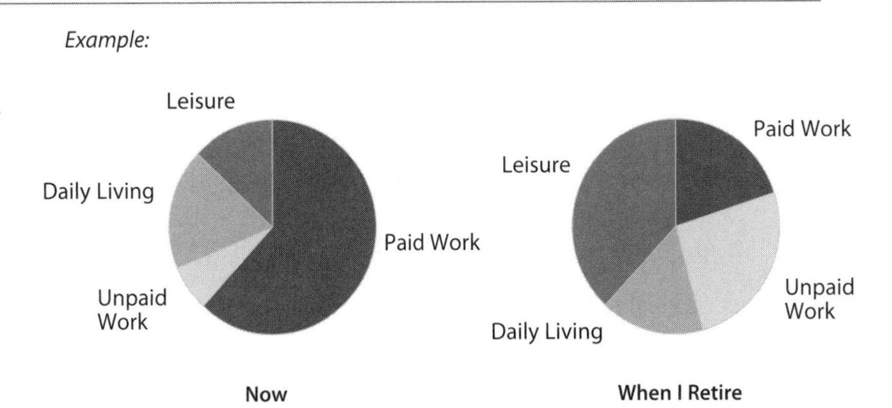

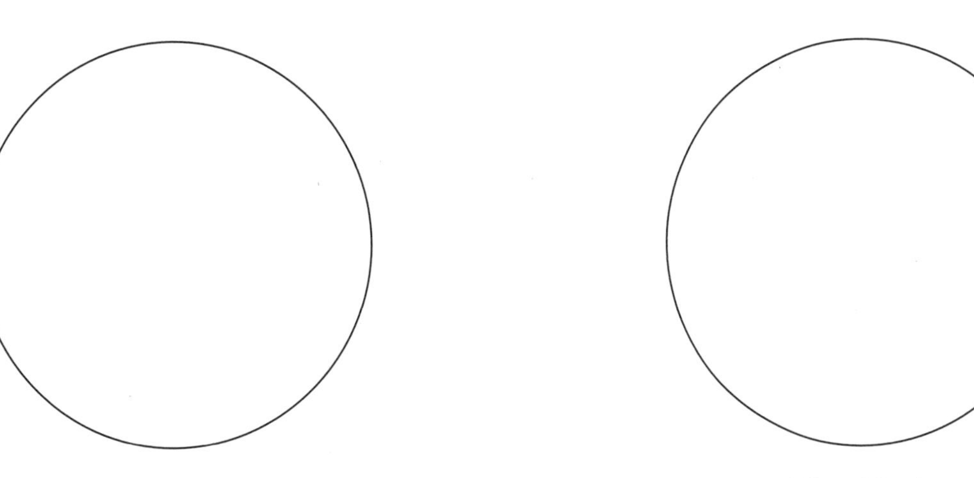

Meaningful Work in Retirement

Almost a quarter of all people between the ages of 65 and 74 are in the workforce, and the percentage is growing. Four out of five employees over 50 say that they will work after traditional retirement age, at least part time, whether for money or enjoyment or both. The good news is that society needs the energy and skills of older workers. Although some large corporations and public institutions are still encouraging early retirements and discouraging older worker hires, human resource managers and volunteer coordinators are beginning to face up to the shortage of mature workers on the horizon.

Our society is going through a change in attitudes about the value of older workers. In 2006, 20 industry associations representing over 5 million businesses organized an alliance to share strategies about how to recruit and retain older, experienced workers (AARP 2006). Retirees have been finding a wealth of opportunities for nontraditional employment that fit the needs of the emerging economy. Many nonprofits are eager for older, mature adults to serve as volunteers.

The predicted labor shortage may play a part in the change. By 2011, when the first boomers turn 65, available jobs could outnumber workers by 4.3 million, and by 2031, that gap could widen to 35 million (Candland 2003). According to a survey of human resource professionals conducted by Deloitte Consulting, baby boomer retirement poses the second-greatest threat to business performance (workers with inadequate skills is first). After years of facing discrimination and layoffs, older workers will soon be courted for expertise. Indeed, the boomer generation is the best educated and most productive generation ever (Civic Ventures 2007).

There is a fertile field for new retirees interested in creating flexible opportunities for meaningful work for themselves and others. Here are some of the options you might consider.

Second Careers

For some, retirement is an opportunity to start a new career. This might be a way to get back to basics or go in a whole new direction. For example, some managers want to divest their supervisory roles as they grow older but hesitate to do so because their pensions may be penalized by a cutback in salary. After retirement, they may find a job doing what they were originally trained for when they started their careers. A hospital administrator goes back to teaching nursing. A workforce center director becomes an employment counselor. With less worry about earning a certain level of income or achieving a level of professional success, some retirees feel the freedom to start new careers that are labors of love.

A number of employers are aggressively recruiting older workers. The Home Depot has participated in a successful pilot program with AARP that steers older workers who enjoy home repair to sales jobs in their stores. Borders bookstores offer health care, dental, and vision benefits to part-time employees working as little as one day a week. The bookseller is also developing a "passport" program that would allow an older worker to work summers in the north and winters in the south. Retirees aren't the only ones who benefit, according to one Borders executive: "We save money by hiring retirees, because our over-50 employee turnover is 10 times less than that for those under 30, and older workers have fewer dependents on their company-provided insurance."

Nontraditional Employment

Retirees are well suited to the creative options available through the growth of nontraditional employment. Workers age 65 and over are actually more likely than younger workers to be engaged in four categories of nontraditional employment:

- Independent contracting (working on a project basis or fee for a particular service rather than as an employee)
- On-call work (such as substitute teachers)
- Temporary work (such as receptionists filling in for sick full-time employees)

- Work provided by contract firms (such as computer programmers working in the office of a customer)

Workers over age 65 are also more likely than younger workers to work part-time. In fact, an estimated one-half of all workers take part-time jobs as they end their full-time working lives—some of them through phased retirement. The likelihood of engaging in home-based work, rather than work outside the home, rises with age. It's common for retirees who become independent contractors to set up offices in the home and take a resulting tax break.

Entrepreneurship

In 1992, the highest percentage of entrepreneurs was between the ages of 25 to 35. Ten years later, the highest percentage of entrepreneurs was between 55 and 65 (U.S. Census Bureau 2002). This statistic suggests that many older workers and new retirees have followed up on their dreams to initiate a new service, open a shop, and lead new programs. Help for business start-ups is available from Service Corps of Retired Executives (SCORE) (*www.score.org*), an organization that provides free and confidential small business advice, and from the Small Business Administration. Entrepreneurship is not limited to for-profit initiatives. Social entrepreneurs develop new products and services that also produce a public good. This is a path with significant potential for retirees.

Volunteering

Many organizations in your community would be delighted with your willingness to assist. Check out your local government or the nonprofit organizations in your neighborhood. Boards, commissions, schools, arts organizations, and children's sports teams are almost always looking for help. If you think you'd like to offer assistance, contact the staff to see if there's a fit.

See chapter 4, "Making a Difference," page 71.

Shifting Interests in Volunteering

When considering the volunteer work they do in retirement, baby boomers tend to have significant expectations. They are looking for:

- **Flexibility.** Most new retirees are not interested in showing up at the same time every week for a long period of time. They want flexibility to travel or to schedule special projects. They want to try out one activity and then go on to another.
- **Opportunities to use their expertise.** Most retirees do not want to perform prescribed tasks over and over again. They prefer to work on a project that makes use of their skills and interests for a specified amount of time. If nothing else, they would like to choose among options for assignments.
- **Ways to work with others.** Many retirees want to volunteer as a team. Working on a volunteer project with a spouse or friends can be a rewarding way to spend time.
- **Signs that they are valued.** Even if they don't receive a paycheck for their efforts, volunteers want to feel they are valued and respected and that their efforts are worthwhile.
- **Innovative incentives.** Volunteers usually receive a plaque and a handshake for their work. Such recognition is a good start, but organizations could offer even better perks to keep valuable volunteers around. New retirees want to see a creative list of incentives, including tax credits, payment for insurance premiums, frequent flyer miles, transportation vouchers, and continuing education.

Organizations that are hungry for volunteers are changing their rules to meet more of these expectations.

Choosing Your Best Path

When Barbara was 56, her husband died unexpectedly, and her entire life changed. She no longer loved her job as an archivist for a major corporation, and with a new understanding of how fragile life is, she was determined to retire sooner rather than later. At 59 $^{1}/_{2}$, when she could tap into her IRA, she retired. However, she didn't have any concrete plans, and to keep busy, Barbara immediately offered to work without pay to archive years of documents that had accumulated in boxes at the local historical society. As expected, she was respected and valued for the unpaid work she did. However, five years later, she realized she hadn't yet allowed herself to explore new territory and seek new opportunities. She was as tied to a schedule as she had been before, only now she wasn't earning any money. Worse, she wasn't having much fun.

Once she got up the courage to truly leave her work, she discovered how delightful real free time could be. In that sixth year, Barbara took three noncredit courses in subjects she had not explored in the past, and she planned out three inexpensive two-week trips. She went to free noon concerts at the local music school, attended art fairs on Fridays when the crowds were small, and even went to movies in the middle of the day. Although she got satisfaction from giving her time to organizations and causes that valued her expertise, she wishes she had realized earlier that she didn't need to work full time in order to retain her identity. Were she to do it all over again, she'd still volunteer her time, but she would have limited it sooner so that she could enjoy all that retirement offered.

Caregiving

Whether it's caring for grandchildren or caring for friends and relatives who are sick or disabled, caregiving is meaningful work with social and economic value for the community.

Caregiving can have psychological, spiritual, and even physical benefits for the caregiver. Allan Luks and Peggy Payne, in *The Healing Power of Doing Good*, say that helping others often gives a "helper's high." They report that helper's high "involves physical sensations that strongly indicate a sharp reduction in stress and a release of the body's natural painkillers, the endorphins. This initial rush is followed by a longer-lasting period of improved emotional well-being." There is also the potential for significant stress.

- **Caring for grandchildren.** Grandparents helping to raise grandkids are increasingly common. Mostly, grandparents provide a few hours of care a week—if they are lucky enough to live near their grandchildren. Men are as likely as women to be involved in this care. Emphasizing the importance of intergenerational learning, several resource organizations provide support for successful grandparenting across the miles that divide many families. The Grandkidsandme Foundation (*www.grandkidsandme.org*) is one example.
- **Caring for the sick and disabled.** Family members, most of whom are women, provide more than 90% of the care provided for the sick and disabled. Caregivers can take advantage of respite care and other assistance. Groups, books, and websites provide support and advice, including ElderCare Online (*www.ec-online.net*).

Finding Opportunities That Match Your Interests

Some retirees are happy spending time on leisure activities for the rest of their lives. Some are focused on starting a business or getting a part-time job even as they process their retirement papers. Most retirees, however, enjoy a time-out for six months or a year and then start looking for additional challenge and meaning. If the following statements reflect how you feel about your retirement, you may be ready to take on new projects.

- One of the best things I can do at this stage is to teach others what I know.
- I would like to apply the skills and knowledge I've acquired over a lifetime to help someone.
- I would love to be part of a movement to make a difference, something bigger than just one person doing his or her best.

Positive and Negative Attributes of Work

These are some of the best benefits people say they get from their work—both paid and unpaid work:

- Feeling appreciated
- Making a useful contribution
- Opportunity to learn and grow
- Co-workers with shared values
- Challenging social interactions
- Flexible schedule
- Good pay
- Pleasant workspace
- Opportunity to use skills
- Structure and expectations

The worst aspects are similarly universal:

- Lack of clarity about job assignments
- Lack of communication about job performance
- Not having the tools or guidance to get the job done
- Office politics that get in the way of productivity

WORKSHEET

Matching My Interests with Work Opportunities

For retirees interested in meaningful work, the task is making the right match. You will want to leave leeway to change your mind. It is an interesting challenge to try to put it all together in a way that satisfies your passion, matches your interests, uses your skills, makes connections with interesting people, helps you learn some new things, and fits your schedule.

1. Think about what you want to do. Why? What? When? Where? With Whom? Map your answers on the worksheet.
2. Draw lines to connect the opportunities that most interest you.
3. Look for an opportunity that combines your first choices.

With Whom?

Example:
Friends and family
People who share my passion for a cause
Community movers and shakers
People on the margins of society

....
....
....
....

Where?

Example:
Within walking or biking distance
Where I already know people
Where I can carpool with neighbors or friends
In a busy, bustling atmosphere or a calm, quiet one
Indoors or outside

....
....
....
....

Example:

To make extra money for travel, hobbies, or basic needs

To use my expertise and skills to mentor or train others

To spend time with others working to achieve goals

To help people who need it

To learn new skills or brush up on old ones

Why?

What?

Example:

Explore something new

Do something with which I'm already familiar

Use the skills I used in previous work

Ideal Opportunity:

When?

Example:

Regular weekly schedule

One-time projects or short-term contracts

Nights only

Challenges to Work after Retirement

Negative Stereotypes

Worker shortages in some fields have opened up a range of work opportunities for retirees (or will in the future). Some potential employers are wary of older workers, but such wariness is generally unfounded. Older workers are, in many ways, a better bet than their younger colleagues. Studies have shown that older workers:

- Learn new technology as quickly as younger workers (if they understand the basics of the equipment)
- Are easier to train because they can rely on similar past experiences to learn
- Take fewer sick days than workers in their 20s
- Have fewer workplace injuries than younger workers
- Stay longer in each job than younger workers
- Have stronger problem-solving abilities
- Have better overall work habits

As is true in any interview for a job, be sure you tell your employer about all of your positive qualities. The interviewer won't take anything for granted.

New Technology

Technological illiteracy is the number one deficiency employers face with older workers. If you plan to apply for a job, get comfortable with a computer and let the employer know you can be trained.

Termination of Older Workers

Employers have traditionally laid off older workers first when they pursue cost cutting, largely because older workers tend to receive higher pay and accrue higher health care costs. This practice will probably continue, but it could be modified if there were changes in health care policies or changes in pension policies that would not penalize lateral moves to lesser-paid jobs in phased retirement plans.

The tide is turning. Employers are beginning to revise policies that have discriminated against older workers. They see the number of baby boomers moving toward retirement, and also see a skills gap between the highly skilled and educated boomer population and incoming young adult workers.

Lack of Professional Development Opportunities

Older workers have often been passed by when it comes to professional development. However, employers are starting to expand education incentives to help with employee retention (even for part-time workers). In return, they will want mature workers to demonstrate their passion for learning, stretching, and doing things better. In *Workforce Crisis*, Ken Dychtwald and coauthors (2006) report that more than ever, professional development with all workers is a business essential. If you wish to participate in development opportunities, it's worth talking about possible alternatives with your employer.

Questions & Answers

Q. Are there surprises I should be prepared for in retirement?

A. Here are some unrealistic beliefs you might run into:

- *Playing golf and bridge and traveling will satisfy indefinitely.* Will you be bored by this routine, eventually? Probably. The process of figuring out how to use your newfound time well will present interesting opportunities for "trial and error" experimentation.

- *You will be eternally grateful because a boss no longer influences what you'll do with your time each day.* It's possible you will instead find yourself floundering. What will you do when you get up? What if you have five hours and no plans?

- *You won't miss your job.* You likely will miss aspects of your work life: the structure, the friendships, the sense of community, the sense of satisfaction and self-esteem (even dignity) that comes from being responsible for a project, for outcomes.

- *You and your partner will enjoy having more time together.* You will have to figure out new patterns, new ways of relating to one another. Repeated discussions will be necessary. What do you want to do together? How much alone time do you need? How much does your partner need? How much time with friends? As always, compromise and conversation will be essential.

- *Your former colleagues will play a major part in your life.* You may visit them at the workplace once or twice, but you'll soon realize that you no longer "belong." Your former colleagues will continue "on the job," but you'll likely find that time spent with them will lessen, dramatically.

Q. I cannot get over feeling guilty for not doing something productive every moment. Any suggestions?

A. You may have struggled to juggle your job and your life at home. The possibility of reading a book during daytime hours, or going to a movie midday during the week, was laughable. A number of recent retirees report that they *still* have a hard time picking up a book, or going to a movie at 11:00 a.m. "There must be something I *should* be doing," they think. "The garage needs organizing, and the refrigerator hasn't had a good cleaning in years. How can I sit here like a sloth, reading while the sun is shining? How can I *spend* money rather than be making it?" In time, the "shoulds" will take their proper place and you will be able to do what you'd like to do, much of the time.

Q. I have a disability. Are there opportunities for me to continue working as I get older?

A. More than 15% of older adults who need and want to be employed are coping with disabilities or with caregiving that keeps them homebound, away from the traditional workplace. Assistive technologies and employer education could expand options for both employment and for volunteering.

continued on page 68

Questions & Answers *continued*

Q. Why should I update my skills?

A. New technologies or processes may act as a barrier to continuing employment or reentering the workforce. Whatever your current status, the future demands technological literacy. Computer literacy courses are available through community education courses, community/technical colleges, and at SeniorNet (*www.seniornet.org*). If you are still employed, ask for time and financial support to update your skills. If you are 62 or older, you may be able to receive special discounts for courses at public colleges and universities.

Q. I am hesitant to start a job or volunteer situation because I am afraid I will lose my flexibility and get trapped in someone else's schedule. Any suggestions?

A. Plan an escape route along with every commitment. Schedule a regular two-way performance review whether you are employed or a volunteer. Move on when it's time. The upcoming labor shortage and the current shortage of volunteers are creating sufficient options that the market is tipped toward retirees exploring new options. Take advantage of the opportunity.

Resources

Work Opportunities

AARP
www.aarp.org/money/careers/findingajob

www.craigslist.org
Craigslist lists local jobs and volunteer opportunities.

www.RetirementJobs.com
Lists job opportunities for people over 50.

U.S. Department of Labor
www.careervoyages.gov
Information about high-growth job opportunities and how to take advantage of them.

Travel

Elderhostel Road Scholar
www.elderhostel.org
Opportunities for educational travel.

Transitions Abroad
www.transitionsabroad.com
Opportunities for work, study, and cultural travel abroad.

Other Resources

Closing Doors, Opening Worlds: Looking beyond the Retirement Horizon
Vern Drilling
Minneapolis, MN: Deaconess Press. 1993.

Creative Planning for the Second Half of Life [Working with Groups]
Burton and Doris Kreitlow
Duluth, MN: Whole Person Associates. 1997.

The Inventurers: Excursions in Life and Career Renewal
Janet Hagberg and Richard Leider
Cambridge, MA: Perseus. 1988.

The Longevity Factor: The New Reality of Long Careers and How It Can Lead to Richer Lives
Lydia Bronte, PhD
New York: HarperPerennial. 1993.

Retire and Thrive: Remarkable People Share Their Creative, Productive and Profitable Retirement Strategies
Robert K. Otterbourg
Washington, DC: Kiplinger Books. 1995.

The ReFirement Workbook
James V. Gambone, PhD, Erica Whittlinger, MBA, and Debby Magnuson
Minneapolis, MN: Personnel Decisions International. 2004.

SeniorNet
www.seniornet.org
Provides adults 50 and over access to and education about computer technology and the Internet.

Service Corps of Retired Executives (SCORE)
www.score.org
Free and confidential small-business advice for entrepreneurs.

U.S. Small Business Administration (SBA)
www.sba.gov
An independent agency of the federal government to aid, counsel, assist, and protect the interests of small businesses.

Vital Aging Network
www.van.umn.edu
Information about employment for seniors and entrepreneurship.

continued on page 70

Resources *continued*

Caregiving

National Alliance for Caregiving
www.caregiving.org

AARP
www.aarp.org/families/caregiving

U.S. Department of Health and Human Services
www.aoa.gov/prof/aoaprog/caregiver/caregiver.asp

National Family Caregivers Association
www.nfcacares.org

The Grandkidsandme Foundation
www.grandkidsandme.org

Volunteer Opportunities and Social Entrepreneurship

(See Resources in chapter 4, "Making a Difference," page 81.)

IN THIS CHAPTER

Chapter 4

Making a Difference

Pursuing goals that improve your community—and the world

THE FIRST DUTY OF A HUMAN BEING IS TO ASSUME THE RIGHT RELATIONSHIP TO SOCIETY—MORE BRIEFLY, TO FIND YOUR REAL JOB, AND DO IT.

—*Charlotte Perkins Gilman, American writer*

Jan Hively
Founder, Vital Aging Network

Julie Roles
Board member,
Civic Organizing Foundation

In retirement, as in all phases of their lives, boomers will have a powerful influence on society. Many boomers say they want to contribute to something beyond themselves—they want to contribute to make a better community or better world. Retirees are in a good position to do just that: they have experience, knowledge, time, energy, and the financial means to help solve problems and improve the quality of people's lives.

There are many ways you can make a contribution to society, but it is wise to consider the ways in which you can have the most impact. The best place to influence is from within the institutions where you are already working, volunteering, or involved.

What Are Your Options?

Acting as a Citizen

In a democracy, everyone—retired or not—has an obligation to be a citizen. The obligation goes beyond voting and paying taxes. It includes acting as a governing member and striving toward the common good.

The common good—what is good for society as a whole—is not easy to know. Reasonable people hold differing views. Citizens must listen to conflicting perspectives, participate in public discussion, come to agreement on the common good, contribute resources to solve problems, and make policies that sustain what is agreed upon as good (Michels 2004). In our society, these skills are neither well developed nor used on a regular basis by the majority of people. But people are increasingly recognizing the need to strengthen our civic infrastructure.

See "Meaningful Work in Retirement," page 60.

A person carries out the role of citizen in the family, in the community, at work, as well as when he or she votes or pay taxes. For instance, within the family a citizen strives to make decisions regarding the use of resources, the relationship to schools, neighbors, government, environment, health care, in the tension between what is good for the individual, the family, the common good, and generations to come.

At work, whether paid or unpaid, a citizen factors in how a decision affects the common good as well as how it affects you and your organization. And you work to develop skills, both in yourself and in others, that build civic capacity. Less visible efforts, like informally mentoring a younger member of a group, are also important.

Acting as a citizen within the institutions and communities with which you are already involved is the best way to make a difference. These are the places where you have authority and you'll have greater influence than in an entirely new arena.

You can have an influence on broader public policy by getting involved in a local or national policy-making group, such as the Minnesota-based Citizens League or Sustainable Seattle; discussing your concerns with elected officials; or writing letters to the editor.

Making a Difference, Whatever You Do

Norman Lear, the producer of the 1970s television program *All in the Family*, talked about his work in a 2006 interview on the PBS program *NOW*. David Brancaccio, the host of the show, noted that all of Lear's programs had an eye toward "mak[ing] the world a slightly better place." Through humor, rather than heavy-handed messages, *All in the Family* tackled a range of difficult, sensitive issues. Lear and those he worked with believed it was their responsibility to make a positive difference in whatever small way they could. "We were parents, we were citizens, we were caring individuals," he said. In those roles, he explained, they cared about doing the right thing, and it affected the decisions they made as writers and actors.

Jobs That Make a Difference

Many retirees use paid work as a platform for making a difference. This might be working in a nonprofit you believe in or starting a second career in a whole new field. There are plenty of opportunities for full-time and part-time work. A business executive may turn her energies to running an organization that helps underprivileged youth. A mortgage banker may plan a second career as a nurse working with South African AIDS patients. Your new paid work may be closely linked to your career—a teacher may decide to tutor underprivileged students in retirement; a construction manager may agree to consult for a Habitat for Humanity affiliate.

Using Skills and Talents to Make a Difference

Bill spent his career in international business, and when he left his job, he was interested in pursuing volunteer projects. Not long after his retirement, he learned of the Solar Oven Society (SOS), an organization that helps provide solar-powered ovens to some of the billions of people in the world who don't have sufficient fuel to cook their meals. He was intrigued and volunteered to share the expertise he'd gained during his career to help the organization achieve its mission.

Using his international business experience, Bill created a marketing plan and implemented it. He also developed a commercial arm of the organization in order to create a steady income stream to sustain SOS.

Bill's skills have been instrumental in helping SOS to improve the lives of people in the poorest regions in the world.

Volunteering and Other Unpaid Work

The Corporation for National and Community Service estimates the value of contributions by volunteers in America at $147.6 billion annually. This is a huge category of giving that includes activities as varied as delivering Meals on Wheels to serving on a nonprofit board of directors.

The diversity of opportunities for volunteers is enormous. Whether you want to do small tasks like stuffing envelopes or substantial work like helping shape the mission and goals of nonprofit organizations, you can find a situation that fits your desires. Organizations are learning how to engage volunteers in ways that take advantage of their capabilities and provide meaningful and fulfilling experiences for both the organization and the individual.

Many organizations are not there yet. In order to get what you're looking for, you may need to push for changes. As organizations begin to adapt to changing demographics, they will increasingly see the value of having smart, diligent volunteers in their ranks who have a sincere interest in their mission and goals—and who have innovative ideas to address the missions of the organizations. David Eisner, chief executive of the Corporation for National and Community Service, has said he is looking forward to the time when nonprofits find volunteers to develop their strategic plans and hire people to do lower-cost clerical work. The baby boomers—and their determined efforts—will be the greatest motivator of this change.

See "Volunteering," page 62.

A New Approach to Using Volunteers

RSVP, a federally funded Senior Corps program, allows volunteers to decide when, where, and for how long they will serve; they also receive travel reimbursement. Volunteers are invited to focus on a prime impact area that matches their passion (environment, ESL, literacy, hunger), and they receive training and resources to improve the return on their investment of time and energy.

Passing the Baton to the Next Generation

The literal meaning of "retirement" is to pull back. While no one expects baby boomers to fade into the background anytime soon, the concept of pulling back is useful in thinking about how one generation makes room for the next.

One of the most useful and rewarding roles to take up is mentoring. As a mentor you make room, offer wisdom, and teach what you know. Passing on what you know builds the capacity of those who follow you and can help to form your legacy.

Civic Leadership

A civic leader has a vision of what can be and takes action to make those aspirations real. You can be a civic leader as a volunteer, as a business leader, as an elected official, as a retired person. A civic leader organizes others to get the power needed to influence the direction of the community. Use the worksheet "Where Can I Have Influence in My Community?" on pages 78–79 to get your thinking going.

Social Entrepreneurship

A social entrepreneur takes civic leadership a step further. A social entrepreneur takes notice of a social problem, comes up with a solution, and implements the solution with an organized business plan. These entrepreneurs are often highly experienced professionals who combine a desire to make a better world with the discipline of a businessperson. The Skoll Foundation, whose mission is to invest in social entrepreneurs, defines a social entrepreneur as a "pioneer of innovations that benefit humanity."

Growing Gardens, Nurturing Community

Theresa was an avid gardener, and she often shared her passion for the activity with others. When she retired, she was eager to have more time to spend in her own gardens, but she also wanted to give others the opportunity to learn about the benefits of gardening. When a plot of empty land went up for sale in a nearby neighborhood, Theresa got a grant from the city to help her purchase it, and she developed it into a community garden. For a minimal fee, anyone can get a small section of the garden to grow flowers, fruits, and vegetables. The garden is especially popular with apartment dwellers and retirees, and cross-generational friendships have formed as the plot owners work side by side throughout the growing season.

The communal gardeners aren't the only ones who benefit: the splash of color has been a beautiful addition to the neighborhood.

WORKSHEET

How Will I Contribute?

Find opportunities that engage your passion, match your interests, use your skills, make connections with interesting people, allow you to learn new things, and fit your schedule.

1. Think about how you want to contribute. Why? What? When? Where? With Whom? Map your answers on the worksheet.
2. Draw lines to connect the opportunities that most interest you.
3. Look for an opportunity that combines your first choices.

With Whom?

Example:

Demographic (your family, older adults, mixed-age group, learners)

Size (large group, small team, by yourself)

Where?

Example:

In the institutions where I already have a role

Location (Latin America, national park, Scout camp, around the corner)

Atmosphere (indoors or outdoors, in an office or community center, in your own home)

Example:

To express gratitude to an organization that has helped you or your family (hospital, cancer association, school, library)

To help people who need help (the homeless, immigrants, shut-ins)

To make things better in the world—build a sustainable community (park trails, housing, small-business development)

Why?

What?

Example:

Use special skills (tennis, accounting, photography, driving, talking with people)

Ideal Way to Contribute:

When?

Example:

Timing (one morning/afternoon a week, evenings, weekends, one or two weeks at a time)

Flexibility (on call, prescheduled regular, or now and then)

WORKSHEET

Where Can I Have Influence in My Community?

Are you interested in providing civic leadership in a bigger way? Use this list to evaluate your community's assets and how you might contribute to a stronger community.

In the first column, mark (✗) your personal priorities. In the second column, evaluate your community's assets. Where is your community strong? Where is it weak? Which of your high-priority assets are weak or lacking? For the items that you marked *Very Important,* make notes in the third column about the specific needs/issues that should be addressed.

	How Important Is This to Me?		Community Strength or Weakness?		What Are the Needs or Issues?
	Not Important	Very Important	Very Weak	Very Strong	
Quality of Life					
Intergenerational interaction	●	●	●	●	
Civic infrastructure	●	●	●	●	
Educational opportunities	●	●	●	●	
Access to the Internet	●	●	●	●	
Creative arts activities	●	●	●	●	
Community respect	●	●	●	●	
Parks and recreation	●	●	●	●	
Other:	●	●	●	●	
Housing Options					
Both renters and owners	●	●	●	●	
Affordable	●	●	●	●	
Accessible	●	●	●	●	
Community activities/services	●	●	●	●	
Assisted living	●	●	●	●	
Long-term care	●	●	●	●	
Other:	●	●	●	●	
Services Supporting Independence					
Transportation	●	●	●	●	
Housekeeping and yard work	●	●	●	●	
Home rehab and repair	●	●	●	●	
Home health care	●	●	●	●	
Access to service information	●	●	●	●	
Telephone/e-mail capacity	●	●	●	●	
Other:	●	●	●	●	

Where Can I Have Influence in My Community? *continued*

	How Important Is This to Me?		Community Strength or Weakness?		What Are the Needs or Issues?
	Not Important	Very Important	Very Weak	Very Strong	
Food and Nutrition					
Food shelves					
Community gardens					
Home-delivered groceries and meals					
Group meals					
Nutrition education					
Other:					
Security (Personal, Economic, Financial)					
Feeling safe at home					
Feeling safe in the neighborhood					
Employment opportunities					
Social services					
Financial and legal services					
Other:					
Health Care					
Affordable health care					
Physical, mental, spiritual activities					
Respite care for caregivers					
Hospice					
Other:					
Other Areas					

Consider how you might make a positive difference in areas that are important to you.

1. Make a list of some of the initial steps you could take to help improve these areas of your community. For example, if you know of other communities that have successfully addressed these needs, think about how they've done so. How might you replicate their efforts—or adapt what they've already done?
2. Do you need to do more research? Where can you get the information you need?
3. Who else might be interested in this area? Who could be an ally? How could you generate interest in this topic among your friends or other community members?
4. Where can you get the resources you will need? Can you write grants? Get government funding? Use your own resources?

(Adapted from Vital Aging Network)

Questions & Answers

Q. Is the Peace Corps an option for adults?

A. Yes. The Peace Corps welcomes volunteers of all ages, even into their 80s. They have found that the experience and maturity of older volunteers are of great value. Check out *www.peacecorps.gov* for information. Here's another option to consider: a few years ago two former Peace Corps volunteers founded Peace Corps Encore (*www.peacecorpsencore.org*), a nonprofit that places former Peace Corps volunteers in short-term overseas assignments.

Q. I have done the "How Will I Contribute" exercise, and I have found the perfect way for me to contribute. Can you give me some pointers for how to approach the executive director about my idea so that I can make it happen?

A. Start with an informational interview. Find out where the organization is trying to go and what its vexing problems are. Once you understand what they need, find the fit. How can you help meet their needs and still meet your criteria? If they see that you have their interests in mind, most organizations will be open to making it work.

Resources

AmeriCorps
www.americorps.org
The domestic Peace Corps.

Civic Ventures
www.civicventures.org
Civic Ventures is a nonprofit organization that is redefining retirement in terms of social and individual renewal. Its website offers the following resources:

- *The New Face of Work* survey documents the desire for meaningful work after age 50
- *Still Working* chronicles the experience of individuals moving into post-midlife careers in education, health care, and the nonprofit sector
- *The Boomers Guide to Good Work: An Introduction to Jobs That Make a Difference* provides options and tips for those looking to apply their experience
- *Realizing an Experience Dividend: Helping the Longevity Revolution Add Up for America*

Corporation for National and Community Service
www.cns.gov
Information about how to engage in service to help strengthen communities. Includes searchable databases for volunteer opportunities.

Experience Corps
www.experiencecorps.org
National program to mobilize the time, talent, and experience of older adults in service to communities. The initial focus has been connecting older adults with children and youth.

Faith in Action
www.fiavolunteers.org
National volunteer movement that helps the aging and chronically ill maintain their independence. The website contains a searchable database that lists programs by state.

Global Volunteer
www.globalvolunteer.org
An organization that matches volunteers with opportunities to work on education, environmental and community aid projects around the world.

Habitat for Humanity
www.habitat.org
A nonprofit organization that helps volunteers build new homes for low-income families all over the United States.

National Senior Service Corps
www.seniorcorps.org
A network of three projects (Foster Grandparent Program, Senior Companion Program, and Retired Senior Volunteer Program). The website posts openings for volunteers, with links to all 50 states. The organization also connects seniors with information about various topics, including education, computers, grants, and volunteering opportunities.

The Points of Light Foundation
www.pointsoflight.org
A nonprofit organization that promotes volunteering and community service through their network of more than 500 volunteer centers across the United States.

Prime Time: How Baby Boomers Will Revolutionize Retirement and Transform America
Marc Freedman
Cambridge, MA: Public Affairs Books. 1999.

continued on page 82

Resources *continued*

Red Cross Volunteers
www.redcross.org
Volunteer opportunities in transportation, disaster relief, health and safety, youth, support, and blood services.

The Skoll Foundation
www.skollfoundation.org
Information about social entrepreneurialism.

Volunteer Match
www.volunteermatch.org
A site that posts listings of volunteer opportunities across the nation that can be viewed by state, agency, or type of service.

Volunteers of America
www.voa.org
Provides access to diverse volunteer opportunities in communities across the nation.

WORKSHEET

Action Plan for Living Your Life

Are you moving in the right direction to achieve your goals? To help you think about the changes you might want to make, mark (✗) the following on the scale between *No Change Needed* to *Needs Immediate Attention.*

LIVING YOUR LIFE	No Change Needed		Needs Immediate Attention
Chapter 1 – Embracing What Matters			
Knowing what matters to me	●	···········	●
Having purpose in my life	●	···········	●
Leaving a legacy	●	···········	●
Chapter 2 – Building Strong Relationships			
Building my social network	●	···········	●
Strengthening relationships with family and friends	●	···········	●
Being part of a community	●	···········	●
Relocating to another city or state	●	···········	●
Chapter 3 – Using Your Time			
Exploring new options for spending my time	●	···········	●
Using my skills, talents, and experience	●	···········	●
Learning something new	●	···········	●
Spending more time in activities I enjoy	●	···········	●
Managing my time	●	···········	●
Doing meaningful work after I retire	●	···········	●
Finding opportunities that match my interests	●	···········	●
Chapter 4 – Making a Difference			
Developing my civic capacity	●	···········	●
Making a difference in my community and the world	●	···········	●

Action Plan for Living Your Life *continued*

What are my retirement goals for living my life? Write your goals here and on "My Retirement Map" on pages 10–11.

What barriers do I need to overcome to achieve my goals?

What am I going to do to achieve my goals? Use the action steps worksheet on the next page to write down the steps and track your progress.

WORKSHEET

Action Steps Worksheet – Goal #1

Steps I Am Going to Take	Target Completion Date	My Progress	Notes
		started complete!	
		started complete!	
		started complete!	
		started complete!	
		started complete!	
		started complete!	
		started complete!	

WORKSHEET

Action Steps Worksheet – Goal #2

Steps I Am Going to Take	Target Completion Date	My Progress	Notes
		started complete!	
		started complete!	
		started complete!	
		started complete!	
		started complete!	
		started complete!	
		started complete!	

Part 2

Maintaining Your Health

Although health is an area we can influence, people often take good health for granted. The choices and decisions you make about what you eat, how often you exercise, and whether you get regular checkups have an effect on the quality of your life.

We often assume an adverse relationship between the quality of our health and aging. While the aging process affects our bodies in many ways, aging does not necessarily mean deterioration in health.

As you consider your physical and mental well-being, you may find there are changes you would like to make to enhance it.

The chapters in this section include:

- **Staying Healthy.** Your day-to-day activities and habits have a major impact on your body and mind. Even small changes can influence your health significantly.
- **Eating for Life.** A good diet improves health. Choosing a good balance of nutritious foods and eating moderately is a key to maintaining a healthy body and weight.

- **Keeping Strong, Fit, and Active.** Cardiovascular exercises and strength training are essential to physical well-being. Exercising regularly will help you stay healthy and independent.
- **Maintaining Mental Fitness.** Good mental health is as important as physical fitness—and it's essential to your well-being. Knowing how the brain works and how to improve your mental health will give you the tools to stay sharp.
- **Creating Your Health Care Team.** You will get better health care if you know what you want and seek it out. With information and resources, you can work with your health care providers to make informed choices and take control of your care.
- **Finding Nontraditional Paths to Health.** Nontraditional therapies and healing practices are increasingly popular additions to conventional care. You need good information to make wise and informed choices.

IN THIS CHAPTER

Chapter 5

Staying Healthy

Establishing healthy habits and preventing disease and accidents

GOOD HEALTH AND GOOD SENSE ARE TWO OF LIFE'S GREATEST BLESSINGS.

—*Publilus Syrus, first-century B.C.E. Roman writer*

Susan Bradley
Health writer

Healthy lifestyle habits and good working relationships with your medical providers increase your chances of enjoying good health, the basis of a successful, productive retirement. Enjoying good health in later years means establishing good habits now. It is never too late to improve your health.

Good health comes from a combination of genetic, environmental, and lifestyle factors. While you can't change your family's medical history or completely control your environment, you can adopt lifestyle practices that promote health and well-being. One estimate suggests that 70% of how well you age is determined by factors you can control (Schneider and Miles 2003). Preventing disease and accidents can make the difference between "getting by" and enjoying a full and rewarding retirement.

Strengthening Healthy Habits

Eat a Healthy Diet and Exercise Regularly

The benefits of eating a healthy diet and getting regular exercise are discussed in detail elsewhere in the workbook. Diet and exercise are important factors in maintaining a healthy body weight. Two-thirds of American adults are overweight. Excess weight contributes to serious health problems, including high blood pressure, diabetes, coronary artery disease, and stroke (Mayo Clinic 2007). A person who eats well and stays active is usually healthier and has a better self-image and a more positive outlook on life.

See chapter 6, "Eating for Life," page 105, and chapter 7, "Keeping Strong, Fit, and Active," page 123.

Manage Stress

Stress is a two-edged sword in modern life. "Good stress," such as hosting a party or preparing for a holiday, can enrich your life and help you feel good about accomplishing something meaningful to you. For many people, a manageable amount of stress improves productivity and adds excitement to our otherwise mundane days. Intense or prolonged stress, however, can cause physical, mental, and emotional problems. Physical problems may include back and neck problems, headaches, indigestion, reduction in immune responses, high blood pressure, and coronary heart disease. Emotionally, stress may cause you to become anxious, angry, depressed, or have trouble sleeping. Mental problems may include difficulty remembering or concentrating, and stress can trigger poor lifestyle choices such as overeating, excessive drinking, or smoking.

Stress can result from many factors, including major life events, minor inconveniences, strained relations with others, poor lifestyle choices, and even environmental factors. None of us has the ability to control all the potentially stress-inducing factors in our lives. We can, however, control how we react to stress so that we minimize its negative effects. In addition to directly addressing the cause of your stress, you can benefit from eating nutritious foods, exercising regularly, limiting caffeine, and getting adequate sleep. Building time into your schedule to relax and to do activities you enjoy can also help you manage stress. If your stress is taking too great a toll on your well-being, you may want to consider seeking professional help (Cohen 2000).

See "Reduce Stress," page 50.

Get Enough Sleep

There are obvious benefits of regular rest—you feel energetic, think more clearly, and look your best. Research evidence has found that adequate sleep is essential to your health. It boosts your immune system, so it can ward off disease and infection. In one study, males (ages 22–61) who were kept awake from 3:00 to 6:00 a.m. had reduced levels of T cells (white blood cells that help the body fight infection) (Claflin 1998).

The human growth hormone (HGH) responsible for increasing bone strength, promoting muscle mass, and discouraging the storage of fat is secreted during the deepest phase of sleep. HGH levels are highest during adolescence and decline as people get older and spend less time in this phase of sleep. There is evidence to suggest that sleeping enough to maintain adequate levels of HGH slows the aging process (Schneider and Miles 2003).

Other studies have found a link between sleep and lifespan. Results show that people who sleep fewer than four hours or more than nine hours per night die sooner than people who sleep between four and nine hours (Komaroff 2005). One six-year study found that men who slept an average of four hours per night were three times more likely to have died during the study than the men who got more sleep.

A person's need for sleep usually stays constant throughout adulthood. A middle-aged person who feels rested after six hours of sleep will likely find six hours adequate during retirement. Older people often get tired earlier in the evening and wake earlier in the morning (Creagan 2001).

Sometimes, in spite of your intention to get proper rest, sleep just won't come. Menopausal women can experience hot flashes and frequent awakenings. In later years, sleep for both men and women can be compromised by health conditions, side effects of medication, more frequent bathroom visits, and circadian rhythms that cause more daytime sleepiness and nighttime wakefulness. If you are troubled by insomnia, try the following behavioral strategies before reaching for a sleeping pill:

- Go to bed! Don't wait until you fall asleep in a chair. Reserve your bed for sleeping, not reading or watching television.
- Reduce distracting noise and consider using "white noise" such as a fan or quiet music.
- Limit or avoid daytime naps.
- Avoid stimulants such as caffeine and nicotine past early afternoon.
- Finish vigorous exercise at least five hours before bedtime.
- Avoid eating or drinking close to bedtime so that you won't need to get up to use the bathroom. (Creagan 2001; Schneider and Miles 2003)

Are You Getting Enough Sleep?

- Do you feel tired when you wake up?
- Do you fall asleep immediately when going to bed?
- Are you sleepy during the day, especially when sitting down to do a quiet activity?
- Do you fall asleep during the evening before your normal bedtime?
- Do you find your energy level is lower than usual?

If you answer yes to any of these questions, your body probably needs more sleep.

(Claflin 1998; Schneider and Miles 2003)

Get Regular Dental Care

Good dental care is a partnership between you (regular brushing, flossing, and limiting exposure to sweet foods and beverages) and your dentist (checking for cavities, giving regular fluoride treatments, and assessing tooth and gum condition). Your dentist can let you know about issues that come up or change as you age.

Gum health is critically important as people age because infected gums can cause tooth loss or systemic bacterial infection. Poorly fitting dentures can damage gums and cause infection. In the worst-case scenario, bacteria from the mouth can travel to the heart and damage the heart valves. Many dentists prescribe prophylactic antibiotics for older patients even for something as minor as teeth cleaning.

Teeth can develop hairline cracks (microcracks) that may become visible. It is also normal for teeth to darken and yellow as the enamel layer wears down and the nerves that nourish teeth diminish (Claflin 1998). Professionally applied or home bleaching agents may improve appearance. Check your insurance coverage before having dental work done.

Take Care of Your Skin

The National Institute on Aging (2005) offers the following advice on taking care of your skin.

- **Dry skin and itching.** There are many causes for dry, itchy skin: overheating in the winter and air-conditioning in the summer; the loss of sweat and oil glands as you age; soaps, antiperspirants, perfumes, or hot baths; dehydration; sun exposure; smoking; or stress. If your skin is uncomfortably dry and itchy, see a doctor. It can affect your sleep or be a symptom of diabetes or kidney disease.

- **Skin cancer.** It is estimated that 40–50% of Americans who live to age 65 will have skin cancer at least once. UV radiation from the sun is the main cause of skin cancer. Anyone can get skin cancer, but the risk is greatest for people who have fair skin that freckles easily.

  All skin cancers can be cured if they are brought to a doctor's attention before they have a chance to spread. Check your skin regularly and see a doctor if any symptom lasts longer than two weeks. The most common warning sign of skin cancer is a change on the skin, especially a new growth or a sore that doesn't heal. Skin cancers don't all look the same and seldom cause pain.

  Remember that UV rays are the strongest between 10 a.m. and 3 p.m. and that harmful rays can pass through clouds and water. Use a sunscreen with an SPF of 15 or higher that is broad spectrum (protects against both UVA and UVB rays) and water resistant. Reapply the lotion as needed. Wear a hat with a wide brim. Look for sunglasses that block at least 99% of the sun's rays. Wear loose, lightweight, long-sleeved shirts and long pants or long skirts.

- **Shingles.** Shingles is an outbreak of a painful rash or blisters caused by the virus that causes chicken pox. The virus lies dormant in the system and can reappear years later as shingles. It is most common in people over age 50, but anyone who has had chicken pox can get shingles. Signs of shingles include burning or shooting pain and tingling or itching, usually on one side of the body or face. A rash appears as a band or patch of raised dots on the side of the trunk or face and develops into small blisters. If you suspect you have shingles, see a doctor right away. Immediate treatment can reduce the length and severity of an attack and may prevent painful aftereffects.

- **Bruising.** Many older people get more bruises, especially on their arms and legs, because the skin becomes thinner with age and sun damage. Loss of fat and connective tissue weakens the support around blood vessels, making them more susceptible to injury. Some bruising is caused by medications or illness. If unexplained bruising occurs, see a doctor.

Keep Your Feet Healthy

Untreated foot problems can impair mobility and lead to significant problems, and the risk of foot problems increases as you age. Problems are caused by circulatory diseases like diabetes, poorly fitting footwear, thinning of the skin and the padding of the feet, foot deformities, and increased susceptibility to infection. To keep your feet healthy, wash, dry, and apply lotion every day; regularly trim nails (cutting straight across and filing off any sharp corners); wear properly fitting, comfortable shoes; and check for cracks, dryness, or ingrown toenails.

Check with your doctor if you have pain; swelling; changes in skin color; deep cracks or breaks in the skin; red streaks; tingling, numbness, or other changes in sensation; or ingrown toenails (Mosby Consumer Health 1997).

Minimizing Unhealthy Habits

Unhealthy habits can undermine your well-being in retirement. This section looks at the harmful effects of addictions and compulsive behavior.

Stop Smoking

If you smoke, the most important lifestyle change is to quit. By doing so, you reduce your risk of stroke; coronary heart disease; chronic obstructive pulmonary disease; asthma; ulcers; peripheral vascular disease; and cancer of the lung, larynx, bladder, pancreas, cervix, esophagus, and mouth; and you arrest (though not reverse) the development of emphysema (Fries 1999; Komaroff 2005).

You will also save money, set a good example, reduce your risk of fire, have a cleaner home and car, and improve relations with people who do not wish to breathe your smoke. As difficult as it may be to quit, there really isn't one good reason why you should continue smoking.

Treat Alcohol Dependency

An estimated 14 million (1 in 13) adults in the United States have problems with alcohol (Cohen 2000), ranging from excessive drinking (causing negative consequences at work, at home, and/or in their community) to dependence (an inability to stop drinking despite negative consequences). Chronic alcohol use is related to cirrhosis of the liver; cardiomyopathy; chronic gastritis; coronary artery disease; high blood pressure; stroke; kidney disease; cancer of the mouth, esophagus, pharynx, larynx, and liver; decreased pancreas function; impotence; and mental impairment (Cohen 2000; Schneider and Miles 2003; Upton and Graber 1993). Alcohol abuse affects work performance, strains relationships with family and friends, and increases the risk of injury from impaired driving, falls, and other accidents.

Eliminate Drug Abuse

Abusing prescription medicines can cause as many problems as using illegal drugs. Some prescription drugs are highly addictive, and overuse can lead to mental impairment and dangerous medical conditions. There is also an increased risk of reactions to other prescription drugs. If you are taking medication past the point of your doctor's recommendation or if drug use is compromising your well-being or your relationships with others, tell your physician.

WORKSHEET

I Want to Quit!

Your responses below will help you make a plan to quit smoking that works for you.

Three reasons why I smoke:

1. ______
2. ______
3. ______

Three reasons why I want to quit smoking:

1. ______
2. ______
3. ______

Three behaviors or activities I will need to change to quit:

1. ______
2. ______
3. ______

The method(s) I plan to use to quit:

______ "Cold turkey" (quitting on my own without medical or group support)
______ Participating in a smoking cessation program
______ Contacting a telephone quitline
______ Using nicotine replacement therapy
______ Using drugs prescribed by my doctor to assist me in quitting
______ Other (list here) ______

Three friends or family members who will encourage me and hold me accountable as I quit smoking:

1. ______
2. ______
3. ______

Three steps I need to take (locate a nearby smoking cessation program, remove ashtrays from my home and car, etc.) before quitting and when I will do them:

1. ______ by ______(date)
2. ______ by ______(date)
3. ______ by ______(date)

The date I am going to become a nonsmoker:

______

Is Alcohol Affecting My Life?

- Have you ever felt a strong need to consume alcohol? ☐ yes ☐ no
- Do you drink alone more often now than you once did? ☐ yes ☐ no
- Have others criticized your drinking habits or said you have a problem? ☐ yes ☐ no
- Have you ever had difficulty stopping an episode of drinking once you start? ☐ yes ☐ no
- Have you experienced negative consequences because of your drinking? ☐ yes ☐ no
- Have you ever hurt yourself or someone else while you were drunk? ☐ yes ☐ no
- Have you ever had nausea, sweating, shakiness, headaches, or anxiety after an episode of heavy drinking? ☐ yes ☐ no
- Do you need to drink more than you used to in order to get drunk? ☐ yes ☐ no

If you answered yes to two or more of these questions, you may be at risk of alcohol abuse. You can talk to your doctor confidentially and ask for information about appropriate treatment services.

(Cohen 2000; Komaroff 2005)

Working with Your Health Care Provider

Good working relationships with your health care providers are an important part of staying on top of your health. By keeping up-to-date with checkups, immunizations, and screening procedures, you and your doctor can keep your body working at its best.

- **Be informed.** Educate yourself by reading books, magazines, newspapers, and websites. Your doctor can provide better help and information if you are knowledgeable about maintaining your health and avoiding disease.
- **Know what's normal.** Give concrete information about the how, when, and where of your symptoms. A vague report that "something doesn't seem right" is less useful than a specific account of how things are now compared to how they used to be. One person might find it normal to have several headaches per week, but for you, that may represent a change that needs attention.
- **Follow through.** Follow the instructions and advice given by your physician. While it is well within your rights to question a doctor's advice or to seek a second opinion, you should have enough confidence in your provider to follow the regimen prescribed for you. You will not fully benefit from your doctor's advice if you follow it haphazardly or not at all.
- **Monitor your health.** Schedule periodic visits for the purpose of monitoring your health apart from specific problems you may be having. *Mayo Clinic on Healthy Aging* suggests you should have a routine medical examination four times in your 40s, five times in your 50s, and yearly in your 60s (Creagan 2001).
- **Don't procrastinate.** Some people put off doctor visits for fear of what the doctor will find. It is always wiser to face a problem before it becomes too advanced to be treated successfully. A visit to the doctor may bring unwelcome news, but it's better to confront it than to live in worry about what might be going on.

See chapter 9, "Creating Your Health Care Team," page 147.

These Symptoms Require Immediate Medical Attention

- *Fatigue* lasting more than one week without a known cause.
- *Cough* lasting more than 10 days, particularly with thick phlegm.
- *Pain* in a specific area lasting more than five days without a known reason.
- *Chest pain* or a heavy feeling in your chest, left shoulder, or jaw: seek emergency care.
- *Blood* in rectum, stool, urine, or phlegm.
- *Lump or bump* that lasts more than a week.
- *Mole* that appears suddenly, changes color, bleeds, or itches.
- *Weight loss* without trying to lose weight.
- *Headaches* in greater frequency or intensity than normal.
- *Signs of stroke* such as numbness or tingling: seek emergency care.

(Creagan and Wendel 2003)

Screening and Testing for Early Detection

Screening

Many tools are available to identify disease risks and recognize early signs of problems. In the past, many people only learned of their coronary artery disease upon their first (perhaps fatal) heart attack. Now diagnostic tests identify problems and allow for corrective, lifesaving interventions.

A screening test should be able to detect diseases that have a possible course of treatment and for which early intervention can lessen suffering or reduce mortality (Margolis 2002). Before a screening test, understand what the test will tell you, whether it is covered by your insurance plan, whether there are any risks or side effects, and whether you need to do anything to prepare for it (Mosby Consumer Health 1997).

Evidence supports screening for coronary heart disease, diabetes, glaucoma, hearing loss, thyroid disease, colorectal cancer, skin cancer, breast and cervical cancer (women), and prostate cancer (men) (Creagan and Wendel 2003).

Self-Examination

While you may rightfully feel that you are not an expert about what to look for, people can and do locate tumors and other problems before health care providers find them. The most common self-assessments are monthly breast exams for women, monthly testicular examinations for men, and regular skin examinations for men and women.

Home Tests

Two common home tests let you check your total cholesterol and blood glucose levels. Unfortunately, the cholesterol test does not distinguish between "good" (HDL) cholesterol and "bad" (LDL). Your doctor should test your cholesterol periodically to get a more thorough profile. Many people with diabetes or blood sugar issues use blood glucose tests. A urine test is less expensive but also less accurate. If your blood pressure is a concern, you can monitor it at home or in pharmacies and stores with pressure cuff monitors (Reader's Digest 2001).

Cancer Detection

The good news on the cancer front is that even the most fatal cancers (lung, breast, colon, and prostate, which together account for more than half of all cancer deaths in the United States) are often curable if detected early (Creagan and Wendel 2003). With the exception of lung cancer, screening tests for these and other cancers are available and hold great promise for early detection. Lung cancer, the leading cause of cancer death for both men and women, is still hard to diagnose early and to treat effectively (Creagan and Wendel 2003).

Health Testing

Are you up-to-date on routine testing? If you have a family history of a condition or are at particular risk, you may need more frequent monitoring.

Test	How Often?	I'm Up-to-Date	Needs Attention
Blood pressure	Every 2 years (more often for those with identified high blood pressure)		
Lipid profile (fasting)	Every 5 years for adults over age 20		
Blood glucose	Every 3 years after age 45		
Thyroid function	Every 5 years after age 35		
Fecal occult blood test	Annually after age 50		
Colonoscopy	Every 3 to 5 years after age 50; digital rectal exam: same interval		
Bone density X-ray	Once for menopausal women or as advised per risk factors		
Skin cancer	Annually after age 40		
Visual acuity	Annually after age 65		
Hearing exam	As indicated		
Glaucoma	Every 2 years after age 50 for whites and 40 for African Americans; annually after age 65		
Dental exam	Every six months		
Men: PSA/rectal exam	Annually after age 50		
Women: Pap/pelvic exam	Annually until three consecutive normal results are obtained; after that at physician's discretion		
Clinical breast exam	Annually starting at age 40 (can be less frequent after 70)		
Mammography	Annually starting at age 40 (unless indicated earlier)		

(Creagan and Wendel 2003; Margolis 2002; Reader's Digest 2001)

Early Detection Stops Colon Cancer in Its Tracks

When she turned 50, Mary Ann's doctor told her it was time to get a baseline colonoscopy. She made a mental note to make the appointment but never got around to it. She had always been quite healthy, and while she had good intentions, she kept putting it off for the future.

Five years later, she knew something was wrong when she found blood in her stool. Tests showed colon cancer. She required major surgery to remove the cancer and a portion of her colon. Mary Ann learned that she was lucky—colon cancer is one of the deadliest cancers when it is not caught early. A routine colonoscopy can make all the difference: it is very effective at early diagnosis, and precancerous polyps are removed as a part of the procedure before they cause problems. If she had done the colonoscopy five years earlier, she would not have needed surgery.

Getting Immunizations

Vaccinations are not just for children. An important part of staying healthy is keeping current with immunizations recommended for middle-aged and older adults:

- **Tetanus/diphtheria.** Vaccinations for tetanus and diphtheria are usually given in the same shot. You should get a booster shot every 10 years (or perhaps sooner if traveling to undeveloped areas). If you suffer a deep puncture wound and your booster is more than five years old, get a new booster within two days.
- **Hepatitis B.** Hepatitis B is usually transmitted through contaminated body fluids. People whose job or lifestyle puts them at higher risk of infection, or who travel to undeveloped areas, should receive three shots over a six-month period for lifetime protection.
- **Hepatitis A.** Hepatitis A is a viral infection of the liver contracted mostly through infected food or water. Travelers to undeveloped areas or people with liver disease or blood-clotting disorders should be immunized with two shots at least six months apart.
- **Influenza.** A flu shot is recommended annually for people over age 50, especially those with chronic diseases like asthma or emphysema.
- **Pneumonia.** Immunization against bacterial pneumonia is recommended for anyone over age 65 and for younger adults with chronic medical conditions. A shot given after age 65 lasts a lifetime, but people first immunized before age 65 should get a booster after six years. Immunization does not protect against viral pneumonia.
- **Chicken pox.** Adult chicken pox can cause brain inflammation, high fever, and nerve damage. If you have never had chicken pox, get a blood test and get vaccinated if needed. Talk to your doctor if you have never been vaccinated for (nor had) measles, mumps, or rubella. (Margolis 2002; Reader's Digest 2001)

Preventing Injuries

In the truest sense of the word, "prevention" means structuring your behaviors and attitudes to avoid disease and promote health. Here are some ways to develop a "prevention mind-set."

Protective Equipment

Prevention becomes especially important as you age because it becomes harder to spring back from injury and disease. Here are some ways you can protect yourself:

- **Seat belts.** You should wear a seat belt whenever you drive or ride in a motor vehicle. Seat belts reduce the risk of death in a serious crash by 50% (Komaroff 2005). Don't rely on air bags; the risk of injury is increased if you are not using a seat belt when the air bags discharge.
- **Helmets.** Wear a helmet, even if you have never had a biking or skating accident. Injuries to an unprotected head can cause bleeding and swelling inside the brain, which can be fatal. In addition to protecting yourself, you will set a good example for others!
- **Eyewear.** Wear safety glasses whenever you do chores or hobbies that could result in eye injury (using a chain saw, woodworking, etching glass, or soldering), or when you work with caustic liquids.
- **Dust masks and respirators.** Use personal dust masks when doing activities that might cause you to inhale dust and other fine particles. Use a respirator when there is a danger of exposure to hazardous gases or fumes.

Safety at Home

For people with declining vision, hearing, balance, mobility, or reaction time, activities such as cooking or standing on a stepstool can bring risks. According to the Consumer Product Safety Commission, 600,000 people over age 65 are seen in emergency rooms each year for injuries sustained while using basic household products (Creagan 2001).

Falls

The number of people who fall each year and the impact of those falls are startling:

- Each year 13,000 deaths and 200,000 hip fractures result from falls.
- One-third of all people over age 65 fall at least once a year.
- Three-quarters of these falls take place at home.
- More than 90% of the falls occur while doing everyday activities. (Creagan 2001; Komaroff 2005)

Because your bones become more brittle as you age, a fall that may not have hurt you in your thirties can be debilitating in your sixties. Trouble spots that can cause a fall include stairs, stepstools and ladders, slippery shower stalls and bathtubs, kitchens or other places where liquid can be spilled, and places where electrical cords, throw rugs, or other impediments could cause you to trip. Think about installing grab bars in the bathroom, removing obstacles from walkways, and increasing light near stairways.

Fire Safety

Most city codes require smoke detectors on every level of a home and in every bedroom because working smoke detectors reduce the chance of dying in a home fire by 50% (Komaroff 2005). Replace batteries every six months and test the detectors occasionally. If you haven't had an electrician check your electrical system in a while, do so.

Smoking greatly increases the risk of fire. If you use a space heater of any kind (electrical, propane, or kerosene), don't place anything too close to it and never leave it unattended. If your home is heated with natural gas and you smell gas, leave immediately and call 911 from a different location. Do not use your phone or turn on lights or other electrical products as doing so could trigger an explosion if gas is leaking.

Each level of your home should have a working fire extinguisher within easy reach. Every member of your household should know what to do if there is a fire. Your first priority should always be to get everyone out of the home. You may have as little as two minutes before smoke and flames make it impossible to get out. Have an exit plan and a place to meet once outside. Remember that your safety is more important than photos and heirlooms. Once you are out of your home, do not re-enter. Even if you think you can avoid the flames, smoke inhalation can kill you rapidly.

Toxins

Check and regularly monitor your home for toxic substances:

- **Carbon monoxide.** A carbon monoxide detector (hardwired, electric, or battery-operated) should be installed on each level of your home.
- **Radon.** Radon is an odorless gas that seeps into the foundations of homes and buildings built on contaminated soil (Komaroff 2005). Contact your public health department to obtain a test kit.
- **Lead.** If you live in an older home and suspect that either water pipes or painted surfaces in your home contain lead, contact a professional. Do not try to correct the problem yourself.
- **Asbestos.** Asbestos was used for fireproofing and insulating until 1974 (Upton and Graber 1993). The good news is that only airborne asbestos fibers are a health risk. Contact a professional if asbestos might be in your home. Never try to remove it yourself.

Food Safety

Seven million Americans get sick from eating contaminated food each year, and nine out of 10 cases of food poisoning could be prevented by proper food preparation (Komaroff 2005). Remember to follow safety practices when preparing and eating food:

- Pay attention to "sell by" and "use by" dates on products. Look for spoilage, contamination, dented cans, or broken seals. Store older food in front of newer supplies. Buy only pasteurized dairy products and fruit juices.
- Keep your refrigerator at 40°F and your freezer at 0°F. Use or freeze fresh meat within two days of purchase. Keep cold food refrigerated; refrigerate leftovers promptly.
- Wash your hands frequently and any utensils or surfaces that come in contact with fresh meats, fish, or eggs. Use hot, soapy water. Wash and scrub fruits and vegetables in warm water.
- Use a meat thermometer to be sure the meat has reached a safe temperature before eating (Cohen 2000; Komaroff 2005).

WORKSHEET

Checklist for a Safe Home

Put a check mark (✗) in front of each safety measure you have incorporated into your life.

Falls	
	Remove cords, and other obstacles from walking paths.
	Use only nonslip throw rugs or purchase nonslip pads to go under rugs without backing.
	Use night lights or other lighting near stairways.
	Apply nonslip adhesives on the floor of your bathtubs and showers. If needed, install grab bars to help you when bathing, showering, or using the toilet.
Fire	
	Check for frayed or damaged electrical cords. If your electrical system has not been checked within five years, schedule an appointment with an electrician.
	Have your furnace and any other gas appliances checked at least every two years.
	Install a smoke alarm in each bedroom and on every level of your home. Check and change batteries every six months.
	Place an accessible, working fire extinguisher on every level of your home.
	Develop and practice a fire escape plan with every member of the family.
	Never put combustible objects near a space heater, and never leave a heater unattended.
Toxins	
	Put a carbon monoxide detector on each level of your home and change batteries if needed.
	If your home might have either lead-based paint or lead pipes, contact a professional.
	If you haven't already done so, get a radon test kit and use it in your home.
Protective Equipment	
	Use your seat belt every time you drive or ride in a motor vehicle.
	Use a helmet when biking, skating, or doing other activities in which you could injure your head.
	Use protective eyewear whenever it is warranted.
Food Safety	
	Take an inventory of your cupboards and refrigerator. Throw away expired or spoiled food.
	Use a meat thermometer.

Questions & Answers

Q. I wish I'd taken better care of myself through the years. Is it too late?

A. Definitely not. There probably isn't anyone who reaches retirement age without some regrets about health and lifestyle choices. You may wish you had exercised more, never smoked, or just taken better care of yourself. While you can't rewrite the past, there are changes you can make that will help you feel better, look better, and have better long-term health. Part of getting older is forgiving yourself for what you did yesterday and focusing on making a better today and tomorrow.

Q. How can I start living more healthily and not just talk about it?

A. Wanting to be healthy and having the will to make it happen can be different things. Practicing a healthy lifestyle requires knowledge, diligence, determination, and attention to detail. Start slowly by adding or changing one thing at a time, and reward yourself when you follow through. Most important, keep at it!

Q. I eat a candy bar or a bag of chips every afternoon. How can I beat the cravings?

A. Research shows it takes 21 days to establish a new habit. Try replacing a bad habit with a good one. Instead of reaching for a candy bar, go for a 30-minute walk. If you can't change a habit, it may have become an addiction. Talk to your doctor about professional help.

Q. If early screening can identify diseases, why don't doctors screen everyone?

A. In a perfect world, screening tests would be used for anyone who might benefit from them, but in the real world, financial considerations are a factor. Also, it doesn't make sense to screen the general population for a disease like tuberculosis when the incidence is so low. Some tests, such as mammograms and chest X-rays, bring risks if they are overused.

Q. After an appointment I often can't remember what the doctor said. Any suggestions?

A. Get your doctor's instructions in writing so that you can refer to them later if you forget or are confused. Take someone to appointments at which you might need help remembering what the doctor says; take notes during the discussion. Try to develop long-term relationships with your doctor and other medical providers. People who know you are better able to understand your concerns.

Q. My husband is terrified of cancer. What can I say to reassure him?

A. While statistics show that heart disease and stroke are actually the leading killers in the United States, fear of cancer is still widespread. Tell your husband that half of all cancers can be avoided through a healthy diet, exercise, limiting sun exposure, and controlling alcohol and tobacco use (Creagan and Wendel 2003).

Resources

American Cancer Society
www.cancer.org

American Diabetes Association
www.diabetes.org

American Heart Association
www.americanheart.org

American Lung Association
www.lungusa.org

American Stroke Association
www.strokeassociation.org

Arthritis Foundation
www.arthritis.org

Consumer Information Center
www.info.gov

Harvard Health
www.health.harvard.edu

The Mayo Clinic
www.mayoclinic.com

National Clearinghouse for Alcohol and Drug Information
www.ncadi.samhsa.gov

National Institutes of Health
www.nih.gov

National Institutes of Health, National Institute on Aging
www.nia.nih.gov

National Sleep Foundation
www.sleepfoundation.org

Smoking Quitline
www.smokefree.gov

IN THIS CHAPTER

Chapter 6

Eating for Life

Staying healthy with a nutritious diet

EAT NOT TO DULLNESS; DRINK NOT TO ELEVATION.

—*Ben Franklin, American author, politician, and scientist*

Arthur Leon
MD and professor
in nutrition and exercise

You have no doubt observed that dietary recommendations have a tendency to come and go with time. In light of ever-evolving scientific findings, you might wonder what you should eat, and whether today's recommendations will still be valid tomorrow.

As in much of life, moderation is the key to a healthy diet. Eating a balanced diet composed of a variety of healthful foods is the best way to give your body the energy and building blocks that it needs. A common-sense approach suggests that your diet should be based on the following principles:

- Eat plenty of whole grain products, vegetables, and fruit
- Keep your diet low in fat, saturated fat, and cholesterol
- Limit your salt and sugar intake
- If you drink alcohol, do so in moderation

Eating a healthy diet in your retirement years is just as important as it has been during the rest of your life. Throughout all of your life, your body grows, develops, heals, restores, maintains, and renews. Good nutrition can slow the aging process and reduce the possibility of potentially disabling medical conditions, thereby improving both the quality and length of your life. In order to work at its best, your body needs proper amounts of various nutrients. Most of these nutrients are found in common foods, and the choices you make determine whether your body gets them or tries to get along without them.

What You Eat Makes a Difference

Early humans, through trial and error, identified foods that were *safe* to eat, but they had no way of knowing what was *nutritious* to eat. It wasn't until the 20th century that scientists identified what the body needs for growth, energy, and tissue maintenance and repair.

Substances that the body needs in relatively large amounts—water, carbohydrates, proteins, and fat—are called macronutrients. Those needed in small amounts—vitamins and minerals—are called micronutrients. Let's look at what some of them do and why our bodies need them.

What You Get from a Healthy Diet

More of what you want:

- Energy
- Desirable body weight
- Good motor and sensory functions and mental processes
- Improved quality and length of life

Less of what you don't want:

- Bone and muscle loss
- Visual problems
- Chronic diseases
- Disabilities
- Anemia and infectious diseases
- Conditions caused by nutritional deficit

The Mainstays of Your Diet

Water

Our bodies are about two-thirds water. Water surrounds and fills body cells and acts as a solvent for circulating nutrients and essential blood proteins. It also transports oxygen to the cells.

A moderately active person in a temperate climate loses about 2.7 liters to 3.7 liters (about 10 to 15.5 cups) of water a day. About 20% of these fluids are replaced with the water in food. The Institute of Medicine (2004) recommends that women consume approximately 2.2 liters (about 9 cups) and men consume about 3.0 liters (about 13 cups) of additional liquids each day.

The actual amount of water you need depends upon the amount of activity you are engaged in, the surrounding temperature, and other factors. Your body needs more water in situations that cause fluid loss, such as diarrhea, poorly controlled diabetes, or the use of diuretics.

Early warning signs that your body is dehydrating are lightheadedness; a dry, sticky mouth; and dark yellow (instead of pale) urine. Mild dehydration can cause fatigue, weakness, dizziness, and rapid heart rate. Severe dehydration causes elevation of body temperature and cardiovascular dysfunctions, which can progress to circulation collapse, coma, and death.

Carbohydrates

Remember two things about carbohydrates:

1. Carbohydrates are either *simple* or *complex*.
2. Complex carbohydrates with high amounts of *dietary fiber* are the most nutritious.

Simple carbohydrates are sugars and refined starches that are quickly digested. Fruits, some vegetables, and dairy products are nutrient-rich simple carbohydrates. Other simple carbohydrates—found in refined flours and grains, cookies, and candy—are "empty" calories without vitamins, minerals, or fiber.

High-Fiber Foods

Complex carbohydrates that are high in fiber are the most nutritious. How many of these foods do you eat each week?

- *Vegetables:* artichokes, asparagus, broccoli, brussels sprouts, cabbage, carrots, cauliflower, corn, green peas, potatoes with skin, popcorn, spinach, sweet potatoes, tomatoes
- *Fruits:* apples, apricots (dried), blueberries, figs, grapefruit, oranges, pears, plums, prunes, raisins, raspberries, strawberries
- *Grains:* brown rice, buckwheat, multigrain bread, oatmeal, spelt, whole barley, bulgur, whole cornmeal, whole grain ready-to-eat cereals
- *Legumes and nuts:* almonds, garbanzo beans, kidney beans, lentils, navy beans, peanuts, pinto beans, pistachio nuts, soybeans, split peas

(*www.mypyramid.gov*)

Complex carbohydrates, found primarily in whole-grain breads and cereals, legumes, and starchy vegetables, are starches that convert slowly to sugar during digestion, allowing an even release of energy to the body. Most complex carbohydrates include vitamins, minerals, and fiber.

Dietary fiber comes from parts of plants that cannot be digested and absorbed by the body. Fiber is important for proper elimination of waste from the body. It also lowers cholesterol levels and appears to reduce the risk of heart disease, type 2 diabetes, and colon cancer. How much fiber do you need? Women need about 25 grams a day and men need about 38 grams a day. There are about 15 grams of fiber in a cup of black beans, 5 grams in a medium pear, and 5 grams in a 3/4 cup serving of high fiber cereal. The amount of fiber in commercial foods is listed on the nutrition label. Another source of information about the amount of fiber in common foods is the USDA nutrition website (*www.nutrition.gov* click on "What's in Foods").

Proteins

Proteins make up three-quarters of the dry weight of our bodies and are composed of 20 different building blocks called *amino acids*. Of the 20 amino acids, the body can produce all but nine. These nine are called *essential amino acids* and must be added through the diet. The deficiency of any essential amino acid limits the body's ability to make new proteins.

The word protein comes from the Greek word meaning "primary," and proteins are essential for the body's growth and repair. Proteins allow critical functions, including:

- Maintenance and repair of cells, including bones, muscles, connective tissue, and organs
- Muscular contractions
- Cardiovascular functions
- Energy metabolism
- Digestion
- Blood clotting
- Fluid balance
- Oxygen transport
- Vision
- Immune defenses
- Appetite and mood control

Dietary proteins vary in quality and biological value. Complete proteins with the highest value are in eggs and milk. Other high-quality proteins are in red meats, fish, poultry, and soybeans. Plant proteins in beans, peas, lentils, whole grains, and vegetables have lower biological values when eaten alone, but can be combined to create dishes that provide the essential amino acids without the saturated fat and cholesterol of animal products. Examples of complementary plant-protein combinations are beans and rice or peanut butter on whole grain bread. Another way to supply essential amino acids is to add small quantities of animal products to plant proteins; for example, chili con carne, macaroni with cheese, milk with cereal, and Asian dishes in which vegetables and rice are supplemented with small amounts of meat, poultry, and/or seafood.

How much protein do you need? The USDA recommended daily allowance (RDA) for an average-sized adult (154 pounds) is 56 grams per day. A 3-ounce serving of lean meat has about 25 grams of protein, an 8-ounce serving of milk has about 8 grams, a half-cup serving of cottage cheese has about 14 grams. Check the USDA nutrition website (*www.nutrition.gov* click on "What's in Foods") for protein content of common foods.

Fats

Fat is a major source of calories and energy in the diet. The familiar fats in our diets, such as butter, margarine, oils, and cream, are part of a larger category of nutrients called *lipids*. Lipids that are solid at room temperature are generally called *fats*; those that are liquid at room temperature are called *oils*.

The two most significant types of lipids in our diets and in the human body are fatty acids and cholesterol.

Fatty Acids

Fatty acids are made up of carbon and hydrogen. Based on the saturation of hydrogen, fatty acids are classified as:

- Saturated (contained in butter, meat fat, cocoa butter, coconut oil)
- Monounsaturated (vegetable oils such as olive oil, avocados, and nuts)
- Polyunsaturated (corn oil, safflower oil, soybean oil, sunflower oil, and fats in fish and fish oils)

The American Heart Association (*www.americanheart.org*) recommends that 30% or less of your daily calories come from fat: 10–15% from monounsaturated fats, 10% polyunsaturated fats, and less than 7% from saturated fats.

Monounsaturated and polyunsaturated fats have a positive effect on cholesterol in the body. Olive oil, a monounsaturated fat, is a cornerstone of the Mediterranean-style diet, one of the healthiest diets in the world.

In contrast, saturated fats raise harmful cholesterol levels and increase the risk of cardiovascular disease. *Trans fats*, formed by the commercial hydrogenation of unsaturated vegetable oils to lengthen shelf life or to make margarines and shortening, also raise cholesterol levels and should be avoided.

Two polyunsaturated fatty acids—linoleic acid and alpha linolenic acid—cannot be synthesized by the body and must be obtained through the diet. These acids help regulate blood flow, blood clot formation, and inflammation:

- *Linoleic acid*, an omega-6 polyunsaturated fatty acid, is found in corn and sunflower oils.
- *Alpha linolenic acid*, an omega-3 polyunsaturated fatty acid, is found in canola, linseed, and soybean oils. Omega-3 fatty acids are partially converted in the body to EPA and DHA fatty acids. These fatty acids contribute to the health of the heart, brain, and eyes. Fatty fish (such as salmon, tuna, and herring) and other seafood are rich in EPA and DHA fatty acids.

Cholesterol

Cholesterol is not essential in the diet because the body can synthesize it from fat, carbohydrates, and protein. Cholesterol is a component in cell membranes and helps to form hormones, bile salts needed for fat digestion, and vitamin D in the skin (upon ultraviolet sun exposure).

Cholesterol in the diet raises health concerns because, like saturated fats, it increases blood cholesterol levels. When levels are too high, cholesterol will build up on the artery walls and can eventually block blood flow and cause heart disease and strokes.

Cholesterol is carried in the bloodstream by lipoproteins. We track two of those lipoproteins—low density and high density.

- *Low-density lipoproteins (LDL)* are often called "bad" cholesterol because they carry cholesterol in the blood.
- *High-density lipoproteins (HDL)* are known as "good" cholesterol because they remove cholesterol from tissues.

Dietary cholesterol comes from animal sources: meats (particularly of organ origin, such as beef liver), dairy products made from whole milk, butter, and egg yolks. The USDA recommends keeping the intake of dietary cholesterol to less than 300 mg/day.

Before you stop eating eggs, keep in mind that the most effective way to lower cholesterol levels is to avoid saturated fats and trans fats in your diet and to instead consume healthier unsaturated fats. Weight loss and exercise also help reduce blood cholesterol levels.

Family History Is Not Destiny

Karen grew up on a farm where meals were filled with meat, gravy, potatoes, fried foods, eggs, and desserts—a diet she kept well into adulthood. However, both of her uncles and her grandfather died fairly young from heart attacks, and she knew she would need to change her diet to avoid a similar fate. Although it was a significant change for her, she started eating leaner meat and then removed red meat from her diet. She cut back on fried foods, chips, and desserts and added more whole grain foods, fruits, and vegetables.

Eating healthily has not always been easy, and Karen knows her weaknesses. She knows her emotions affect the way she eats, and she tries to stay tuned to her stress. It's a challenge and she's not perfect, but she's done well over time.

Now 60 years old, Karen has no major health issues—her cholesterol and blood pressure are normal.

Vitamins and Minerals

Our bodies need tiny amounts of vitamins and minerals for production of enzymes, hormones, and other substances that help regulate growth and development, generate energy, and maintain the functioning of the immune and reproductive systems. The USDA provides recommended daily allowances (RDAs) for vitamins and minerals.

The word "vitamin" comes from *vita*, the Latin word for "life." Vitamins cannot be synthesized in the body and must come from plant and animal dietary sources or supplements.

Minerals, the other class of micronutrients, make up about 4% of the weight of the human body and are found in both plant and animal products in a balanced diet. These essential elements keep our bones and teeth strong; send oxygen to tissues and muscles; maintain our heartbeat, nerve impulses, and muscle contractions; regulate our body fluids; activate antioxidants; and allow our blood to clot.

Essential Vitamins

The RDAs for most vitamins are measured in milligrams. Some are measured in micrograms (1 microgram = 1/1000 of a milligram).

- **Vitamin A** helps with night vision, maintenance of healthy eyes and skin, and immune system functions.
  RDA: 900 micrograms for men; 700 micrograms for women.
  Plant sources: sweet potatoes, carrots, spinach, broccoli, squash, mangoes, peaches.
  Animal sources: beef liver, milk, and other dairy products.
  Vitamin A overload: Two to four times the RDA can be toxic.
- **Vitamin C** forms connective tissue collagen, the most abundant protein in our bodies and the main fibrous component of bone, tendons, cartilage, teeth, and scar tissue.
  RDA: 90 milligrams.
  Plant sources: citrus fruits, strawberries, peppers, tomatoes, cabbage family vegetables.
  Animal sources: none.
  Vitamin C deficiency: Can cause inflamed and bleeding gums, scaly skin, decreased wound-healing rate, easy bruising, nosebleeds, weakened enamel of the teeth, swollen and painful joints, anemia, decreased ability to ward off infection, and scurvy (mainly in older, malnourished adults).
- **B vitamins** help generate energy for cellular activity, support proper functioning of the brain and nervous system, and help in growth of red and white blood cells. There are eight B vitamins, but B_6 and B_{12} are the most important to include in your diet.
  Vitamin B deficiency: There are limited amounts of B vitamins in the body (with the exception of B_{12}), and depletion can happen in a matter of weeks. Deficient amounts of B vitamins can cause fatigue; loss of appetite; skin rashes; inflammation of the lips, mouth, and tongue; sensory loss; numbness and muscle weakness; anemia; heart failure; and serious mental changes, including depression, memory loss, and dementia.

Essential Vitamins *continued*

Vitamin B_6 is important for protein metabolism, synthesis of hemoglobin and brain neurotransmitters affecting mood and appetite, and reduction of blood homocysteine levels (a risk factor for heart disease).
RDA: 1.7 milligrams for men; 1.5 milligrams for women.
Plant sources: whole grain cereals, white and sweet potatoes, seeds, and beans.
Animal sources: poultry, beef steak and liver.
Vitamin B_6 deficiency: See preceding.
Vitamin B_6 overload: Two to four times the RDA can be toxic.

Vitamin B_{12} is needed for normal nerve cell activity, DNA replication, and production of the mood-affecting substance called SAMe (S-adenosyl-L-methionine).
RDA: 2.4 micrograms.
Plant sources: none.
Animal sources: meat, fish, poultry, milk and other dairy products.
Vitamin B_{12} deficiency: Initial signs of deficiency are disturbances in the lower extremities caused by nerve and spinal cord damage, including tingling and numbness, loss of "position sense," and balance disturbance (making walking difficult). Other symptoms include loss of appetite and diarrhea. This condition, if unrecognized and untreated, will progress to *pernicious anemia*, a potentially fatal disease that causes serious mental or neuropsychiatric problems like memory loss, disorientation, and (on occasion) dementia. Vegetarians who do not eat meat, eggs, or dairy products are particularly vulnerable to B_{12} deficiency, especially late in life. People over age 50 should take vitamin B_{12} as a supplement.

- **Vitamin D** promotes healthy bones and teeth by helping the body to absorb and use calcium and phosphorous. It helps prevent osteoporosis and age-related fractures.
  RDA: Because of changes in absorption rates, the RDA for vitamin D increases with age. Ages 51–70: 10 micrograms; older than age 70: 15 micrograms.
  Plant sources: fortified cereals.
  Animal sources: fatty fish or fish liver oils; fortified milk; egg yolks.
  Other sources: also formed by exposure of skin to ultraviolet from sunlight.
  Vitamin D deficiency: Can lead to muscle and joint pain and the progressive loss of muscle mass and strength. People over age 50, people with dark skin, and people in areas with insufficient sunlight should consume vitamin D–fortified foods and/or supplements.
  Vitamin D overload: Two to four times the RDA can be toxic.
- **Vitamin E** is an antioxidant protecting cell membrane lipids, red blood cells, and essential fatty acids from oxidative damage.
  RDA: 15 milligrams.
  Plant sources: vegetable oils, whole grain products, nuts and seeds, and margarine.
  Animal sources: none.
  Vitamin E deficiency: rare.
  Vitamin E overload: May affect blood-clotting functions.

Why Minerals Matter

- **Calcium** builds and maintains bones and teeth, regulates nerve transmission and muscle contraction and tone, and helps blood clot.

  RDA: 1,200 milligrams.
  Plant sources: green leafy vegetables, dried beans, peas, fortified soybean milk.
  Animal sources: milk and other dairy products, canned fish with small bones such as sardines.
  Calcium deficiency: Can lead to osteoporosis and bone fractures. Use of supplements can compensate for diminished ability to absorb dietary calcium as you age.

- **Iron** transports blood proteins, helps in energy metabolism, and is essential for proper brain development and functioning.

  RDA: 8 milligrams.
  Plant sources: whole and enriched grain products, seeds and beans, spinach, dried fruit.
  Animal sources: beef liver and steak, dark meat of poultry, shellfish, egg yolk.
  Iron deficiency: Causes anemia, the most common nutrient deficiency worldwide. It is important for older people with low iron to be checked for blood loss, particularly from a malignancy in the gastrointestinal tract.
  Iron overload: An inherited gene mutation found in about 7% of North Americans causes the body to absorb too much iron. This can damage the liver, pancreas, heart, kidneys, and other organs.

- **Sodium** helps maintain proper body fluid, osmotic pressure, body water distribution, and blood pressure; it is needed for nerve impulse transmission, muscle contractions, and heartbeat regulation.

  RDA: no RDA but minimum of 500 milligrams/day; maximum of 2,400 milligrams/day (1 teaspoon table salt).
  Dietary sources: table salt, food flavor substances and condiments, many processed foods, such as snacks, canned goods, smoked meats and fish, dill pickles, and spaghetti sauce.
  Sodium overload is common in American diets and causes hypertension. This can be a particular concern as you age and are at increased risk of having a stroke.

- **Potassium** maintains body fluid balance and blood pressure; regulates nerve impulses, muscle contraction, and heartbeat.

  RDA: no RDA, but for a healthy diet: 2,000–4,000 milligrams/day.
  Plant sources: potatoes, tomatoes, citrus fruits, bananas, spinach, beans.
  Animal sources: fish, shellfish, milk.

Dietary Considerations as You Age

By now, you have likely established eating habits that have served you well (or not so well) with respect to your health. It stands to reason that in your retirement years, your eating habits probably will bear a strong resemblance to those you have practiced to this point in your life. You most likely have identified foods and eating practices that make you feel healthy and well, as well as those that bring less favorable results. Remember that it is never too late to make positive changes in your diet! You will enjoy both immediate and long-term effects of nutritional and dietary improvements.

As your body ages and as you experience lifestyle changes during retirement, you may need or want to modify your approach to diet and nutrition in order to maintain optimal health. For example, if while working you were accustomed to eating a large lunch and then burning many calories in the afternoon doing your job, you may need to cut back your calorie intake to match your declining activity level once you retire. Conversely, if you worked in a sedentary desk job and seldom took time to exercise, having more time during retirement for physical exertion may cause you to lose weight. You are the best judge of how you look and feel, so you will need to be attuned to how the quantity and quality of what you eat affect your well-being.

Physical Considerations

It is a fact of life that your metabolism begins progressively slowing down after age 40. As part of the aging process, your body burns fewer calories at age 65 than it did at age 35 to do the same activities. With a slower metabolism, you will need to work harder to keep your weight in check if your food intake remains the same. You also may experience diminished taste and appetite as you age, thus making eating less appealing. If you need to take medications that suppress your appetite, or have medical conditions that make it hard for you to eat a balanced diet, it may become a challenge for you to take in the calories and other nutrients you need. Finally, changes in enzymes and the responsiveness of your intestines may affect the absorption of essential vitamins and minerals. If you do not currently take a multivitamin and mineral supplement to make up for possible gaps in your diet, you may wish to consider doing so.

Emotional and Lifestyle Considerations

You may find that retirement requires some difficult emotional adjustments. For example, you may feel lonely or unproductive once you leave a stimulating work setting. Feeling down or depressed may affect your eating habits, whether it be through overeating, undereating, or making poor food choices. Where, when, and what you eat during retirement may change just by virtue of operating on a different daily schedule. Should you become divorced or widowed, your eating habits may be affected due to the emotions and lifestyle changes that may result. Whatever evolving landscape you encounter, it's up to you to find a way to practice healthy eating habits. Be sure to seek professional help if needed to ensure your emotional and physical well-being.

What Makes a Healthy Diet?

Most Americans do not eat enough fruits, vegetables, whole grains, and fat-free or low-fat milk and milk products. Not only are these foods nutritious, they may reduce the risk of chronic disease. Here's a quick look at what you should eat each day (based on USDA recommendations).

Fruits and Vegetables

Two cups of fruit and two and one-half cups of vegetables a day

Eating a variety of vegetables (dark green, orange, legumes, starchy vegetables, etc.) and fruits provides a rich source of vitamins A, C, and K, iron, calcium, and potassium and other minerals, as well as dietary fiber. They also are low in calories and have no saturated fat or cholesterol.

Grains

Three or more one-ounce servings a day

At least half of the daily grain intake should come from whole grains. In addition to energy, grains provide B vitamins, minerals, dietary fiber, and some protein. Whole grains must be listed as such on the label.

Dairy

Three one-cup servings of fat-free or low-fat milk (or the equivalent of other dairy products) a day

Dairy products (milk, yogurt, cottage cheese, etc.) are a great source of high-quality protein, vitamins A and D (enriched milk), and all of the B vitamins except for folate and B_{12}. This group is also the best source of calcium and phosphorous.

Meat

Less than six ounces a day (about two servings)

All of the animal muscle meat sources are rich in sources of high-quality protein, iron, zinc, phosphorous, and vitamins A and B (including the hard-to-get B_{12}). However, all are high in dietary cholesterol, and red meat and the skin of poultry contain unhealthy saturated fat. Choose only the leanest cuts of red meat and broil or grill it to drain off the fat.

Serving Sizes

The labels on many packages define serving size. For foods that don't provide serving information, here are suggested sizes:

Fruit	A serving of fruit is equal to one piece of fresh fruit, one-half cup of chopped fruit, or three-fourths cup of fruit juice.
Vegetables	A serving of vegetables is one-half to one cup of raw or cooked vegetables or two cups of leafy greens.
Grain	A serving of grain is equal to one slice of white or whole grain bread, one-half to one cup of prepared cereal, or one-half cup of cooked pasta or rice.
Milk and Other Dairy	A serving of dairy is equal to one cup of milk or one and one-half ounces of cheese.
Meats, Nuts, Eggs, and Beans	A serving of meat is two to three ounces, or about the size of a deck of cards. Serving sizes for other proteins include two tablespoons of nut butters, two eggs, and one-third cup of dry beans.

(www.mypyramid.gov)

Eggs

Two or three a week (one to two servings)

Although the whites of eggs provide excellent-quality protein and the yolks are rich sources of vitamins and minerals, the yolks also are major sources of cholesterol in the American diet. Egg substitutes are lower in cholesterol.

Legumes/Beans

One to three servings a day

Legumes, beans (especially soybeans), nuts, and seeds can be combined with whole grain products to equal the quality of meat protein. Legumes, beans, seeds, and nuts also provide vitamin E and fiber (absent from animal protein sources), plus some B vitamins and minerals.

Fats

Use sparingly

Healthy sources of fat (polyunsaturated omega-3 and -6 fat and monounsaturated fat) come from fish, poultry without the skin, and vegetable oils.

WORKSHEET

Tracking My Diet for a Week

Record everything you eat and the serving sizes for a week. Total your servings in each of the recommended food groups. Compare your choices with the recommendations described in the previous pages.

Day	Morning	Midday	Evening	Total Servings
Sunday				____ Fruits ____ Vegetables ____ Grains ____ Dairy ____ Meat/eggs/legumes
Monday				____ Fruits ____ Vegetables ____ Grains ____ Dairy ____ Meat/eggs/legumes
Tuesday				____ Fruits ____ Vegetables ____ Grains ____ Dairy ____ Meat/eggs/legumes
Wednesday				____ Fruits ____ Vegetables ____ Grains ____ Dairy ____ Meat/eggs/legumes
Thursday				____ Fruits ____ Vegetables ____ Grains ____ Dairy ____ Meat/eggs/legumes
Friday				____ Fruits ____ Vegetables ____ Grains ____ Dairy ____ Meat/eggs/legumes
Saturday				____ Fruits ____ Vegetables ____ Grains ____ Dairy ____ Meat/eggs/legumes

Tracking My Diet for a Week *continued*

Over the week did I eat excess fat? Sugar? Sodium?

Did I get enough fiber?

Did I get enough water and other liquids?

What changes do I want to make for a healthier diet?

Healthy Eating Habits

Healthy eating sounds simple: eat the right things, in the right amount. But for most of us that's not easy to do. The truth is, we often eat for reasons other than good nutrition: boredom, loneliness, anxiety, stress, and cravings are all nonhunger prompts that send us to the kitchen. Or we fill up on high-calorie foods and then don't have appetite left for more nutritious fruits, vegetables, and whole grains.

An occasional treat is no problem, but if you find yourself repeatedly making choices that don't fit a nutritious diet, consider getting some help. Find a nutritionist or personal trainer, or join a support group like Weight Watchers. A healthy diet is important enough that you should find a way that works for you.

WORKSHEET

Eating Habits I Want to Change

Do your eating habits work against you? For example, do you eat when you're not really hungry or are there particular foods that trigger overeating or undereating? Think of a healthier alternative. (*Example*: What: eat unhealthy snacks; When: after dinner; Why: boredom; Alternative: take a walk.)

What?	When?	Why?	Alternative?

Questions & Answers

Q. How much salt can I have in my diet?

A. Probably less than you think. Consume no more than 2,300 milligrams (about 1 teaspoon) of sodium per day. Choose and prepare foods with little salt and eat potassium-rich foods like fruit and vegetables. People with hypertension, African Americans, and middle-aged and older adults should try to consume no more than 1,500 milligrams (about half a teaspoon) of sodium per day.

Q. What effect does alcohol consumption have on health?

A. Alcohol appears to reduce risk of coronary heart disease when consumed in moderation. However, heavy alcohol consumption increases the risk for liver disease. It also increases the risk for high blood pressure, certain cancers, accidents, and violent behavior.

Q. Are raw eggs dangerous?

A. You should not eat raw eggs or foods made with raw eggs because of the risk of salmonella bacteria. People whose immune systems are compromised should not eat or drink unpasteurized milk, raw or undercooked meat and poultry, raw or undercooked fish or shellfish, unpasteurized fruit juices, or raw bean sprouts.

Q. What happens if I have too much protein in my diet?

A. Many Americans eat too much protein. Only 30% of daily calories should come from protein. Too much protein in your diet can cause osteoporosis, gout, arthritis, kidney stones, high blood pressure, and heart disease.

Q. Can you give me some guidelines for fat in my diet?

A. It's important to have some fat in the diet, but keep total fat intake to between 30% and 35% of calories. Most of those fats should come from polyunsaturated and monounsaturated fatty acids, like those in fish, nuts, and vegetable oils.

Q. How do I know if something is whole grain?

A. Check the ingredient list on the label. The whole grain should be listed first and as a whole grain.

Q. Has the food pyramid changed?

A. Yes. The U.S. Department of Agriculture changed the pyramid in spring 2005 and created a website (*www.mypyramid.gov*) that gives in-depth information on selections from each major food group. It includes examples of foods, daily quantities, and tips for preparation and serving. This information can be used to design your own customized eating plan, a great way to make the "Dietary Guidelines for Americans" work for you.

continued on page 120

Questions & Answers *continued*

Q. What is the best way to achieve and maintain a healthy weight?

A. To *lose weight*, aim for a slow, steady loss by decreasing calorie intake while maintaining adequate nutrient intake and increasing physical activity.

To *prevent gradual weight gain* over time, make small decreases in food and beverage calories, and increase physical activity.

To *maintain body weight* in a healthy range, balance calories from foods and beverages with calories expended by physical activity.

Overweight adults with chronic disease and those who are on medication should consult a health care provider about weight loss strategies before starting a weight reduction program to ensure appropriate management of other health conditions.

Q. Can you explain body mass index?

A. Body mass index, or BMI (see table on page 121), is a way to judge a person's weight relative to his or her height and to define overweight and obesity.

continued on page 121

Body Mass Index

BMI	19	20	21	22	23	24	25	26	27	28	29	30	35	40
Height (in.)	Weight (lb.)													
58	91	96	100	105	110	115	119	124	129	134	138	143	167	191
59	94	99	104	109	114	119	124	128	133	138	143	148	173	198
60	97	102	107	112	118	123	128	133	138	143	148	153	179	204
61	100	106	111	116	122	127	132	137	143	148	153	158	185	211
62	104	109	115	120	126	131	136	142	147	153	158	164	191	218
63	107	113	118	124	130	135	141	146	152	158	163	169	197	225
64	110	116	122	128	134	140	145	151	157	163	169	174	204	232
65	114	120	126	132	138	144	150	156	162	168	174	180	210	240
66	118	124	130	136	142	148	155	161	167	173	179	186	216	247
67	121	127	134	140	146	153	159	166	172	178	185	191	223	255
68	125	131	138	144	151	158	164	171	177	184	190	197	230	262
69	128	135	142	149	155	162	169	176	182	189	196	203	236	270
70	132	139	146	153	160	167	174	181	188	195	202	207	243	278
71	136	143	150	157	165	172	179	186	193	200	208	215	250	286
72	140	147	154	162	169	177	184	191	199	206	213	221	258	294
73	144	151	159	166	174	182	189	197	204	212	219	227	265	302
74	148	155	163	171	179	186	194	202	210	218	225	233	272	311
75	152	160	168	176	184	192	200	208	216	224	232	240	279	319
76	156	164	172	180	189	197	205	213	221	230	238	246	287	328

(The Partnership for Healthy Weight Management at *www.consumer.gov/weightloss*)

< 18.5 = Underdeveloped
18.5–24.9 = Normal
25–29.9 = Overweight
30–34.9 = Class 1 Obesity
35–39.9 = Class 2 Obesity
40 or more = Class 3/Severe Obesity

A BMI of 25 to 29.9 is considered overweight and over 30 is obese. Risk of serious health problems increases progressively by BMI levels over 25 and by excessive waist circumference. If a person's waist circumference is more than 35 inches for a woman or more 40 inches for a man, the overweight status is upgraded to obese. If someone has diabetes, cardiovascular disease, or has multiple risk factors for these conditions, the person's overweight status again is upgraded to obese. The health risks of being overweight include hypertension, cholesterol problems, type 2 diabetes, heart disease, stroke, and several forms of cancer.

Resources

Centers for Disease Control and Prevention
www.cdc.gov/nutrition
Information about nutrition and good health.

Dietary Guidelines for Americans
www.health.gov/dietaryguidelines
This appendix to the Dietary Guidelines for Americans lists information about many foods, including the number of calories, amount of fiber, and many nutrients.

HealthierUS.gov
www.healthierus.gov
Information to help Americans make healthier choices.

MedlinePlus
www.medlineplus.gov
Health and nutrition information from the National Library of Medicine and the National Institutes of Health.

Nutrition for Life
Janice Thompson and Melinda Manore
San Francisco: Pearson/Benjamin Cummings. 2007.

Nutrition.gov
www.nutrition.gov
Food and nutrition information.

Quick Easy Cookbook
American Heart Association
New York: Clarkson Potter. 1995.

USDA Food and Nutrition Service
www.fns.usda.gov
Food and nutrition assistance programs.

USDA Food Safety Education
www.fsis.usda.gov/Food_Safety_Education

USDA MyPyramid.gov
www.mypyramid.gov
Interactive planning tool that helps you make healthy food and exercise choices.

IN THIS CHAPTER

Chapter 7

Keeping Strong, Fit, and Active

Improving health, well-being, and quality of life through physical activity

THOSE WHO THINK THEY HAVE NOT TIME FOR BODILY EXERCISE WILL SOONER OR LATER HAVE TO FIND TIME FOR ILLNESS.

—*Edward Stanley, English politician*

Luke Carlson
Certified health and fitness instructor

Physical activity can keep you healthier, stronger, and more independent as you age. You cannot afford to make it optional in your life. Exercise is not just for people who are fit, young, and athletic; people who enjoy exercise; or people who are just interested in losing weight. It is not just for the summer months, after the holidays, or before vacations. Exercise is for virtually everyone, throughout the life span, and needs to be as much a part of your daily routine as brushing your teeth.

A physically active lifestyle, including both planned exercise and daily physical activity, is a powerful way to improve physical and mental health, potentially expand the lifespan, and improve your quality of life. However, as with most major life changes, consult with your physician before significantly increasing your activity level or starting an exercise program.

Why Is Physical Activity Important?

Physical activity is any body movement that uses your muscles to expend energy. Exercise is planned, structured, and repetitive bodily movement to improve or maintain physical fitness (Whaley, Brubaker, Otto, and Armstrong 2006).

Physical activity and exercise decrease the risk of developing many chronic diseases and premature death. Cardiovascular exercises improve the functions of your heart and respiratory system. Strength training enhances physical strength and coordination. Flexibility and stretching exercises increase range of motion and the ability to perform daily activities.

How much physical activity do you need? To stay healthy, the surgeon general recommends 30 minutes a day, continuously or in 10-minute or longer increments. If you are attempting to maintain a particular weight or lose weight, the amount should increase to 60 to 90 minutes per day. This physical activity doesn't have to come solely from an exercise program, but can come from activities of daily living: raking leaves, taking the stairs instead of the elevator, vacuuming, or walking briskly from the car to the grocery store.

A Physically Active Lifestyle

The choices you make about how you use your time make a difference in your physical fitness. Reduce sedentary activities such as sitting behind a desk, watching TV, and using a computer. Making an intentional choice to "move rather than be moved" can make a difference. Don't stand still if you can move; don't sit if you can stand; don't lie down if you can sit.

The Benefits of Physical Activity and Exercise

The many benefits associated with physical activity reinforce the importance of maintaining an active lifestyle. Regular exercise *improves*:

- Blood pressure
- Cognitive function
- Cholesterol
- Diabetes
- Insulin sensitivity
- Short-term memory
- Quality of life

At the same time, exercise *decreases the risks* of:

- Heart and vascular diseases
- Type 2 diabetes
- Bone loss in postmenopausal women
- Falls and fractures
- Depression
- Obesity
- Fatigue in cancer patients.

(Nied and Franklin 2002)

Strength Training

Strength training, also known as resistance training or weight training, has evolved from an activity for bodybuilders and football players to one that should be part of every exercise program. Strength training improves health and mobility throughout your life.

After age 50, strength declines by 15% per decade; after age 70, it declines by 30% per decade (Nied and Franklin 2002). This loss of muscle and strength is due to the physiological changes of aging and, for many people, an increasingly sedentary lifestyle. Loss of muscle and strength makes daily activities (like walking and using stairs) and exercise more difficult. A negative cycle is created. Strength and muscle decrease with age, which makes physical activity difficult, which increases the risk of negative health outcomes, which make physical activity almost impossible.

Strength training breaks this cycle by reducing the loss of muscle strength and mass, allowing you to participate in other cardiorespiratory or aerobic exercise.

Strength Training Guidelines: Quality over Quantity

The quality of the strength training exercise performed is of far greater importance than the quantity or amount of exercise performed. Here are some guidelines:

- **Exercise two to three times a week on nonconsecutive days.** Your muscles don't get stronger while strength training, but rather while you rest and recover from strength training. Wait a minimum of 48 hours before the next workout. Each workout should last between 20 and 30 minutes.

Research-Based Reasons for 50-Plus Strength Training

All the benefits of exercise listed previously plus:

- Staying strong
- Keeping your metabolism running
- Maintaining muscle mass
- Reducing body fat
- Reducing arthritic pain
- Reducing lower back pain
- Reducing depression

(Westcott and Ramsden 2001)

Do I Have to Join a Health Club?

You can get the benefits of strength training and exercise wherever you choose, but to ensure safety and optimal improvements, consider strength training with supervision from a personal trainer or fitness instructor at your local health club, YMCA, or community center.

Joining a health club or fitness facility gives you access to quality exercise equipment in a safe environment. Research shows that home-based strength training can be less effective than supervised strength training because supervised strength training ensures the proper form, volume, and intensity.

- **Train the major muscle groups**, including buttocks, thighs, chest, upper back, shoulders, arms, abdomen, and lower back. Work from large muscle groups to smaller muscle groups. It is important to train all muscle groups rather than just the "problem" groups that you feel need improvement. (See the illustrations on pages 127 and 128 for sample exercises.)
- **Start with a weight that allows you to do 8–12 repetitions.** Complete one set of 8–12 repetitions of each exercise for the first two weeks of training. After two weeks, or when you can perform 12 repetitions of a particular exercise, increase the weight used by two to five pounds for the next workout. Perform the exercise to the point where another repetition in good form is not possible. If you cannot reach 8 repetitions, reduce the weight for the next workout. Many people use the same weight for every workout. That is a mistake. For muscles to get stronger, they must be progressively overloaded. This means that at each workout you need to perform either more weight or more repetitions than the previous workout.

- **Concentrate on form while performing all repetitions in a slow and controlled manner.** This is an effective and safe way to minimize momentum and maximize muscle tension. Guidelines for performing a proper repetition are as follows:
  - Breathe throughout the entire exercise, paying special attention to exhaling during exertion (while pushing or pulling). Never hold your breath while strength training.
  - Raise the resistance (weight) in a slow and controlled way (approximately 2 seconds).
  - Pause in the contracted position.
  - Change directions slowly and smoothly without speeding up.
  - Lower the resistance in a slow and controlled way (approximately 4 seconds).
  - Move through the greatest range of motion that comfort allows.
  - Avoid creating leverage by altering body position.
  - When using exercise equipment, avoid excessively squeezing the machine/equipment handles.
- **Exercise with a training partner or personal trainer.** Working with someone else will provide consistent feedback and motivation.
- **Record workout data.** Record the order of exercises, weight/resistance used, and the number of repetitions performed in a log.

Example:

Weight/Resistance — Number of Repetitions

Exercise	Setting	Date 4/15	Date 4/17
Leg press	3	10 / 8	
Leg curl	4	25 / 10	
Leg extension			
Heel raise/calf raise			

Exercise	Setting	Date	Date	Date	Date	Date	Date
Leg press							
Leg curl							
Leg extension							
Heel raise/calf raise							
Shoulder shrug							
Shoulder press							
Pull-down							
Chest press							
Abdominal							
Low back extension							

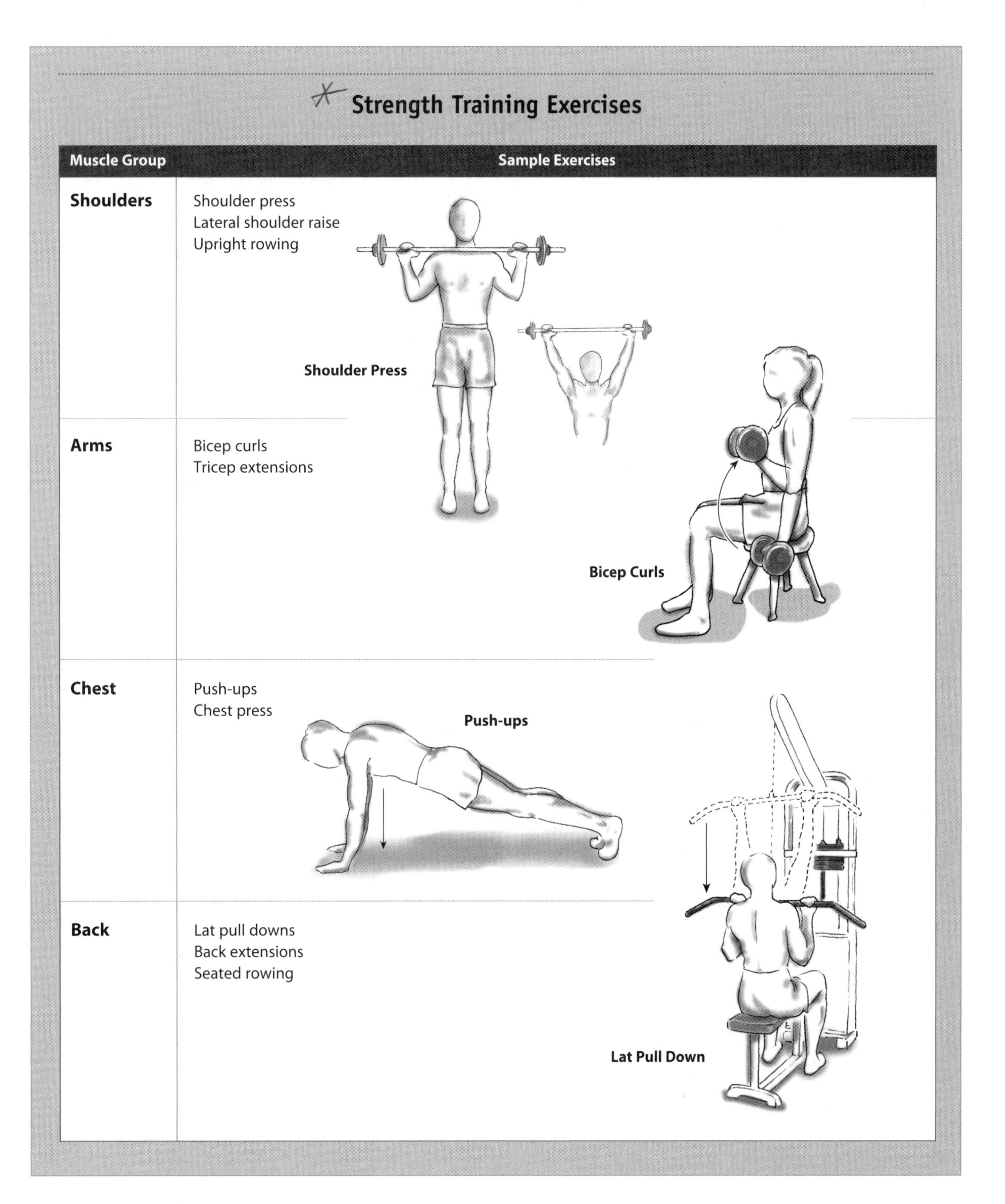

Strength Training Exercises

Muscle Group	Sample Exercises
Shoulders	Shoulder press Lateral shoulder raise Upright rowing
Arms	Bicep curls Tricep extensions
Chest	Push-ups Chest press
Back	Lat pull downs Back extensions Seated rowing

Strength Training Exercises *continued*

Muscle Group	Sample Exercises
Abdomen	Crunches Sit-ups Leg raises
Buttocks	Lunges Leg press
Legs	Leg press Leg extensions Lunges Squats

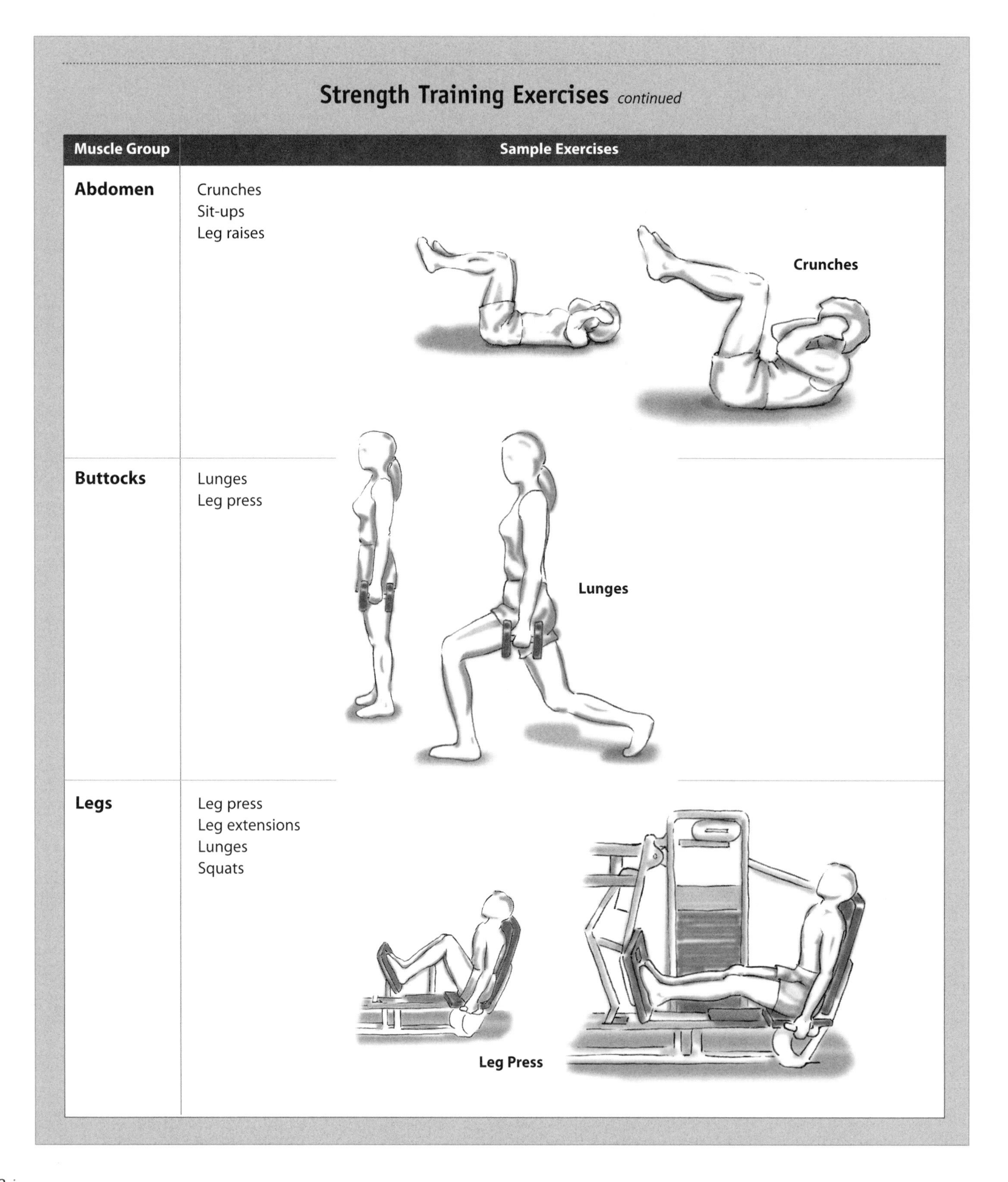

Strength Training and Benefits at the Beach

Kathryn, a 63-year-old recent retiree and grandmother of five, began a strength training regimen when her doctor recommended the twice-a-week program to improve her muscle and bone strength and to prevent muscle loss.

While the health benefit was the reason she started, Kathryn is most excited about her ability to enjoy weekends at her lakeshore home with her family. Last summer the walk up and down the hill to the beach tired her. She often found herself watching her grandkids play on the beach and in the water as she sat on the cabin porch. This summer has been different. Kathryn's improved muscle strength lets her walk easily up and down the hill, lift her granddaughter above her head, and even canoe across the lake with her daughter. The stamina acquired through strength training twice a week for 20 minutes has improved Kathryn's independence, mobility, and energy levels. Strength training has allowed her to continue to enjoy the life and the activities she loves.

Cardiorespiratory Exercise

The other essential part of an exercise regimen is cardiorespiratory or aerobic exercise. Cardiorespiratory exercise improves the functions of the heart, blood vessels, and respiratory system. It helps control weight and improves health. Here are some guidelines:

- **Choose rhythmic activities that involve large muscle groups.** Excellent choices are walking, jogging, swimming, and using exercise machines, including elliptical trainers, bikes, and stair steppers. Joint pain during one form of cardiorespiratory exercise does not mean you should avoid all cardiorespiratory exercises. Consider activities that are lower impact and "easier" on joints and connective tissue, such as swimming.
- **Perform aerobic exercise 20 to 60 minutes per day.** Understand the relationship between duration and intensity. If you exercise for 20 minutes (a relatively short duration), your intensity level should be relatively high. If you exercise for 60 minutes (a long duration), your intensity may be low or moderate. Either will yield benefits in fitness.
- **Monitor your intensity.** Use the formula (220 – age) to get an estimate of your heart rate maximum. You should be able to talk comfortably throughout the exercise session. If you cannot carry on a conversation, decrease the intensity. If you can whistle, your intensity level is too low.
- **Try to burn 150 to 400 calories** per day through cardiorespiratory exercise (Whaley et al. 2006). You can see how many calories particular activities burn at *www.healthcalculators.org/calculators/calories_burned.asp*.

WORKSHEET

My Physical Activity and Exercise Plan

Example:

	Sunday	Monday	Tuesday	Wednesday	Thursday	Friday	Saturday
Cardiorespiratory exercise *Recommended: 3–5 times per week for 20–60 minutes*		30 min. elliptical trainer	45 min. stair climber	20 min. jog	45 min. stair climber	30 min. elliptical trainer	75 min. walk
Strength training *Recommended: 2–3 times a week for 20–30 minutes*		25 min. workout				25 min. workout	
Daily physical activity *Recommended: As much as you can*	45 min. gardening			2 hours golf	45 min. tennis		

My Physical Activity and Exercise Plan *continued*

Weekly Physical Activity and Exercise Log

Track your physical activity and exercise for one week.

	Sunday	Monday	Tuesday	Wednesday	Thursday	Friday	Saturday
Cardiorespiratory exercise							
Strength training							
Daily physical activity							

How well am I meeting my physical activity goals?

What changes do I want to make?

Flexibility and Balance

Flexibility training, or stretching, improves the range of motion in your joints and is widely thought to improve your ability to perform daily activities, although research does not support this belief (Whaley et al. 2006).

When stretching:

- Include two or three 15-second stretches for each major muscle group
- Stretch to the point of tension but not pain
- Avoid bouncing
- Stretch when muscles are warm, especially after a strength training or a cardiorespiratory exercise session

Surprisingly, research indicates that stretching before exercise or physical activity does not prevent injury or soreness (High 1989; Shrier 1999).

Practices such as tai chi, yoga, and Pilates increase balance and flexibility, reduce stress, and encourage a general sense of health and well-being.

Preventing falls is an important consideration for older adults. Proper balance involves complex sensory and motor interactions and can be influenced by medications, vision, and environmental hazards, as well as muscle function. There is evidence that balance-coordination exercises such as tai chi reduce the risk from falls (Wolf et al. 2003). A well-rounded exercise program that includes walking, strength training, and balance training may be your best insurance against falls (Exercise and Physical Activity for Older Adults 1998).

It is important to note that flexibility and balance training does not provide the level of health benefits that strength training and cardiorespiratory training provide. Strength and cardiorespiratory training should have the highest priority in your exercise plan.

Questions & Answers

Q. When is someone too old to begin exercising?

A. Exercise can have a profound impact on your quality of life regardless of your age. Research endorses the safety and benefits of exercise for individuals in their 60s, 70s, 80s, and beyond. Increasing physical activity in any way is good.

Q. I walk and swim regularly. Do I need strength training?

A. Walking and swimming are excellent forms of cardiorespiratory or aerobic exercise. However, these activities do not target and strengthen the major muscle structures. Both cardiorespiratory exercise and strength training should be part of your exercise regimen.

Q. Will strength training make me bulky?

A. Many women are concerned about this. Women generally do not have the genetic characteristics, specifically the testosterone, to develop large or bulky muscles. Following a well-designed strength training program can strengthen muscles without creating increased muscle bulk.

Q. Can I use strength training to target problem areas?

A. This is referred to as "spot reduction" and is a myth. Strength training exercises do not remove or reduce fat or "flab" from a particular area. They develop muscle and strength in that area.

Q. If one set is good, are two or three sets better?

A. With strength training, more is not better. Research indicates that one set is as effective as two or three (Carpinelli and Otto 1998).

Q. I have a chronic disease. Should I still exercise?

A. Talk to your doctor first, but with adaptations to the exercise routine, most people suffering from chronic diseases can continue to exercise safely. A clinical exercise physiologist can be consulted to determine the best approach for your particular situation.

Q. I have not been doing regular exercise. How do I get started?

A. Start slowly and progress to the frequency, duration, and intensity level detailed in this chapter. Keep in mind that the level of exercise outlined in this chapter is designed for maximum benefit. Any amount of exercise is better than no exercise. Make exercise a daily habit. Set specific, realistic, and measurable goals for yourself along the way.

Q. Are free weights better than machines?

A. Free weights and machines are equally effective in improving strength. Machines offer the advantage that they are often safer to use.

Resources

American College of Sports Medicine
www.acsm.org
Information about scientific research and practical applications of sports medicine and exercise science.

The Mayo Clinic
www.mayoclinic.com
Fitness information and exercise advice.

National Osteoporosis Foundation
www.nof.org
Information about preventing osteoporosis and promoting lifelong bone health.

The National Blueprint
www.agingblueprint.org
A comprehensive source about increasing physical activity among adults age 50 and older.

University of Maryland
www.healthcalculators.org/calculators/calories_burned.asp
A calorie counter for estimating the number of calories you burn when you move.

IN THIS CHAPTER

Chapter 8

Maintaining Mental Fitness

Taking steps to keep your mind sharp and your well-being intact

A SAD SOUL CAN KILL YOU QUICKER THAN A GERM.

—John Steinbeck, American novelist

Catherine Johnson
PsyD LP, licensed psychologist

Good mental fitness is as much a part of successful retirement as physical fitness. In fact, neither is possible without the other. Keeping your mental processes sharp, staying physically healthy, enjoying productive activities, and keeping up satisfying relationships can all increase your sense of well-being. You also need self-awareness and a willingness to make emotionally healthy choices.

Sorting out the feelings, thinking, and behaviors that support the life you want to live is a constant process. Just the process of working toward goals can keep your mind healthy and move you closer to finding meaning and satisfaction in retirement.

Aging and Mental Health

Brains Never Stop Growing

Brain development continues throughout a lifetime, longer than was once thought (Albert and McKhann 2006; Nussbaum 2003). Our brains are not stiff and fixed, but are changing all the time. Stimulating your mind creates new connections among brain cells. By reading this page you are both stimulating your neuron (brain) cells to lay down new connections and increasing your memory. Reading and other mental activities actually improve brain function and reduce the effect of normal age-related changes. They may also reduce your risk for Alzheimer's disease and other dementias.

How Brains Age

Not everyone experiences age-related changes in brain function, but many of us see some changes around age 70 (Albert and McKhann 2006; Rowe and Kahn 1998). You may:

- Learn and react at a slower rate.
- Find doing two or more things at once is harder and you are less able to handle distractions.
- Have to practice something you want to remember.
- Lose some ability to recall names, numbers, or locations.
- Lose some ability to follow complex language and logic.

Fortunately, these changes come at a time when it's possible to live at a less frantic pace. You don't have to absorb quantities of information or do six things at once. You can combine your acquired knowledge, wisdom, and creativity to achieve your goals.

The More We Change, The More We Stay the Same

With age, your focus moves to your inner life, the part of you that has been underground while you developed your public personality. You may think less about satisfying others and more about who you are and what you will provide to the next generation that is meaningful and worthy of your legacy (Sperry and Prosen 1996).

Although values and focus might change, personality is pretty constant across the life span. If you were open, agreeable, and conscientious at age 30, chances are you are now and will be at any age. If you don't like some part of your personality, you can change, but you must take intentional action to make it happen (Costa and McCrae 1991).

Alzheimer's Association 10 Warning Signs

If you have noticed several of these symptoms, see your primary care physician:

- Increased memory loss
- Difficulty performing familiar tasks
- Language problems
- Disorientation to time and place
- Poor or decreased judgment
- Problems with abstract thinking
- Misplacing things
- Changes in mood and behavior
- Changes in personality
- Loss of initiative

(Alzheimer's Association 2006)

WORKSHEET

Thoughts about Aging and Retirement

Make a list of all the things you've heard about aging and retirement from television, movies, books and other print media, and conversation. They can be positive or negative.

Now look at your list and cross out everything that doesn't sound like you. Circle anything that applies to you or that you worry about. These are the predictors of your future self.

If there's anything circled that you do not like, actively work to change it. Write one personal change you'd like to make and the steps you will take to make that change.

Change:

Steps I'll take:

Making Plans for a Better Future

Sam, a photographer for a local newspaper, decided to retire early. While he loved the first few months, he found himself growing bored with his schedule. His friends from the newspaper were still working and didn't have much time to spend with him, and he found that he wasn't disciplined enough to work on his photography consistently. He became sullen and withdrawn, and friends and family worried about him.

Although Sam had never suffered from depression before, the sudden shift to retirement had made him unhappy. He decided to spend a few sessions with a life coach, who helped him make a new plan for his retirement. His coach helped him realize that he had to engage his mind and connect with others, and he needed to find activities that met those needs. As part of that goal, he joined a history book club and began teaching a community education class on photography. He joined an art co-op, which gave him space to work, and more important, a community that would help inspire him and keep him focused on his goals. His new activities provided intellectual challenge, social connection, and fulfillment, and he found that he enjoyed his day-to-day life much more.

Keys to Mental Fitness

Find a Sense of Well-Being

Mental health reflects the degree to which you feel positive and enthusiastic about yourself and life. Well-being is more than the absence of problems (which can start at any time) or the presence of a good mood (which could end at any time). Most of us want to continue to feel and be effective as we age. Carol Ryff (1995) suggests habits that will help you achieve that goal:

- Have purpose and meaning
- Strive for continual personal growth and development
- Nurture warm, intimate relations with others
- Cultivate a sense of freedom, self-confidence, and control
- Accept yourself as you are
- Develop a mastery about daily life

You may already have healthy habits in these areas (or will as you create your retirement plan). Habits that improve your mental health move you closer to overall health and wellness. For example, being around friends can enhance memory and reduce stress, contributing to both mental and physical health.

Accept Who You Are

Self-acceptance is the door to personal freedom, self-actualization, and fulfillment. This brings an acceptance of others, flexibility, and an inner peace. Sometimes it helps to step outside of your moment-to-moment feelings and observe yourself in your life. Once you are aware of your thoughts (your interpretation of an experience), your feelings (your emotional response to an experience), and your behaviors (your pattern of responding to an experience), you can see whether they are in line with your true self. If they are not, you can change how you think, feel, and behave to more closely reflect who you are. Doing so leads to self-fulfillment and a healthier, happier life.

Challenge Your Mind

If you think that old dogs can't learn new tricks, you have swallowed a myth that isn't true. If you want to keep your mind fit, you have to keep learning. You will find abundant lifelong learning opportunities at your local colleges and universities and other organizations. Reading stimulates the mind. So does traveling, evaluating investment options, learning to dance, taking classes, doing crossword puzzles, and planning for your retirement.

See chapter 3, "Using Your Time," page 49.

Character Traits for Aging Well

- Courage: Keep fears in check
- Simplicity: Travel light
- Wisdom: Avoid too much nostalgia or remorse
- Humor: Let your wit out

(President's Council on Bioethics 2005)

WORKSHEET

How Do I Stimulate My Mind?

Name three things you do every day that stimulate your mind.

1. ______________________________
2. ______________________________
3. ______________________________

What are three mentally challenging activities you do less often but enjoy?

1. ______________________________
2. ______________________________
3. ______________________________

Name three mentally stimulating activities you look forward to trying when you have more time.

1. ______________________________
2. ______________________________
3. ______________________________

Stay Healthy

Physical health, especially heart health, is important to your brain. The brain uses 25% of the blood from each heartbeat.

Reduce Stress

Chronic stress, real and perceived, may accelerate age-related damage to your brain and body. While eliminating all stress is not an option, you have a choice about how you react to a real or perceived problem or crisis. Your attitude toward the situation can lessen the impact of stress on your life. The goal is to change your reaction to stressful events from biological activation (fight or flight) to biological relaxation. If you set realistic goals, prepare in advance for situations you know will be stressful, and ask for help, you are on your way to managing the stress of life (and the stress of transitioning into retirement). Progressive relaxation, meditation, visualization, yoga, and biofeedback training are some strategies for reducing stress.

For a Healthy Mind, Body, and Spirit

- Keep learning
- Do not smoke
- Get regular physical exams
- Exercise regularly
- Have fun, relax, and be around people
- Be financially stable
- Resolve conflicts
- Be spiritual and thoughtful
- Keep your diet healthy
- Stay in touch with family and friends
- Build new relationships
- Don't retire from life.
- Find your purpose.

(Albert and McKhann 2006; Nussbaum 2003)

See chapter 5 "Staying Healthy," page 89.

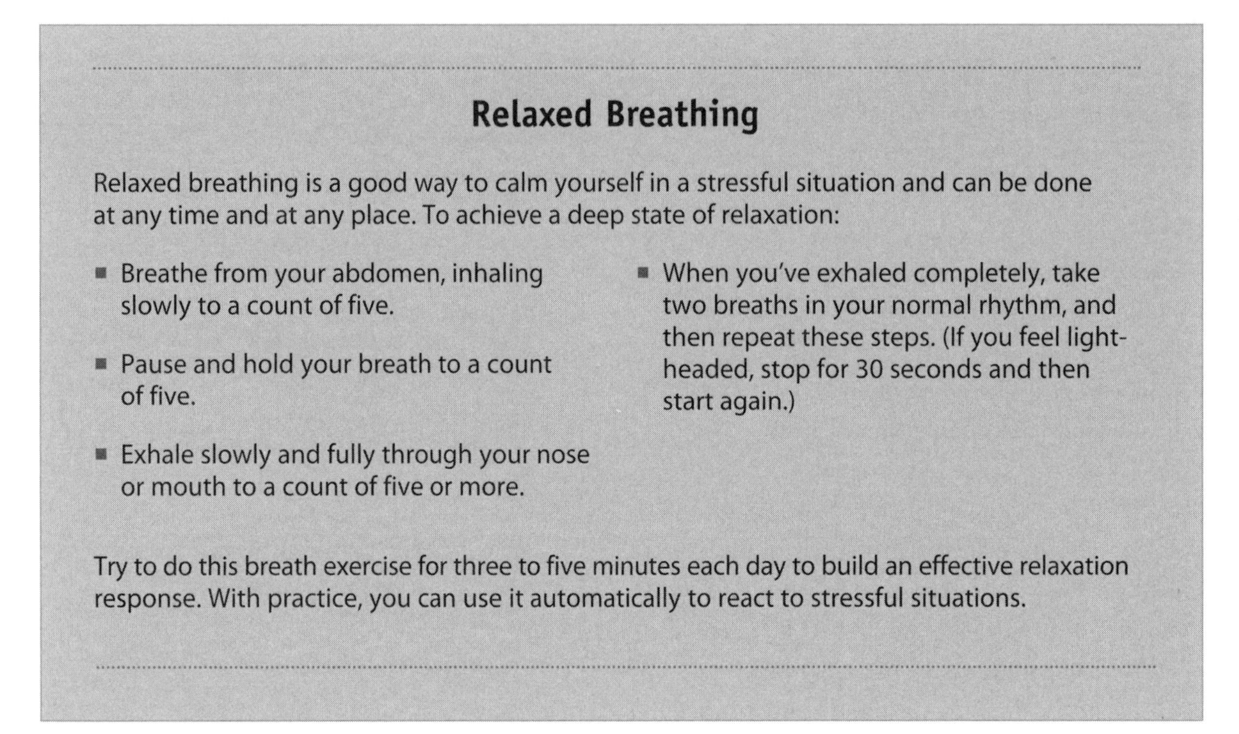

Relaxed Breathing

Relaxed breathing is a good way to calm yourself in a stressful situation and can be done at any time and at any place. To achieve a deep state of relaxation:

- Breathe from your abdomen, inhaling slowly to a count of five.
- Pause and hold your breath to a count of five.
- Exhale slowly and fully through your nose or mouth to a count of five or more.
- When you've exhaled completely, take two breaths in your normal rhythm, and then repeat these steps. (If you feel light-headed, stop for 30 seconds and then start again.)

Try to do this breath exercise for three to five minutes each day to build an effective relaxation response. With practice, you can use it automatically to react to stressful situations.

Making Positive Changes

The choices you make in your life affect your physical, emotional, and psychological health. You can choose the thoughts, feelings, and behaviors that will lead to achieving your full potential.

- **Be accepting and nonjudgmental.** We are naturally and culturally taught to judge each experience on a scale from good to bad. An alternative perspective is to view each life experience as just what it is, without judgment (Chopra 1994). For instance, compare how you'd react to a fender bender in the next lane to how you'd react if you were in the car hit from behind. In the first case you might think, "Nobody's hurt," or "No real damage." But in the second case, you think, "My car is damaged!," "My insurance will go up!," or "I'll be late!" It's the same situation, but your view affects how you respond. Try to be nonjudgmental of yourself and others.
- **Behave "as if."** Changing the way you behave can change the way you think and feel. This is called *acting opposite*. Laughing or smiling can actually put you in a better mood (Linehan 1993).
- **Use rational problem solving.** Mapping out the facts, alternative options, possible solutions, and the pros and cons of each solution helps you find the best solution.

- **Follow a plan.** Create a plan to respond to an issue or problem. You are more likely to follow through with a plan if you:
  - Imagine implementing the plan
  - Create a public pledge by telling others
  - Attach a timeline to the goal
  - Commit the goal to paper (Sharma 1997)
- **See yourself reaching your goals.** When you imagine doing something, you are more likely to accomplish it. This includes life goals. The resource section at the end of this chapter has sources for visualization exercises to improve performance or reduce stress (Sharma 1997).

Learn to Resolve Conflict

Effective people skills help you build relationships and make repairs in a way that is respectful to yourself and others. When facing conflict, try to find common ground:

- Find a time to talk with the other person that allows both of you to discuss the issue.
- Describe the situation objectively. Avoid verbal attacks, judgments, or manipulative statements as you present the issue.
- Express your feelings or opinions—don't assume the person knows how you feel or think.
- Assert yourself. Clearly ask for what you want.
- Explain why getting what you are asking for is beneficial to both of you.
- Listen to what the other person has to say. Be courteous. Don't interrupt. Be patient.
- Focus on your objective even if the other person becomes defensive. Appear confident.
- Ignore threats, attempts to change the subject, or comments to divert you.
- Be willing to negotiate. Be willing to reduce your request or ask the other person to offer a solution.
- Acknowledge the other person's feelings, wants, challenges and opinions.
- If it's appropriate, be lighthearted and use humor.
- Be fair.
- Apologize when needed, but keep your self-respect. Don't overapologize; stick to your values and be truthful.

(Bourne 2000)

See "Challenges in Relationships," page 41.

WORKSHEET

Improving My Mental Fitness

What changes do I want to make to improve/maintain my mental fitness?

Change	Steps I Will Take	Progress

Questions & Answers

Q. Are mental health problems inevitable as I age?

A. No. Mental health problems are not a consequence of aging and may be a symptom of disease. Paying attention to mental health changes is as important as monitoring your physical and financial health.

Q. Will it be harder to deal with change as I get older?

A. You will probably respond to change as you did at other times in your life (Sperry and McNeil 1996). If change was especially challenging for you in the past, you will want to monitor your response and get help if needed.

Q. What if the change includes loss?

A. The hard fact is that retirement and aging can bring unpleasant changes. Leaving a job, the death of a loved one, divorce, relocation, or illness can cause a range of physical and emotional reactions. Here are some ways of dealing with loss:

- Share your feelings with trusted friends or family members.
- Join a support group.
- Take special care of your physical health; eat right and rest.
- Recognize that grieving a loss takes times. Be gentle with yourself.

Q. I'm always losing my car keys. How can I tell if it's forgetfulness or the beginning of Alzheimer's?

A. Many of us misplace our car keys or forget something at the grocery store, and that is normal for us. If you notice *increased* memory loss or disorientation, however, talk to your doctor. These are not signs of normal aging but symptoms of disease. Early detection and diagnosis are important to managing Alzheimer's disease and other dementias.

Q. I just turned 60 and can't shake the feeling that my life is over. I've never felt this way before. What can I do?

A. If you are experiencing distress that consistently interferes with everyday life, talk to a physician or a psychologist. Mental suffering can be treated with medication, psychotherapy, or both. Signs include:

- Persistent sadness, emptiness, and hopelessness
- Loss of interest in once-pleasurable activities
- Difficulty concentrating, remembering, or making decisions
- Decreased energy, sleep, or appetite disturbances
- Thoughts of suicide
- Excessive worry or nervousness
- Aches and pains that don't go away when treated

Q. Does aging mean losing my desire for intimacy?

A. The basic human need for affectionate human contact continues throughout life. Sex, romance, and intimate relationships can continue into your later years and become deeper, fuller, and more satisfying. The desire for intercourse and the amount of sexual activity may decrease, but the desire for sexual contact and intimate touch remain fairly constant across the life span.

Resources

Alzheimer's Disease Education and Referral Center
www.nia.nih.gov/alzheimers

Alzheimer's Association
www.alz.org

The Anxiety & Phobia Workbook
E. J. Bourne
Oakland, CA: New Harbinger. 2000.
Breathing exercises and other step-by-step directions for relaxation and visualization.

Awareness
A. de Mello and J. F. Stroud
New York: Doubleday. 1990.

Chopra Center
www.chopra.com
Dr. Deepak Chopra's insight into spirituality, relationships, health, and success.

DrWeil.com
www.drweil.com
Dr. Andrew Weil's site offers information on common mental health issues.

The Miracle of Mindfulness
T. Nhat Hanh
Boston: Beacon Press. 1999.

National Institute of Mental Health
www.nimh.nih.gov

Wherever You Go, There You Are: Mindfulness Meditation in Everyday Life
J. Kabat-Zinn
New York: Hyperion Books. 1995.

IN THIS CHAPTER

Chapter 9

Creating Your Health Care Team

Taking responsibility for your health by being informed and getting involved

NEVER GO TO A DOCTOR WHOSE OFFICE PLANTS HAVE DIED.

—*Erma Bombeck, American humorist*

Many of us grew up assuming that the doctor knew what we needed. We accepted "doctor's orders" without question. Today, it is widely understood that you are in the best position to manage your health. To take charge of your health, it is critical that you become knowledgeable about the health care system—from finding a provider to choosing a health plan.

Become an informed decision maker. You cannot make good choices if you don't have accurate information. Navigating the health system is challenging and, if you are not well, you may want a family member, friend, or health professional to serve as an advocate. Forming a health care team may not be easy, but it increases the likelihood that you will get the care that you need.

Mary Jo Kreitzer
Founder and director
Center for Spirituality and Healing

Start by Staying Healthy

Most of us think of ourselves as healthy when we are not physically sick. Increasingly, experts are recognizing that for overall health and wellness, you need to pay attention to the mind, body, and spirit.

See chapter 5 "Staying Healthy," page 89.

Positive health choices like regular exercise, eating well, managing stress, and avoiding tobacco make a difference. Mayo Clinic physician Edward Creagan, in his book *How Not to Be My Patient* (2003), offers tips for living long and well. He calls them a "prescription for survival."

- Form stable and long-term relationships
- Maintain ideal body weight
- Eat a plant-based diet and make sensible food choices
- Engage in regular physical activity
- Don't smoke
- Use alcohol in moderation
- Foster a sense of spirituality
- Find meaning and purpose in life (Creagan 2003)

Becoming an Informed Decision Maker

You need information to make good choices. There was a time when patients were expected to be passive and were often discouraged from asking questions, seeking information, and raising concerns. Today, more people are looking for a different relationship with their health care provider, whether that provider is a physician, nurse-practitioner, or chiropractor.

Increasingly, people see their health care provider as a valued source of information, able to both provide care and help them navigate the health care system. As you partner with your provider, it is your job to be:

- *Informed about your health and health care options.* Ask questions and do research.
- *Intentional about what you want.* Discuss with your provider which options best fit your needs.
- *Involved in decisions.* Although you may rely on health professionals to advise you, you have the final say.

The resources section at the end of this chapter lists credible Internet sites and print resources.

Finding a Health Care Provider

The best time to look for a health care provider is before you need one. Health plans or managed care organizations have directories or websites with listings of primary care providers (physicians or nurse-practitioners) and medical specialists. The directory may include biographical information and areas of specialization within the providers' practice.

When choosing a doctor, nurse-practitioner, or other health care professional, consider these factors:

- **Qualifications.** Look for a health care provider who is certified (received advanced training) in your area of care. For older adults, look for a doctor who is board-certified in geriatrics. Nurse-practitioners may also be certified in areas such as adult health, family health, women's health, and geriatrics.You may also want to find out how many years the provider has been in practice. If you are having a procedure done, find out how many similar procedures the provider has performed.
- **Hospital affiliation.** Doctors have privileges to practice only at certain hospitals. In choosing a medical provider, consider the hospitals they are affiliated with and ask for information on patient satisfaction, safety and quality, the amount of experience with certain procedures, infection rates, patient fall rates, access to complementary or integrative therapies, and cost.
- **Care philosophy.** Getting information on health care providers' philosophy of care is not as easy as reviewing their qualifications. You might ask if they work well within an interdisciplinary team, whether they are oriented to health promotion and prevention as well as disease management, and whether they consider less intensive or aggressive approaches before advancing to more expensive and technology-oriented approaches.
- **Access.** How easy is it to get an appointment? If you have a question, can you call and talk with someone?
- **Team members.** Who else works in the office? If your provider is unavailable, who would you see?
- **Reimbursement.** Is this health care provider covered by your insurance? Does the provider accept Medicare and Medicaid?

See "Working with Your Health Care Provider," page 95.

Communicating with Your Health Care Provider

Before an Appointment

Good communication begins when you set up an appointment. Be clear about why you are scheduling the appointment. Provide enough information for the scheduler to know whether you need a short or longer appointment. For example, rather then saying, "I need to see the doctor," it is more helpful to say, "I have been feeling dizzy for a week," or "I have had a cold for 10 days and now have a fever." If you don't feel comfortable giving this information to the receptionist or if you are unsure whether you need to see a health care provider, ask to speak to a nurse.

When you meet with your health care provider, use your time wisely. Most doctors' appointments are limited to 15 minutes. Generally, a visit begins with the health care provider asking a question such as "What brings you here today?" or "How are you feeling?" It is helpful if you are prepared to tell your story. You may want to write this down in advance of the appointment. Be sure to include:

- Your symptoms
- When the symptoms began
- What makes the condition better or worse
- Questions or concerns

It is not helpful or practical to go in with a long list of questions. Decide what it most important to you. Bring in a list of medications you are taking, including prescription drugs and over-the-counter medications, vitamins, herbs, and nutritional supplements. Include the name, dose, and how often you take it. Even if you are anxious or embarrassed, don't wait until the end of the visit to bring up the real reason you are there.

Understand Your Medications

Whether you are taking a prescription medication or an over-the-counter drug, you should know the following:

- What is being prescribed or recommended and why
- How and when the drug should be taken
- Any side effects
- How to tell if the drug is working
- Whether the medication might interfere with any other prescriptions or substances
- What to do if you forget to take a dose
- How much it costs and what insurance covers
- Alternative medications to consider

At a Routine Checkup or Health Exam

If you have an appointment for a routine checkup or health exam, you should know the following before leaving the doctor's office:

- What was the result of the exam? Were any problems identified?
- If laboratory tests or other tests were done, when and how will you get the results? Will you also receive an interpretation of the results—in other words, how will you know if they are normal?
- Are there screening or diagnostic tests that should be scheduled? If so, when and how often?
- What recommendation does the health care provider have for helping you maintain or improve your health or prevent disease?

At an Appointment to Discuss a Health Concern or Problem

If your appointment was scheduled to discuss a specific health care problem or concern, you should know the following before leaving the doctor's office:

- The diagnosis or how the diagnosis will be made
- Your treatment options
- What you can do to manage your health condition
- Where you can get more information

Discussing Insurance Coverage

You will want to know how much of your care is covered by insurance, whether you have private insurance, Medicare, or Medicaid. If you have questions about your coverage, talk with a customer service representative from your health plan or someone in the business office of your clinic or hospital. Your health care provider is unlikely to know the details of your insurance coverage.

What Will My Insurance Cover?

- Does the care I'm considering need preapproval by my insurance company or health plan? ☐ yes ☐ no
- Do I need a referral from my primary care provider? ☐ yes ☐ no
- Is there a copayment? ☐ yes ☐ no
- Is there a deductible? ☐ yes ☐ no

- What services, tests, or other costs will be covered?

- How many visits are covered and over what period of time?

- What additional costs (laboratory tests, equipment and supplies, etc.) will be covered?

- Do I need to see a health care provider from a network? If so, where can I get a list of those providers?

- Do I have any coverage for out-of-network providers? What are the out-of-pocket costs?

- What dollar or calendar limits are there?

(Center for Spirituality and Healing, University of Minnesota 2006)

About Your Medical Records

If you are seeing a new provider, it is a good idea to bring a copy of your medical records and test results. Consider putting together a three-ring notebook or filing system so that you can have all of your records and notes in one place. It is also a good idea to periodically review and verify the accuracy of medical records. Your name should appear on all of the forms, tests, and correspondence. Make sure that the diagnoses and procedures are correctly listed.

Many medical records are maintained online. Electronic medical records eliminate the need for physical transportation and avoid the problem of lost or misfiled charts. There are strict procedures for maintaining confidentiality and limiting access to your information. If you are concerned about this, ask questions about how data privacy is assured. Even if the information is stored online, you can always ask for a printed copy.

About Hospitalization

Ironically, hospitals are not always safe and healthy environments. According to a study by the Institute of Medicine called *To Err Is Human: Building a Safer Health System* (Kohn, Corrigan, and Donaldson 1999), as many as 98,000 people die each year because of medical errors. An even greater number suffer complications due to poor or inadequate care. The issue is so significant that the organization that accredits hospitals has published a brochure, "Speak Up: Help Prevent Errors in Your Care" (Joint Commission on Accreditation of Healthcare Organizations 2002), with information on how to avoid being the victim of medical errors.

Seigal and Yosaif (2003), in their book *Help Me to Heal: A Practical Guidebook for Patients, Visitors and Caregivers*, say the key to a healthy hospitalization is becoming an empowered patient. They offer suggestions for hospital stays, including:

- Have someone with you.
- Make sure your health care providers know your history and are communicating with each other.
- Ask questions about anything that you are unsure of.
- Don't hesitate to request a second opinion.
- Make sure the environment is clean.
- Make sure health care providers check your wristband and verbally confirm who you are.
- Don't eat hospital food if it doesn't smell or taste right.
- Before you are discharged, make sure that you understand how to care for yourself and any plans for follow-up treatment.

Making a Medical Decision

In deciding on a course of action, whether that includes having surgery, taking a drug, or seeing an acupuncture provider, you may want to consider several factors:

- Will this treatment, approach, or procedure improve your health, prevent disease, cure your condition, or improve your symptoms?
- Are there dangerous or harmful side effects?
- Is there scientific evidence that this course of action works?
- Can you afford it? Will it be covered by insurance?
- How easy will it be to find or use the approach you are considering?
- What might stop you from doing this?
- Is the choice compatible with your personal values, beliefs, and preferences? Does it "feel right"?

WORKSHEET

Making a Health Care Decision

Do you have a health care decision to make? It could be anything: exercising more, quitting smoking, taking a drug to lower your cholesterol, or weighing options for treating a particular disease. Use this worksheet to record what you know about the situation and to evaluate your options.

My decision to:

The benefits:

The risks:

Evidence:

Cost or insurance issues:

Access issues:

Obstacles:

Does it feel right?

Taking Control of Your Health Care

Marnie has spent plenty of time in hospitals but it's never slowed her down, and it's taught her a lot about taking charge of her health care.

Marnie's first surgery was in 1953 after she shattered her leg in a ski accident. Now 74 years old, Marnie has a rod through her tibia, a replaced knee and hip, and a fused right ankle. But that hasn't stopped her—she won a gold medal in a national ski race two years ago.

Marnie offers the following tips to be sure you're getting good care:

- Educate yourself. Do some research about your disease or procedure.
- Write down your questions or concerns before you visit the doctor.
- Take someone with you to doctor appointments, and take notes.
- It is important to be comfortable with and trust your doctor. If you don't, find another doctor.
- Always ask your doctor what drugs you will be taking, why, and how often.

Preparing an Advance Directive

An advance directive tells your health care team the parameters of care you would like to receive if you become unable to make medical decisions. When you are admitted to a hospital, you will likely be asked if you have an advance directive. If you don't have one, the hospital can provide you with information on preparing one. Advance directives include information on:

- Care you would like to receive if you have an illness from which you are unlikely to recover
- Treatment that you don't want to receive
- Treatment that you do want to receive no matter how ill you are

Laws about advance directives differ by state, so be sure to follow your state law in preparing an advance directive. There are different kinds of advance directives.

- *Living wills* are used when you are terminally ill and not expected to live more than six months. In a living will you can describe care you want to receive in various situations (oxygen tubes, feeding tubes, etc.). A living will does not identify who will make decisions for you should you be unable to act on your own behalf.
- A *power of attorney* states who you have chosen to make health care decisions for you if you are unconscious or unable to make decisions on your own.
- A *do not resuscitate (DNR) order* means that you do not want to receive cardiopulmonary resuscitation if your heart stops or if you stop breathing. If the hospital staff does not have a DNR order, they will begin lifesaving measures.

While advance directives are most often written by older people or people who are seriously ill, it is a good idea for all adults to have advance directives. It is also important that you discuss your advance directives with your family and health care team. Having advance directives can offer both you and your family peace of mind in that it makes it very clear what is important to you and increases the likelihood that your preferences will be followed.

See chapter 17, "Passing On What You Have," page 251.

Influencing Health Care Policy

You can influence public policies that affect your health care. In 2003, the Minnesota Citizens Forum on Health Care Costs held a series of meetings to listen to Minnesotans' ideas about health care. The group identified the following characteristics as being desirable in a health care system:

- Accessible to all
- Fair
- Safe, high-quality care
- Personalized
- Affordable
- Rewards personal responsibility
- Understandable

Use the worksheet on page 157 to help you think about how you might influence health care policy in your community.

WORKSHEET

Rating the Health Care System

Consider each of the following characteristics. Rate (✗) how important you consider each characteristic and how well the health care system in your community fulfills that characteristic.

	Not Important	Somewhat Important	Very Important	Is the System Adequately Meeting These Needs?
Accessible to all	●	········	●	☐ yes ☐ no
Fair	●	········	●	☐ yes ☐ no
Safe, high quality-care	●	········	●	☐ yes ☐ no
Personalized	●	········	●	☐ yes ☐ no
Affordable	●	········	●	☐ yes ☐ no
Rewards personal responsibility	●	········	●	☐ yes ☐ no
Understandable	●	········	●	☐ yes ☐ no

How can I influence change in the areas in which I have identified needs?

Questions & Answers

Q. When should I get a second opinion? What if the opinions are different?

A. If you have questions or concerns about a diagnosis, it is entirely acceptable to ask for a second opinion. Most physicians are very supportive and understanding of why patients may want to do this. Choosing a provider for a second opinion requires going through the same steps as choosing a primary care provider. Make sure of insurance coverage in advance. Competent and skilled providers may have different opinions, and it doesn't mean that one is right and the other wrong. In the end, you need to sort out which approach is a better fit for your goals, values, and preferences.

Q. I've heard of people having health care advocates. What does an advocate do?

A. Health care advocates can help you navigate the system and can also be a companion as you move through a health care experience. An advocate can be a family member, friend, or professional health care coach who acts on your behalf. If you are anxious, concerned, have a language barrier, are facing a challenging or uncertain diagnosis, or anticipate discussing treatment options, it helps to have someone with you to remember what was said or discussed. It's a good idea to have him or her write down what was discussed or done. An advocate can help guard your interests, expectations, preferences, and needs, and can help assure that all caregivers are communicating and focused on the same goals.

Q. I'm going to need surgery this year. What kinds of things should I look for in a hospital?

A. You can contact each hospital directly and ask questions or find a website that compares information on hospitals. Look for quality and safety indicators like nurse-to-patient ratio, rate of patient falls, and infection rates. Find out the volume and types of procedures or surgeries done at each hospital. You want to choose a hospital that performs a high volume of the procedure you need. You may also want to know if a hospital has a pain management program and if it offers complementary or alternative therapies.

Q. How hard is it to prepare an advance directive?

A. Advance directives do not have to be complicated documents. They can be short and simple statements about what you want done or not done. For information on preparing an advance directive, you can contact your physician, state health department, or an attorney. Aging with Dignity (*www.agingwithdignity.org*) offers "Five Wishes," an easy-to-use format that will help you put on paper what you want to happen. But be sure that whatever you prepare is valid in your state.

Questions & Answers *continued*

Q. What if I need treatment but don't have insurance?

A. If you do not have insurance coverage and need care, you will need either to make immediate payment or arrange to make payments over time. You can ask if the fee can be negotiated or if they offer a "sliding fee" that adjusts charges based on your income and ability to pay.

Q. I have a new insurance plan and a new health care clinic. Can I get my records from my former clinic?

A. Yes. You have a right to your medical information and can get copies of everything. Ask your health care providers. You may need to pay a small fee to cover duplication costs.

Resources

American Medical Association
www.ama-assn.org/go/doctorfinder
Free physician selection service.

Center for Spirituality and Healing, University of Minnesota
"Navigate the Healthcare System"
www.csh.umn.edu/health

"Taking Charge of Your Health"
www.takingcharge.csh.umn.edu
Information on how to navigate the health system and make informed health care choices.

The Joint Commission on Accreditation of Health Care Organizations
www.jointcommission.org/GeneralPublic/Speak+Up/
Information on how patients can prevent health care errors by becoming active, involved, and informed participants.

The Mayo Clinic
www.mayoclinic.com
Information on many health topics.

Medline Plus
www.medlineplus.org
Information from the National Library of Medicine, the National Institutes of Health, and other trusted sources.

WebMD
www.webmd.com
Comprehensive health information.

IN THIS CHAPTER

Chapter 10

Finding Nontraditional Paths to Health

Complementing conventional health care with nontraditional therapies

THE GREATEST DISCOVERY OF ANY GENERATION IS THAT HUMAN BEINGS CAN ALTER THEIR LIVES BY ALTERING THE ATTITUDES OF THEIR MINDS.

—*Albert Schweitzer, German Nobel Peace Prize winner*

Mary Jo Kreitzer
Founder and director
Center for Spirituality and Healing

Like food co-ops and garden composting, nontraditional medicine has moved from the fringes of our society nearer to the mainstream. In 2004, 62% of Americans used some form of nontraditional therapy, whether for chronic conditions, to improve health, or for more natural and less invasive therapy. The most commonly used therapies were natural products such as herbs and nutritional supplements, deep-breathing exercises, meditation, chiropractic care, yoga, prayer, massage, and diet-based therapies (Barnes et al. 2004).

As therapies are proved safe and effective, many are being adopted into conventional care, and new therapies are continually emerging. People are demanding both access and choice, and need information so that they can make wise and informed decisions. It is likely that, as research continues to validate the use of nontraditional approaches, more clinics and hospitals will offer nontraditional services and insurance will cover more of the cost.

Complementary therapy, alternative therapy, and integrative therapy are all terms that describe nontraditional medicine. For simplicity, we will refer to all of these therapies as nontraditional therapies.

What Therapies Should I Consider?

There are at least 1,800 different nontraditional therapies. We will look at six that are widely available: chiropractic care, tai chi, meditation, yoga, herbal therapies and nutritional supplements, and acupuncture.

See "Flexibility and Balance," page 132.

Chiropractic Care

Doctors of chiropractic (DCs) are licensed health care providers who focus on the musculoskeletal and nervous systems of the body. Chiropractors use a drug-free, hands-on approach. They are trained to recommend therapeutic exercises and dietary and lifestyle changes to support general health. People often seek chiropractic care after an injury.

A visit to a chiropractor will likely begin with a health history and a physical examination. Chiropractors may also take X-rays and do laboratory tests. Based on these findings, a variety of techniques may be used to treat your condition, including exercises, application of heat or cold, manual adjustment, or nutrition recommendations and instructions for self-care. Chiropractic adjustments are most often made to the spine, although they can also be used to treat other areas. A chiropractic adjustment ranges from mild pressure to manual manipulation and is done to restore structural alignment or improve joint function. Adjustments can be made while you are lying down, sitting, or even standing. A series of adjustments may be recommended.

Finding a chiropractic doctor is much like finding other health care providers. Your insurance provider may list chiropractors who are part of its network. You may want to ask your primary health care provider for a referral or get a recommendation from someone you trust. Remember to ask questions about his or her experience in caring for your condition, what the therapy will involve, how much it will cost, and whether it will be covered by your insurance. While individual insurance plans differ in specifics, most health plans, including Medicare, provide some coverage for chiropractic care.

Tai Chi

Tai chi is a low-impact and inexpensive therapy that can help people relax and feel peaceful. It includes balance training, which can reduce the incidence of falls. A traditional Chinese martial art, tai chi is viewed by some as an exercise or dance, while others report that it helps them relax or find peace of mind.

There are many styles of tai chi, but all focus on meditation, breathing exercises, and slow, graceful movements. Tai chi is usually learned in a group setting, although there are videos and DVDs with good instruction. A tai chi session typically lasts between 10 and 30 minutes and moves through a series of specific postures or forms.

The advantage of a class is that you can get feedback and ask questions. Classes are offered in community centers, hospitals, churches, and health clubs. Classes often meet for four to six weeks, and participants are encouraged to practice daily on their own. In looking for a class, find a teacher who is experienced and who does a good job both explaining and demonstrating the movements. You can always ask to observe a class before joining. Tai chi does not require any particular equipment or special clothing.

A published study of tai chi involved 200 people over the age of 70. Investigators compared a group attending tai chi class twice a week for 20 minutes and practicing on their own with a discussion group and a group receiving computerized balance training. The results were dramatic. People enrolled in the discussion group and computerized balance training did not reduce their numbers of falls. Those attending the tai chi class reduced the number of falls by 47.5% and were less fearful of falling (Wolf et al. 2003).

Tai chi provides considerable benefit with little risk. There are no adverse effects of tai chi reported in the scientific literature.

Meditation

Meditation is a self-directed practice for relaxing the body and calming the mind. People in many cultures have used it since ancient times. Research studies have found that meditation helps people manage pain, reduce anxiety and depression, reduce blood pressure, and improve sleep (Kreitzer 2002).

There are many forms of meditation. Tai chi is considered to be a type of moving meditation, as is the Japanese martial art of aikido. Walking a labyrinth can be a meditative practice. Yoga involves postures and breathing that prepare a person for meditation. However, the most common forms of meditation used in the United States are sedentary and generally require only a quiet place to sit on a chair, bench, or pillow.

Three types of meditation practices will be described in this chapter: mindfulness meditation, relaxation response, and centering prayer.

An increasingly popular form of meditation is called *mindfulness meditation*. The goal of mindfulness meditation is often described as "nonstriving and nondoing." Meditators become detached observers of the stream of changing thoughts, feelings, drives, and visions. While focusing on breath, attention freely shifts from one thought to the next. In this form of meditation, no thought or sensation is considered an intrusion or is judged. People are encouraged to meditate 20–30 minutes per day.

Dr. Herb Benson, founder of the Mind-Body Institute at Harvard Medical School, has developed an approach that he calls the *relaxation response* (1975). Using this technique, people find a quiet place where they will not be distracted or interrupted and choose a focus that will be used whenever they meditate. The focus may be a sound, word, or phrase that is repeated silently or aloud. People are encouraged to spend 15–30 minutes a day meditating in this manner.

Centering prayer is a practice developed by the Rev. Thomas Keating (1995). It is a discipline designed to draw our attention from the ordinary flow of thoughts and reduce the obstacles to contemplative prayer. In centering prayer, people find a comfortable position, close their eyes, and focus on a sacred word. As thoughts come to mind, they are encouraged to consider them debris floating down a river and to detach and focus on the river itself. Keating says that at least 20–30 minutes is needed for most people to establish inner silence and go beyond superficial thoughts.

As with tai chi, meditation classes are taught in many schools, community centers, clinics, and hospitals. There are books and CDs that teach meditation techniques and support meditation practice. Meditation is not a skill that can be learned overnight; it takes practice.

Acupuncture for Strength

Conway has been diabetic for many years, and, along with other health complications, his balance is often affected. After falling in his home and tearing his rotator cuff, Conway had shoulder surgery and several weeks of inpatient rehabilitation. While he was recovering from surgery, his legs weakened to the point that he couldn't get into the car without lifting his right leg with his hands and swinging it into the vehicle.

A neighborhood friend told Conway she had gotten relief from severe back pain with acupuncture. Conway was intrigued and decided to try it.

He got a referral from his doctor and went to a local acupuncture clinic, where he learned more about the procedure. The acupuncturist placed the needles starting at Conway's neck, down his back, buttocks, and legs. The procedure was comfortable and almost relaxing.

After just three sessions, Conway noticed an improvement in leg strength. With two more sessions, his legs (especially the right one) were strong enough to lift him in and out of the car.

Yoga

Yoga is an ancient practice that began in India about 5,000 years ago. It is not a religion; rather it is considered a spiritual path that is compatible with many belief systems. The word "yoga" means union or joining together of the individual and universal spirit. Anyone, regardless of health or beliefs, can benefit from yoga. Regular practice heals and strengthens the body, sharpens the mind, and calms the spirit (Cameron 2006).

An estimated 15 to 20 million Americans practice yoga. That number is expected to increase. Hatha yoga, one of several yogic traditions, is the most common form of yoga practiced in the United States. Even within the hatha yoga tradition, there are many different styles of yoga: Iyengar, Ashtanga (also called Power Yoga), and several forms of "gentle" yoga (Integral, Kripalu, and viniyoga). Gentle forms of yoga are a good fit for people with acute or chronic health conditions. Hatha yoga involves stretching and strengthening poses, breathing practices, and meditation techniques.

A recent summary of research findings across many different types of patients with various health conditions found that yoga decreased stress, improved sleep and mood, reduced blood pressure, decreased anxiety, improved balance and movement, decreased fatigue, and enhanced overall quality of life (Cameron 2006).

Talk to the teacher before signing up for a yoga class. Ask about the teacher's training, experience, knowledge, and what the class will involve. You might ask the teacher to describe a typical class session or you can ask to observe a class. Some classes are geared to groups like older adults, children, pregnant women, or people with chronic illnesses. Some teachers also give private lessons. Ask about charges for the class and whether you should bring equipment (such as a mat) to class.

Yoga is considered a safe practice with few risks. Yoga should not be painful, and teachers will discourage you from straining to do yoga poses and breathing. You can avoid any adverse effects by approaching yoga gently and in moderation. If you are on medication, discuss it with your teacher, as some medications may affect your stability or increase your health risks should you fall out of a pose.

Herbal Therapies and Nutritional Supplements

Herbal therapies, such as ginkgo, saw palmetto, or valerian, come from plants or substances derived from plants. Nutritional supplements include vitamins, minerals, and amino acids. They come in many forms, including tablets, gelcaps, liquids, powders, and food bars.

See "Vitamins and Minerals," page 111.

People use herbal therapies to treat symptoms, prevent disease, and to improve their overall health and well-being. Adverse reactions to herbal therapies are low and usually mild with little risk of serious consequences. This is not to say that herbal therapies never produce serious adverse reactions. In 2004, the Food and Drug Administration pulled ephedra, an herbal stimulant used in weight loss products, from the market after several fatalities were reported.

Some early studies of herbal therapies that suggested promising results were later discounted when large clinical trials were conducted. On the other hand, new research is constantly emerging that helps us sort out what is effective and what is not. The websites of the National Institutes of Health (NIH) and other government agencies are excellent sources of information. There are also a number of nonprofit companies that provide independent and unbiased information. A company's website is not always a good source of objective information regarding its herbal products. See the resources section of this chapter for a list of reliable online sites.

Acupuncture

Acupuncture involves the insertion of very fine needles into the skin at specific points to manipulate *qi* (pronounced "chee"), or vital energy. Acupuncture is used to treat many conditions, including chronic pain, nausea associated with chemotherapy, migraine headaches, and substance abuse. The NIH database contains clinical research studies on acupuncture that document safety and effectiveness. A recent NIH study tested the effectiveness of acupuncture in treating osteoarthritis. In that study, participants with osteoarthritis of the knee were randomly assigned to one of three groups. One group received acupuncture (six two-hour sessions over 12 weeks) and the other two groups received either placebo acupuncture or health education. The group that received acupuncture reported better function of the knee (movement) and less pain (Berman et al. 2004).

An acupuncture treatment can last from a few minutes to more than an hour, depending on the type of treatment and condition of the patient. Most treatments take about 20 minutes. The needles are usually made of stainless steel and are not reusable. Most people do not find the treatments painful or unpleasant, describing them as a dull aching or mildly electrical sensation that spreads through the body in waves. After a treatment, many people feel relaxed and refreshed. People typically receive a series of 10 treatments.

All states currently license acupuncture providers, and most states require national board certification as a prerequisite for state certification or licensure. State laws vary, so consult with your state department of health to understand regulations in your area.

Talking to Your Health Care Provider

Many people do not feel comfortable talking with their physician or nurse-practitioner about nontraditional therapy. They fear disapproval, discouragement, or that their health care provider won't know enough about nontraditional therapy to help. You must talk with your health care provider about your use of nontraditional therapy. Not all nontraditional therapies are safe or effective, and some may be dangerous, depending on your health condition and other drugs or treatments you are receiving. More doctors, nurses, and pharmacists are learning about nontraditional therapies in their health-professional training. It is important that you have an open enough relationship with your health care provider to be comfortable asking questions about whatever is on your mind, including the use of nontraditional therapy.

See chapter 9, "Creating Your Health Care Team," page 147.

Accessing Services

If you have decided to use a nontraditional therapy, finding a provider requires the same steps as finding a doctor or nurse-practitioner. Begin by talking with your primary health care provider or someone who is knowledgeable about nontraditional therapies and ask whether he or she has recommendations.

Check with your insurance company to see if the treatment is covered by your insurance. While third-party payers cover some nontraditional therapy services, most require some out-of-pocket payment. After your first visit, you can decide whether the treatment plan seems reasonable and acceptable, whether you feel comfortable with the provider, and whether you want to continue.

What do they mean by...

Naturopathy? Naturopathy is a holistic system of care that includes nutrition and lifestyle counseling, dietary supplements, medicinal herbs, exercise, and homeopathy (highly diluted medicinal remedies).

Energy therapies? Reiki, healing touch, and therapeutic touch are based on the belief that there is an energy field around the body that can be manipulated or changed to improve health and well-being. Some energy therapists use light touch, whereas others move the hands around the body while not actually touching it. Another kind of energy therapy uses magnets and electromagnetic fields.

Aromatherapy? Aromatherapy is the use of essential plant oils to treat ailments such as nausea, fatigue, infections, and burns. The oils can be inhaled or applied (diluted) by compress, spray, bath, or massage. Essential oils are available in markets, co-ops, and pharmacies, and are also being used in some hospitals and clinics.

WORKSHEET

How Do I Want to Use Nontraditional Therapies?

	I Have Tried It	What Worked?	What Didn't Work?	I Would Like to Try It for . . .
Chiropractic care				
Tai chi				
Meditation				
Yoga				
Herbal therapies				
Acupuncture				
Other				

How Do I Want to Use Nontraditional Therapies? *continued*

What questions do I have about nontraditional therapies?

How will I get my questions answered?

What steps do I want to take to integrate nontraditional therapies into my wellness plan?

Questions & Answers

Q. Why are people turning to nontraditional therapies?

A. The majority of users have a chronic health condition and are looking for ways to better manage symptoms (such as pain) that do not respond to conventional medicine. Some use nontraditional therapies to maintain or improve their overall health. Others want natural or less-invasive therapy and find nontraditional therapies closer to their personal values or preferences.

In a study focusing on the use of nontraditional therapy by Medicare enrollees who were also enrolled in a supplemental plan offered by Blue Shield of California, the most commonly cited reasons for using nontraditional therapy were back problems, chronic pain, general health improvement, and arthritis. Of those who used nontraditional therapy, 80% reported improvement in their symptoms after receiving nontraditional therapy (Astin et al. 2000).

Q. Do most users of alternative therapies reject conventional medicine?

A. No. Study after study has found that most users of nontraditional therapies are not rejecting conventional medicine. Rather, they want to combine the best of nontraditional therapy and conventional care. In fact, one study found that less than 5% of people using nontraditional therapies do so "instead of" conventional medicine (Astin 1998).

See "Making a Medical Decision," page 152.

Q. How can I decide whether to try a nontraditional therapy?

A. When making any treatment decision you should talk to your health care provider and then consider the risks, benefits, and evidence supporting the use of the therapy.

Q. I am interested in herbal therapy. How can I be sure I'm buying high-quality herbs?

A. Look at the labels for the symbol or seal from either United States Pharmacopeia (USP) or NSF International. These organizations certify that the product contains the ingredients listed on the label in the declared strength and amount, does not exceed contamination limits, and complies with good manufacturing practices.

Q. How can I be sure a therapy is safe?

A. To find out if a nontraditional therapy is safe for you to use, you should talk to your health care provider. There are some herbal therapies such as gingko that may improve memory. Gingko, however, may also increase bleeding time and would be unsafe to take before surgery or if you are already taking a blood thinner. There are other herbal therapies that may be unwise or even unsafe to take as they may interfere with a prescription or nonprescription drug that you are taking.

continued on page 171

Questions & Answers *continued*

Q. How can I tell if a therapy is effective?

A. There is no simple answer to this question. There is strong evidence that some interventions, such as acupuncture, are effective in treating conditions like chronic pain and migraine headaches. Acupuncture is also safe in that complications or negative side effects from its use are very rare. There is also strong evidence supporting the use of many mind-body interventions, including guided imagery, relaxation therapies, and meditation. The evidence supporting use of homeopathy is less developed, and there are few rigorously executed research studies that demonstrate effectiveness. On the other hand, there is also very little evidence that there is risk in using homeopathy.

Q. In the United States, nontraditional health care has been a sort of grassroots movement. Are mainstream institutions starting to use it?

A. They are. In 2002, 16.6% of hospitals were offering nontraditional therapies, 75% offered community nontraditional therapy education programs, and 49% provided nontraditional therapy information on their hospital websites. Of those hospitals not offering nontraditional therapy services, 24% had plans to do so (Ananth 2002).

Long-term care facilities are integrating nontraditional therapy into residents' plan of care. Acupuncture is used for pain management; biofeedback for urinary incontinence, pain and anxiety; massage for edema; and chiropractic care for back pain and arthritis (D'Eramo 2001).

Resources

Dietary Supplements and Botanical Medicine

American Botanical Council
www.herbalgram.org

NIH Office of Dietary Supplements
ods.od.nih.gov

NSF International
www.nsf.org
(Click "Consumer" then "Dietary Supplements.")

United States Pharmacopeia
www.usp.org

USDA Center for Food Safety and Applied Nutrition
www.cfsan.fda.gov

Other Nontraditional Therapies

Center for Spirituality and Healing, University of Minnesota
www.takingcharge.csh.umn.edu/therapies
Information on nontraditional therapies.

Medline Plus
www.medlineplus.org
Information from the National Library of Medicine, the National Institutes of Health, and other trusted sources. A recent addition is extensive information on herbal medicines from the Natural Standard database.

The National Board of Chiropractic Examiners (NBCE)
www.nbce.org/publications/pub_main.html
Studies on chiropractic practices.

National Cancer Institute
www.cancer.gov
Information for patients and families, including information on complementary and alternative medicine.

National Center for Complementary and Alternative Medicine
www.nccam.nih.gov
National Institutes of Health information on the safety and effectiveness of nontraditional treatments.

WORKSHEET

Action Plan for Maintaining Your Health

Are you moving in the right direction to achieve your goals? To help you think about the changes you might want to make, mark (✗) the following on the scale between *No Change Needed* to *Needs Immediate Attention.*

MAINTAINING YOUR HEALTH	No Change Needed	Needs Immediate Attention
Chapter 5 – Staying Healthy		
Losing excess weight	●	●
Getting enough sleep	●	●
Reducing stress in my life	●	●
Quitting smoking	●	●
Reducing my alcohol consumption	●	●
Addressing drug abuse / addictive behavior	●	●
Getting up-to-date on screening and testing	●	●
Getting immunizations	●	●
Preventing injuries	●	●
Chapter 6 – Eating for Life		
Eating a healthy diet	●	●
Getting the right vitamins and minerals	●	●
Chapter 7 – Keeping Strong, Fit, and Active		
Learning about physical activity	●	●
Exercising regularly	●	●
Chapter 8 – Maintaining Mental Fitness		
Doing activities to keep my mind sharp	●	●
Following keys to mental fitness	●	●
Making positive changes	●	●
Chapter 9 – Creating Your Health Care Team		
Finding a health care provider	●	●
Communicating with my health care provider	●	●
Making informed health care decisions	●	●
Preparing an advance directive	●	●
Chapter 10 – Finding Nontraditional Paths to Health		
Exploring complementary, alternative, or integrative therapies	●	●

Action Plan for Maintaining Your Health *continued*

What are my retirement goals for maintaining my health? Write your goals here and on "My Retirement Map" on pages 10 and 11.

What barriers do I need to overcome to achieve my goals?

What am I going to do to achieve my goals? Use the action steps worksheet on the next page to write down the steps and track your progress.

WORKSHEET

Action Steps Worksheet – Goal #1

Steps I Am Going to Take	Target Completion Date	My Progress	Notes
		started complete!	
		started complete!	
		started complete!	
		started complete!	
		started complete!	
		started complete!	
		started complete!	

WORKSHEET

Action Steps Worksheet – Goal #2

Steps I Am Going to Take	Target Completion Date	My Progress	Notes
		started complete!	
		started complete!	
		started complete!	
		started complete!	
		started complete!	
		started complete!	
		started complete!	

Part 3

Managing Your Money

Managing money for retirement is much like managing money at any other time of your life—with some added considerations. As you move away from work-related income and toward a greater reliance upon savings and pension-related income, you are losing a primary source for adding to your wealth. For most people, retirement is the time in life when you spend down your wealth. That means a limited pool of money and concerns about whether you will have enough.

Money gives you options—to do more things, have more comforts, gain new experiences, and contribute in different ways. Money is a tool, no more and no less. To use it effectively, start by thinking about your goals. It is difficult to get to your destination if you do not know where you are going. As longevity increases and medical costs continue to rise, getting a handle on your finances becomes even more important. Society has a role as a safety net, but the net will not stretch far enough if individuals do not do their share.

So where do you start? Most people want to know if they will have enough money. And while the answer may be a simple yes or no, determining that answer can be complicated. Following the steps in this section will help you make sure you have the money you need throughout your retirement.

Planning has its challenges, both intellectual and emotional. Meeting your goals may require change. Change is scary, even if it's good.
The payoff is that a good plan gives you the information you need to make meaningful choices in your life and puts you in control.

You will notice that there is a great deal of detail involved in this section. There is no way around it. Financial planning requires getting numbers down on paper. If your situation is complicated or if this is all new to you, some of the worksheets in the next few chapters may seem tedious. But thoroughness is critical. Take your time. Get help if you need it. Many of the worksheets build on each other, so you will want to complete them in the order that they are presented. You may find a computer spreadsheet program, such as Microsoft Excel, helpful.

The chapters in this part of the workbook include:

- **Knowing How You Want to Live.** Start by understanding what matters to you and how you want to live your life.
- **Taking Inventory of Your Resources.** This chapter examines how you spend your money, your sources of income, what you own, and what you owe. Just getting these numbers down on paper can help you see if you are earning and spending money in a way that supports the kind of life you want to live.

- **Investing Basics.** This overview will help you understand how different types of investments produce income.
- **Making the Most of Your Investments.** Your tolerance for risk and other factors make some investments better for you than others. This chapter will discuss those factors and strategies for increasing investment returns and managing risk.
- **Managing Tax Obligations.** Lowering the taxes on an investment increases your spendable income. This chapter helps you understand your options.
- **Making Your Money Last a Lifetime.** This chapter helps you answer the burning question: Will I have enough? This will help you estimate what you will need to live the life you want.
- **Passing On What You Have.** Estate planning means having your legal affairs in order at the time of your death. But it also means being prepared in case you become disabled or unable to manage your own financial, legal, and medical affairs.
- **Pulling Together Your Financial Plan.** This chapter brings all your planning together to help you create a blueprint you can follow to achieve your goals and secure your future.

IN THIS CHAPTER

Chapter 11

Knowing How You Want to Live

Matching your finances to your lifestyle

IT'S GOOD TO HAVE MONEY AND THE THINGS THAT MONEY CAN BUY, BUT IT'S GOOD, TOO, TO CHECK UP ONCE IN A WHILE AND MAKE SURE THAT YOU HAVEN'T LOST THE THINGS THAT MONEY CAN'T BUY.

—*George Horace Lorimer, former editor of the* Saturday Evening Post

In the "Living Your Life" section of this book, you have an opportunity to think about what matters to you and how you want to live your life. Once you know how you want to live, you can develop a financial plan that will help you achieve your goals.

See chapter 1, "Embracing What Matters," page 17, and chapter 3, "Using Your Time," page 49.

Defining Your Goals

It is easier to achieve financial goals if you connect them to things that are important to you. Putting your current goals down on paper is the best place to start planning your financial future. Your goals and priorities will likely change over time. That's okay.

Mark Fischer
Certified Financial Planner

WORKSHEET

What Are My Retirement/Life Goals and What Will They Cost?

List your retirement/life goals. Be as specific as you can. If you have already prepared an action plan in the "Living Your Life" or "Maintaining Your Health" sections, the goals you identified there might be helpful as you list your goals here. Remember, this is just how you would answer the question right now. Your goals might change in the future.

Put down a ballpark figure to get a sense of what it will cost to live the retirement life you imagine. Use a monthly, annual, or one-time amount—whatever will help you get a sense of the overall picture. Don't labor over the costs here. In later chapters we will look more closely at what you can predict for your actual cost and income in retirement.

Retirement/Life Goals	Priority (1 = High; 2 = Med.; 3 = Low)	Estimated Cost
______________	______	______
______________	______	______
______________	______	______
______________	______	______
______________	______	______
______________	______	______
______________	______	______
______________	______	______
Accomplish ______________	______	______
______________	______	______
______________	______	______
Travel (number of trips, length, location) ______	______	______
______________	______	______
______________	______	______
Doing these things that I love ______	______	______
______________	______	______
______________	______	______
Spending time with ______	______	______
______________	______	______
______________	______	______

Setting Priorities and Making Choices

Some of the things that are most important to you require substantial resources; others require fewer resources. If you have limited resources, first consider doing the things that are the most important to you but require the least resources to achieve.

Everything in your life is about making choices. Sometimes making choices that support the kind of life you want to lead means making changes in your life. This can be challenging, but if your goals are tied to what matters to you, it will be easier to make the necessary changes.

See "Making Positive Changes," page 142.

Money Talks

Dawn and Jerry retired at the same time. Both had long careers, and because of good planning they were able to retire early. Now they could engage in the activities they liked and pursue their dreams.

Dawn and Jerry each had their own approach to money management, and their different styles were causing some stress in their lives. Jerry wanted to discuss their finances often, sometimes daily, while Dawn felt overwhelmed discussing money that often.

To meet each of their needs—Jerry's to stay on top of their financial plan and Dawn's for some space between discussions—they reached a compromise. Jerry and Dawn agreed to keep their money talks to a two-hour session once a week. They reviewed their budget, upcoming expenses, investment concerns, travel plans, and long-range goals. Revisions or changes were made as needed.

Jerry and Dawn are happy with their compromise on money discussions. Dawn isn't feeling stressed talking about finances every day, and Jerry has come to like the weekly conversations. He plans ahead for discussing any concerns that come up. And the stress level for both is down.

Questions & Answers

Q. I don't have retirement goals. The only way I am going to have enough money is to keep working.

A. Putting off retiring can be a good strategy to give you an opportunity to save more. Keep in mind that you won't be able to work forever. And even if you continue to work, having goals for this part of your life will help you make it more fulfilling.

Q. I want to get my finances under control, but I can't seem to get started. How do I get unstuck?

A. Take some time to think about what's standing in the way. Sometimes people get overwhelmed by trying to achieve too much too quickly. So instead, they just do nothing. The worksheets in this section will help you take one piece at a time and slowly complete the entire puzzle. At the end of this part of the book we will help you make an action plan for yourself. Once you write it down, hold yourself accountable for making progress.

IN THIS CHAPTER

Chapter 12

Taking Inventory of Your Resources

Determining where you are financially—and what you'll need to get where you want to go

CAN ANYBODY REMEMBER WHEN THE TIMES WERE NOT HARD AND MONEY NOT SCARCE?

—*Ralph Waldo Emerson, American essayist and poet*

The most fundamental law of economics is that all resources are limited. You must make choices about how to allocate your resources to accomplish your objectives. Knowing what your resources are will give you more control over your life. It will help you to avoid problems and allow you to take advantage of opportunities.

Start by looking at your current income and expenses. In this chapter, we will also look at what you own (your assets) and what you owe (your liabilities). You will have an opportunity to look at the income you expect in the future. In the next chapter, we will start to look at how to invest the money you save in a way that will help you meet your goals.

Mark Fischer
Certified Financial Planner

Getting Your Financial Bearings

Current Income and Expenses

Examining your current income and expenses is a good place to begin to understand your financial standing. Are you living within your means? Do you have the right balance between spending for now and saving for the future? Does what matters to you guide your spending?

Listing your income and expenses will help you in two ways. First, it will show you where your money is really going. Second, it will help you channel money from less important expenses to those that will provide more meaningful experiences.

WORKSHEET

My Current Income and Expenses

What are your sources of income (look at the past 12 months)? Paycheck stubs, income tax forms, and bank statements are a good source for the numbers. You may find a computer spreadsheet program, such as Microsoft Excel, helpful.

Current Income	Monthly Amount	Annual Amount
Earned Income (gross amount)		
Job 1 ______	______	______
Job 2 ______	______	______
Business ______	______	______
Other Noninvestment Income		
Social Security ______	______	______
Pension ______	______	______
Annuities ______	______	______
Investments		
Dividends ______	______	______
Interest ______	______	______
Capital gains ______	______	______
Other		
Gifts ______	______	______
______	______	______
______	______	______
Total Current Income	______	______

My Current Income and Expenses *continued*

Now identify how much money you spend in different categories. Your checkbook(s) or credit/debit card statements will contain much of the information you need for your estimates. If you are using a computerized bookkeeping program, you can use those figures.

When you are done, you will have many entries, including most of those listed below. You can break the entries down into a more detailed list. Approximate numbers will work well in this tabulation.

Current Expenses	Monthly Amount	Annual Amount
Essentials		
Food ______	______	______
Housing ______	______	______
Utilities ______	______	______
Taxes ______	______	______
Clothing ______	______	______
Transportation ______	______	______
Insurance ______	______	______
Maintenance/repairs ______	______	______
Medical/dental ______	______	______
Medication ______	______	______
Other		
Entertainment ______	______	______
Vacations ______	______	______
Education ______	______	______
Gifts ______	______	______
Charity ______	______	______
Other ______	______	______
______	______	______
______	______	______
Total Current Expenses	______	______

My Current Income and Expenses *continued*

Net Cash Flow

The difference between your income and expenses is your *net cash flow.* Calculate your net cash flow below.

Total Income	–	Total Expenses	=	Net Cash Flow
________	–	________	=	________

If the net cash flow is a positive number, you are saving money. If it is negative, you are borrowing money or withdrawing money from savings.

When you calculate net cash flow, ask yourself if the result is reasonable. Does it match what you know is true about your finances? If not, you may have miscalculated your income or expenses. Go back over the numbers until your cash flow matches what you know to be true about your financial situation.

How am I doing?

Am I making and spending money in a way that supports what I say is important?

What changes do I want to make?

What Have You Saved So Far?

Savings are a cornerstone of financial well-being in retirement. The earlier you save, the better. Still, it is never too late to start saving or to step up your savings rate. Your accumulated savings and what you own (your assets) minus what you owe (your liabilities) is your *net worth.*

WORKSHEET

My Current Net Worth

Today's Date ______________________

Assets	
Type of Account or Property	**Amount**
Checking accounts ______________	______________
Savings accounts ______________	______________
401(k) plan ______________	______________
IRAs ______________	______________
______________	______________
Roth IRAs ______________	______________
Other investment accounts ______________	______________
______________	______________
Life insurance (cash value) ______________	______________
Home (market value) ______________	______________
Automobile (current value) ______________	______________
Personal property ______________	______________
______________	______________
Other ______________	______________
Total Assets	______________

My Current Net Worth *continued*

Liabilities		
Type	**Lender**	**Amount Owed**
Home mortgage	____________	____________
Second mortgage	____________	____________
Credit card balances	____________	____________
Car loans	____________	____________
Education loans	____________	____________
Other ____________	____________	____________
____________	____________	____________
	Total Liabilities	____________

Net Worth

Your net worth is the difference between your total assets and your total liabilities. It is a summary of your money resources at a moment in time. Calculate your net worth below.

Total Assets	–	Total Liabilities	=	Net Worth
____________	–	____________	=	____________

What Income Do You Expect in the Future?

You probably already know something about the income you will have when you retire. List what you know below. You will take a more detailed look at your income in chapter 16. In chapter 11, you had an opportunity to estimate what your dreams will cost. Together, these numbers give you a ballpark sense of your ability to achieve your goals.

WORKSHEET

My Future Sources of Income

Type	Source	Monthly Amount	Annual Amount	When Available?
Social Security	______	______	______	______
Pension	______	______	______	______
Earned income	______	______	______	______
Investment income	______	______	______	______
Inheritance	______	______	______	______
Other ______	______	______	______	______
______	______	______	______	______
______	______	______	______	______

Your Nonfinancial Resources

When you think of your resources, you may think only about money. Money is important, but you have other resources you can use to accomplish your goals: relationships, skills, time, and energy. Sometimes, these resources can be used in combination with or in place of money to help you achieve your retirement objectives.

For example, let's assume that you want to go to Mexico but don't have the money or the mobility to take the trip you want. With your skills and connections in mind, you might find a way.

You have the time and flexibility to go when you want. You have two granddaughters who are excited about working with you. One is an experienced traveler who can help you find less expensive flights and opportunities to combine travel and volunteer service. The other is willing to go with you and help you get around. Her mother, your daughter, would not want the granddaughter to go by herself. But everyone is excited about her going with you. The volunteer work there will provide free housing and meals for part of the trip plus the opportunity to get to know the residents.

WORKSHEET

What Nonfinancial Resources Do I Have?

Look at your retirement/life goals. List some of the ways you might be able to use skills, energy, and connections to achieve these goals with less money than you initially thought.

Questions & Answers

Q. Is managing my cash flow all about cutting expenses?

A. No, it is about matching cash flow with desired lifestyle. This comes from identifying spending alternatives and choosing them based on their costs and how they will help you accomplish your goal of a meaningful lifestyle.

Q. Will I have to work during retirement?

A. That depends on your desired lifestyle and its income requirements. If you do work, look for a job that provides not just income but also activities and outcomes that are meaningful to you and to others.

Q. Should I spend investment income now or reinvest it for later?

A. Figure out how much total return and investment principal you can take out without jeopardizing future income before you make a decision. See chapter 16.

Q. Can I count on Social Security?

A. You will probably have Social Security income in some form. However, Social Security by itself will probably not be enough to maintain your meaningful lifestyle. Second, Social Security may be less generous in the future because of funding issues.

IN THIS CHAPTER

Chapter 13

Investing Basics

Knowing your options and making wise financial choices

BEFORE YOU INVEST, INVESTIGATE.

—*William Arthur Ward, American scholar and author*

W

Investments are a way to turn net worth into additional income. A good investment strategy is crucial to a sound financial plan.

To make good choices about investments, you need to understand how investments produce income. Each type of investment (stocks, bonds, cash instruments, real estate) produces income in a different way. Each has its own risks—and potential rewards.

Investments are created and sold because companies need investors' money to pay company bills and to expand. Companies are willing to pay for the use of that money.

Mark Fischer
Certified Financial Planner

Total return from an investment includes dividends, interest paid by the investment, and asset appreciation—also called capital gains. A capital gain is the difference between the price at which you purchased an investment and the price at which you sold it. For example, if you buy a stock at $30 per share and you sell it at $42 a share, you have a $12 capital gain. If the value of an investment decreases, there is a capital loss and the total return is decreased.

Risk affects total return in this way: The higher the risk of an investment, the greater the potential losses. However, higher-risk investments may also have a greater potential return. Lower-risk products offer lower potential returns but less chance for loss. To be worth it, a riskier investment must have the potential for higher returns.

Types of Investments

Contracts/Bonds

A contract is a promise to pay interest for use of your money and, eventually, to pay your money back. Certificates of deposit (CDs), money market accounts, bank savings accounts, bonds, and derivatives are contracts. The contract's value depends on the quality of the promise. For example, when you deposit money in a bank savings account, you are essentially giving the bank use of your money. The bank pays you interest for the use of your money, and will give it back whenever you want it. FDIC insurance backs up a bank's promise (up to $100,000), so this loan is very safe. The rates paid are therefore relatively low.

When institutions lend money to other institutions, promising to pay the money back years later, the loan contracts are called bonds. When you invest in a bond, you receive a set interest rate. At the maturity of the bond you receive your principal as well as the interest that has accrued. In general, government bonds are safer than corporate bonds and therefore pay less. Governments, unlike companies, can find the money to pay interest and dividends by raising taxes or even printing the money.

Generally, interest rates affect bond prices in an inverse way—when interest rates rise, bond prices fall, and vice versa.

Stocks

The other major category of investments is stocks: the ownership of shares of companies. Stocks are also called equities or securities. In general, stocks are riskier than investment-grade bonds and other contracts. Therefore, they have a higher potential for returns—and potential losses.

Which Bonds Pay the Highest Rates?

There are two major factors that affect risk and, therefore, the bond payment rate. The first is the safety and quality of a bond. The lower the rating and quality, the higher the total return (payments plus appreciation of the bond) if held to maturity. A lower-rated bond has a greater risk of default and, therefore, a greater risk that you will not get your money back. Firms such as Standard and Poor's and Moody's rate bonds, so you can get a sense of the risk you might be taking with a particular bond. The range of bonds between AAA and BBB are of the highest quality and are considered investment-grade bonds.

The second factor is time. The longer the bond term, the greater the risk and, therefore, the higher the rate of return is likely to be.

Owning shares of stock in a company entitles you to a share of the company's profits, paid out in dividends, and a share of the total value of the company. The major risk in owning shares of companies is that a company will stop earning money and stop paying dividends. If the future prospects for the company look good, the value of its shares will be high, and vice versa.

It is easy to believe that the past returns of a particular investment are a good benchmark for future returns. However, future returns are always uncertain. There are many unexpected events in the economy, politics, industries, and companies that affect a company's performance. Companies frequently publicize their expectations for future earnings. A good or bad surprise can have a large effect on prices because it may be an indication of future earnings changes. Stock prices can shift quickly if the earnings expectations change.

Stock Classifications

Stocks investments are sometimes broken down into subgroups by sector, size, location, or style of investment. Knowing these classifications will help you create a diversified portfolio.

Sector: A sector is a group of companies in the same industry, such as chemical, manufacturing, Internet, or telecommunications companies.

Size: Common classifications by size are large companies, medium-sized companies, small companies, and very small (micro) companies.

Location: The most common classifications based on location are domestic and foreign stocks.

Style of investment: There are three style classifications: growth (companies with high past performance and high expectations for increased earnings), value (companies with more modest past performance and expectations for earnings that are lower than growth investments), and blend (a mix of the two).

Aggregated Investments

You can own individual stocks, bonds, or real estate. Another way is to purchase an investment that holds pooled assets. Doing so allows you to diversify your investments effectively at a reasonable cost.

There are many ways to aggregate investments. One of the most common ways is in a mutual fund. When you own a mutual fund, you own a fraction of the whole portfolio, typically composed of hundreds of stocks or bonds or a combination of them. There are thousands of different mutual funds. Each has its own objectives and processes for investing.

Mutual funds differentiate themselves from each other in a variety of ways. Some contain a single asset class or sector or style of investment. A few call themselves "socially conscious" because they exclude categories of investments such as tobacco companies, companies making war armaments, or companies that exploit their employees.

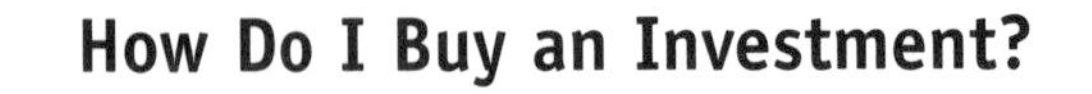

How Do I Buy an Investment?

New to investing and wondering how you purchase an investment? Here are three ways:

- Work with an investment advisor or stockbroker who will help you buy an investment. (See page 221 for more about finding the help you need.)
- Buy the investment yourself with an online brokerage account. Some of the largest are Charles Schwab, TD Ameritrade, Scottrade, and Fidelity. These discount brokers do not offer the level of investment advice of a full-service brokerage company or investment advisor, but fees are substantially less.
- Buy directly from the company that sells the investment. Many mutual fund companies have full-service websites that allow you to purchase shares in hundreds of their funds. Two of the largest are Vanguard and Fidelity. Many companies have direct stock purchase plans that allow you to buy stock directly from the company.

Whether you decide to invest yourself or hire someone to help you, make sure you do your research. If you don't want to manage your money, spend time finding someone who will help you invest your money to meet your goals. (See more about finding the help you need on page 221.) If you invest yourself, be sure you know the risks and the costs as well as the potential payoffs.

Variations on Mutual Funds

There are many variations on mutual funds. Some of these require relatively large minimum investments. Be sure that you have a good understanding of how the investment works before you invest.

Separate accounts (sometimes called subaccounts) are pools of investments managed by insurance companies instead of mutual fund companies. They are sometimes available in the form of annuities or life insurance.

Exchange-traded funds (ETFs) and unit investment trusts (UITs) have fixed portfolios of investments. You buy and sell them on a stock exchange much like a stock. They have lower overall costs, offer greater control over the sell and buy price, and have tax advantages. You pay commission costs when you buy and sell.

Managed accounts, also called managed money or wrap accounts, are pools of money managed on an individual basis for a single investor by a money manager.

Partnerships are smaller groups of investors who pool their money and share the profits.

An Inventory of My Investments

In chapter 12, you listed your assets, including those in investment accounts. Next you want to understand exactly what type of investments you own in each of your accounts. We will help you do that in two steps. First, look at the type of investment (cash, stocks, bonds, other). Then analyze the asset classes of your stock investments and look at the style of the investments.

You can find information about your investments in your monthly account statements or, for mutual funds, in the prospectus. If you have access to a website associated with your account, you will also find the information there. Lipper (*www.lipperweb.com*), Morningstar (*www.morningstar.com*), and Value Line (*www.valueline.com*) provide independent sources of information.

While some investments will be easy to characterize, others will be more challenging. Characterizing mutual funds, for example, can be difficult because many mutual funds contain multiple asset classes. For example, a fund can consist of 10% cash, 70% U.S. large companies, and 20% foreign large companies.

Include savings in bank accounts, CDs, and money market accounts as well as mutual funds and brokerage accounts. But keep in mind that these investments are just one part of your overall financial picture, which may also include Social Security, pensions, and other sources of income.

Step 1 – How Much Do I Have in Each Type of Investment?

List the investments you have in each of your accounts separately. Here is an example. Start your inventory on page 200.

Example:

Type of Investment

Account Name Ace Securities - Traditional IRA Account

Account Number 00023

Investment	Cash	Stocks	Bonds	Other	Total Amount	Annual Return
Company A - 200 shares		$24,400			$24,400	
A-1 Mutual Fund		$6,354	$1,035		$7,389	9.3%
AAA Bond Index Fund			$16,585		$16,585	5.4%
Cash	$2,567				$2,567	3.5%
Total	$2,567	$30,754	$17,620		$50,941	
Percentage	5%	60%	35%		100%	

An Inventory of My Investments *continued*

Date of Inventory_______________________________

Type of Investment						
Account Name						
Account Number						
Investment	Cash	Stocks	Bonds	Other	Total Amount	Annual Return
Total						

Account Name						
Account Number						
Investment	Cash	Stocks	Bonds	Other	Total Amount	Annual Return
Total						

An Inventory of My Investments *continued*

Account Name						
Account Number						
Investment	**Cash**	**Stocks**	**Bonds**	**Other**	**Total Amount**	**Annual Return**
Total						

Add sheets for additional accounts, if needed (available at *www.mappingyourretirement.org*).

When you have listed all your investments, add the figures in the cash, stocks, bonds, and other columns and record the totals below.

	Cash	**Stocks**	**Bonds**	**Other**	**Total Amount**	**Annual Return**
Total						
Percentage of total (Amount divided by total of all investments)						

Next let's look at the diversification within your stock investments.

An Inventory of My Investments *continued*

Step 2 – How Are Your Stocks Diversified by Asset Class and Style?
In this part of the worksheet, list stock investments only (use the list you created in the preceding section to get started). There are many ways to classify stock investments. This worksheet concentrates on asset class by size and location (U.S. large and small companies and foreign large and small companies) and the style of investment (growth, blend, or value).

Date of Inventory____________________________

Diversification by Asset Class and Style

Account Name

Account Number

	Asset Class						Type of Investment			
Stock Investment	U.S. Large	Foreign Large	U.S. Small	Foreign Small	Other	Total	Growth	Blend	Value	Total
Total										

Account Name

Account Number

	Asset Class						Type of Investment			
Stock Investment	U.S. Large	Foreign Large	U.S. Small	Foreign Small	Other	Total	Growth	Blend	Value	Total
Total										

An Inventory of My Investments *continued*

Account Name										
Account Number										
	Asset Class						**Type of Investment**			
Stock Investment	U.S. Large	Foreign Large	U.S. Small	Foreign Small	Other	Total	Growth	Blend	Value	Total
Total										

Add sheets for additional investment accounts, if needed (available at *www.mappingyourretirement.org*). When you have listed all your investments, add up the columns and record them below

	Asset Class						**Type of Investment**			
	U.S. Large	Foreign Large	U.S. Small	Foreign Small	Other	Total	Growth	Blend	Value	Total
Total										
Percentage of total stocks (total divided by total of all stock investments)										

This inventory shows you how your investments are currently diversified. In the next chapter you will have a chance to consider how you might want to change your diversification plan to better meet your goals.

Questions & Answers

Q. How can I find information about how my investments are performing?

A. The three most common standard references are Lipper (*www.lipperweb.com*), Morningstar (*www.morningstar.com*), and Value Line (*www.valueline.com*). They are also available at public libraries. There may be a charge for use of their databases.

Q. When is the best time to buy investments?

A. The best time is when you have the money. On average, investment values grow over a period of time, so waiting could reduce the return.

IN THIS CHAPTER

Chapter 14

Making the Most of Your Investments

Maximizing your wealth by balancing risk and reward

GOOD FORTUNE IS WHAT HAPPENS WHEN OPPORTUNITY MEETS WITH PLANNING.

—*Thomas Edison, American inventor*

Mark Fischer
Certified Financial Planner

The most common question people ask about their retirement finances is, "Will I have enough?" Answering this question is more complicated than it seems, because your needs and expenses will likely change throughout retirement, and the income you receive from investments and other sources will likely fluctuate as well.

While there is uncertainty in some areas, there are things you can control. By carefully managing certain aspects of your financial life, you will maximize your chances of getting what you need from your investments to lead a life that is meaningful to you.

This chapter will focus on a systematic approach to investment, addressing risk management, diversification, and quality of the individual investments. Attending to these issues will help you achieve your financial goals and, in turn, your life goals.

Balancing Risk and Returns

You are probably as concerned about the return *of* your investment as the return *on* your investment, as the American humorist Will Rogers used to say. If you are unable or unwilling to replace investments after a decline, you may be particularly concerned about risk.

One approach to reduce risk is to choose only safer investments—those with guarantees or low volatility. Remember, however, that safer investments generally produce less income. That may or may not be acceptable, depending on how much income you need for your lifestyle.

One strategy that may increase investment income is to combine higher-paying investments in such a way that their overall risk is reduced while still maintaining most or all of their return. This strategy is commonly called diversification. Asset allocation, combining investments based on their classifications (U.S. large companies, long-term corporate bonds, etc.), is the most common way to diversify a portfolio.

There is no single combination of investments that is best, although some combinations are more effective than others in obtaining a good mix of investment return and risk. Usually an investor determines his or her tolerance of risk and then constructs a portfolio with the highest potential return for that amount of risk.

The Importance of Reliable Income

The volatility of your portfolio has a surprisingly large effect on its performance. It is very difficult to recover from a significant drop in price. Consider these changes in an investment:

50% decrease in value:	$1,000 → $500
50% increase in value:	$500 → $750

Note that you are not back to where you started.

The Cost of Procrastinating

Time can work for you or against you. The great thinker Albert Einstein identified compound interest as the greatest invention of all time. Starting to save early will have a huge effect in the amount of money you end up with—through the compounding of your returns. If you have more money, you will have more and better opportunities available to you. Putting off for tomorrow what you should do today will only decrease the compounding.

It is easy to get stuck. You may want to avoid a bad decision. However, keeping the status quo is a decision too, and it may not be the best one.

Here is another example of the effect of volatility:

Start	Portfolio		Year 1	Year 2	Year 3
$1,000	A	Return	10%	10%	10%
		Value	$1,100	$1,211	$1,332
	B	Return	40%	-25%	15%
		Value	$1,400	$1,050	$1,207

The average return in each of the portfolios is 10%. However, Portfolio A, the more stable one, ended up with about 10% more money than the volatile one. Depending on the size of your portfolio, high volatility can make a huge difference over the course of a lifetime.

Combining Investments to Reduce Risk

You can think about a diverse portfolio the way you might think of a balanced meal. In a balanced meal, you would have something from each major food group. In a balanced portfolio, you should have diversity in sectors and asset classes. The total number of investments is not critical; the diversity is. For example, a portfolio composed of four technology-oriented mutual funds is no better diversified than a meal made up of nothing but four kinds of cheeses.

The key to effective diversification is to include a variety of asset classes in your portfolio—the asset allocation approach. For example, if your portfolio consisted of stock in a single computer software company, your investment would be very volatile. If you diversified by including other computer software companies, you would have removed the risk of owning a single stock while still capturing the return from part of the technology sector. If you now added other kinds of technology stocks, the risks would be reduced more. Adding other sectors would reduce the risk more. And adding stocks from other countries could reduce the risk further.

Knowing what you own in your portfolio is important to evaluate the effectiveness of your diversification. In the worksheet in chapter 13, you identified the characteristics of your investments (stock or bond, size, location, and investment style).

Diversification has two benefits—reducing risk and giving you the potential for higher returns. Adding a riskier investment to a portfolio can increase the overall return of the portfolio without markedly increasing the overall risk from volatility.

As an example, consider the effect of adding stocks from smaller U.S. companies to a portfolio composed only of stocks of large U.S. companies. Large and small companies behave differently in different phases of the economic cycle. When the economy gets tight, smaller companies may not have the resources to weather a storm and as a result they can underperform large companies. When the economy begins to boom, smaller companies may be more nimble and take advantage of opportunities more quickly. Movement in their prices will not necessarily be in sync—sometimes while one is falling in price, the other is rising. To some extent, a combination of the two will have less volatility than either by itself.

Also consider the law of diminishing returns. When you add a relatively small number of risky investments to a portfolio, they can increase the return without significantly increasing the portfolio volatility. Adding many risky investments, however, may increase the return only slightly while substantially increasing the volatility.

There is no perfect combination. The best you can do is to have a diverse portfolio that offers the possibility of growth at a risk level you can manage. Beware of using historical numbers to determine the best mix. *Past performance does not guarantee future performance.* Different mixes can and will work differently in the future.

Using Life Goals to Make Investment Choices

Your goals will play a key role in the way you think about investing your money for retirement. These two examples show different (and somewhat extreme) ways of managing risk to achieve different goals.

James has been a diligent saver throughout his life, and thanks to excellent return from investments in his company's stock, he realizes that he has made more than enough money to reach his retirement goals, which include volunteering at the local Humane Society, serving on the board of his church, and taking long hikes and camping trips along the Appalachian Trail. Because he knows he has enough and because he doesn't want worries about his financing keeping him up at night, he moves much of his portfolio into low-risk bonds, CDs, and annuities that offer guaranteed income.

Maura and Tim, meanwhile, have more costly retirement goals: they'd like to do extensive traveling before they settle down in the arts community of Santa Fe to buy and run a bed and breakfast inn. To earn the amount of money they'll need to achieve these goals, they're working hard to put much of their extra money into foreign stocks and U.S. small company stocks. They're hoping that in the 10 years between now and their planned retirement, they'll reap significant rewards, even if they have to weather downturns in their portfolio. They recognize that there is risk involved in this strategy, and know that they may need to hold off retiring or re-evaluate their plans if the stocks do not do as well as they've estimated.

Developing Your Diversification Plan

Successful investing is the result of mixing and matching investments so that they provide enough income for you to live the life you want.

The biggest decision in constructing your portfolio is the percentage of stock you will own. The greater the percentage of stock in your portfolio, the greater your potential return and the higher the risk. Investors are sometimes grouped into different categories based on the amount of stock in their portfolio: aggressive, growth, balanced growth, conservative, and very conservative. In these diversification plans, the portion of your portfolio that is not invested in stocks is invested in bondlike vehicles, cash vehicles such as money market accounts or CDs, and other investments, including real estate. Most people are in the three middle categories.

Your situation and your risk tolerance determine the type of investor you are. If you do not need income from your investments now and you can be philosophical about 15–30% drops in the stock market, then you may be a growth investor. If you lose sleep over 5–10% drops or you need substantial amounts of your principal over the next few years, you are probably a conservative investor.

Note that all of these portfolios, even for very conservative investors, can contain some stock. This is because, historically, all-bond portfolios not only have had a lower return than those with 30% stock, they also have had higher risk, as measured by changes in portfolio value (Goetzmann and Ibbotson 2005).

Aggressive investors will likely own more small companies and international investments within the stock portfolio than conservative investors. Their nonstock investments may include more real estate, leasing, and commodity investments (gold, wheat, oil, etc.) than a conservative investor would hold. A conservative investor, by contrast, may focus his or her investments in large, established companies. Nonstock investments might include insured savings accounts such as CDs and money market accounts.

The graphs on this page and the next show some typical mixes for different types of investors.

Mix of Investments by Type of Investor

Stock/Nonstock Mix

	Very Conservative	Conservative	Balanced Growth	Growth	Aggressive
Stock	Up to 30%	50 to 60%	70%	85%	95%
Nonstock investments (bonds, cash, other)	At least 70%	40 to 50%	30%	15%	5%

Sample Diversification Mixes by Type of Investor

Stock Allocation by Size and Location

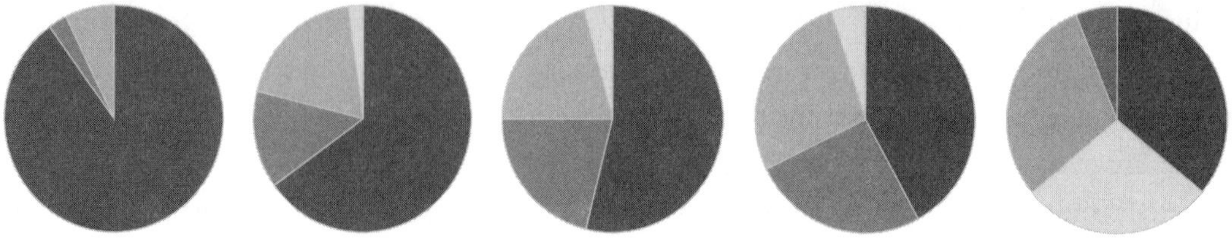

	Very Conservative	Conservative	Balanced Growth	Growth	Aggressive
U.S. large	90%	65%	54%	42%	36%
Foreign large	3%	14%	21%	26%	28%
U.S. small	7%	19%	21%	27%	30%
Foreign small	0%	2%	4%	5%	6%

Stock Allocation by Style of Investment

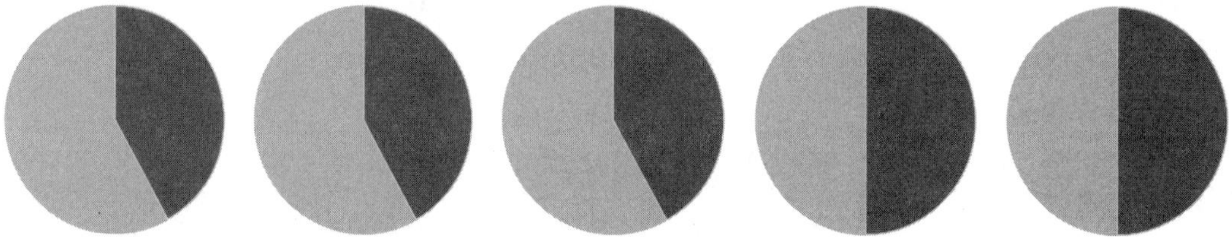

	Very Conservative	Conservative	Balanced Growth	Growth	Aggressive
Growth	35–50%	35–50%	35–50%	40–55%	40–60%
Value	50–65%	50–65%	50–65%	45–60%	40–60%

There are many asset classes that you might consider when diversifying your portfolio, but a portfolio that has large and small U.S. companies and large and small foreign companies provides adequate diversification for most people.

Unfortunately, no one can say exactly what type of return to expect for each portfolio. It is important to remember that diversification does not guarantee a profit or protect against loss. While it is possible to reduce your risk by using asset allocation, based on the Nobel Prize–winning "modern portfolio theory," it is still not possible to predict the future (Bowen and Goldie 1998).

The nonstock portion of your portfolio should also be diversified and can include bonds of different maturity and safety as well as real estate and other investments.

In the real world, all of these asset allocation mixes may be somewhat more conservative than you think—if you are eligible for Social Security payments or a pension. Each of these provides income independent of stock market fluctuations. They add stability to your income stream.

Cash on Hand

Make sure you have enough cash so that you can comfortably handle routine expenses. The typical guideline is 3–6 months of spending, although up to 12 months can be beneficial if you're living on investment income and trying to ride out a dip in your investments. Many people divide cash into two components—money for everyday spending and an emergency fund. If your income and expenses are quite regular and predictable, you can get by with less cash. For emergencies, you need another pool of money or a plan to get hold of additional money if you need it, without having to pay substantial penalties or fees.

Management Costs

Managing investments is not free. Costs are sometimes divided into two types: the cost of an initial or final transaction (for buying and selling) and the ongoing cost (for managing the investment and furnishing reports about what is happening on the inside of the investment).

The transaction costs are higher if you need help identifying or purchasing the investments. If a broker or investment advisor helps you, you typically pay them a commission or fee, either when an investment is bought or when it is sold, or both. Costs can range from 0% to 6% for the transaction. If the investment requires special setup, such as for real estate deals, the costs can be somewhat more.

Mutual funds and other aggregated investments require management. Even a "no-load" mutual fund—a mutual fund that has no transaction cost—charges annual fees for managing the investment. The typical mutual fund charges from .02% to more than 2% per year in management fees. In addition, mutual funds have their own transaction costs, which are over and above those stated in their prospectus (the disclosure document for funds). Because actively managed mutual funds average a 78% turnover of their portfolios each year, as much as 1% may be added to the annual costs (Bogle 2003).

Managed money accounts can have lower costs. Unlike mutual funds, their percentage of ongoing costs is generally reduced as the account size increases. Partnerships typically cost more to set up and manage. They are typically used to own less traditional investments, such as some real estate, future commodity contracts, leasing investments, oil and gas ventures, and others.

Nontraditional Approaches to Managing Risk

Over the past several years, new strategies for managing risk have been developed. Many of these use a hybrid approach, where a single investment contains a mix of stocks and contracts. Here are some examples:

- **Stock portfolios with option contracts.** The option values automatically move in the opposite direction of stocks to cushion the effect of market declines while reducing returns only slightly.
- **Annuity contracts with guarantees.** Annuities are investment contracts managed by an insurance company.
    - *Equity-indexed annuities* do not contain stocks, but their earnings can track certain stock indexes. They guarantee that an investment will never lose value. Their total return is generally limited and somewhat reduced from a pure stock portfolio.
    - *Variable annuities with guarantees.* Variable annuities contain separate accounts. They can put floors on the income you will receive in the future. For example, you will receive an income based on the growth of your investments but no less an amount than you would have received if your investments had grown at a 5% rate per year. (Any such guarantees are based upon the claims-paying ability of the issuing insurance company.)
- **Structured notes.** You hold the investment (traded like a stock) typically for four to seven years. At the end of that time you receive a return that tracks stock index(es) or is a fixed return at a low rate (1–3% per year), whichever is higher.

Some of these hybrid products have guarantees on the payout of income. They guarantee either the payout rate (for example, 5–6%) or the length of time, or both. It is likely that there will be an explosive growth of new financial products over the next few years that will be designed to produce the income retiring baby boomers will need.

Be careful in your evaluation of these hybrid products. They can be very complicated. Most will have a prospectus or an offering statement that describes how they work. Read it. Equity-indexed annuities are not considered securities and do not have prospectuses. Read their disclosure forms carefully so that you know the features and limitations of the products.

Make sure you understand the restrictions in accessing your money in these nontraditional approaches and how their costs will affect your eventual returns and income. The cost of guarantees will reduce the long-term total returns, compared to a pure stock portfolio. But they can be very competitive with a variety of safer investments—having a higher (potential) return with little if any more risk. They may also be competitive with a conservative or balanced portfolio described on pages 210 and 211.

Active and Passive Management of Investments

There are two major schools of thought about how to manage investments—active management and passive management. *Active management* means that a money manager selects investments in an attempt to provide higher returns than a particular benchmark. *Passive management* means building a portfolio with investments that match a particular market index or a combination of market indexes. Some say that money managers make a positive difference and, therefore, they advocate active management. Others advocate passive management, believing that money managers are not essential. Here are the arguments for each.

Active Management

- Many managers are very bright and hardworking and have superior research and technology to identify the best investments. They can and do find them.
- Active management is more fun. You get credit for being smart enough to find the best investment or investment manager.

Passive Management

- Passive funds have lower costs, which subtract less from the total return. This leaves more money for investments.
- On average, passive investments perform better than actively managed investments, probably because of their lower costs (Carhart 1997).
- It is not possible to pick the individual investments with the best potential. Current prices already reflect investors' expectations. It is only the unpredictable changes that make a substantial difference in performance.
- It is not possible to pick tomorrow's top active managers. In fact, actively managed investments with good past track records do not on average outperform managed investments with poorer past track records.

Keeping Your Costs Low

Although investment performance may be beyond your control, there are steps you can take to make sure you're getting the most for your money. One way is to control your costs.

Costs generally come in two forms: management expenses and "loads" (essentially sales commissions). The lower these fees are, the more money that will go into your pocket. After all, even if you earn 8% on an investment, if you are paying 2% in loads and fees, your effective return is 6%. (That's a 25% hit on your return!)

When you choose an investment, be sure you understand the costs as well as the overall effectiveness of the investment.

Most passive funds choose investments to match an index. For example, dozens of mutual funds are composed of the same stocks in the same amount as the Standard & Poor's 500 Index, which consists of the 500 largest publicly traded companies. There are hundreds of other funds that are matched to other indexes, both U.S. and foreign.

You can use either an active or a passive approach to construct a diversified portfolio. The difference is the investment styles of the individual funds. You must be careful that an active manager sticks with the diversification you want.

Beware of "closet indexing"—the worst of both alternatives (Seeking Alpha 2006). If you own a variety of actively managed funds within one asset class, they may own so many different companies that they are effectively indexed. But you are paying much higher costs for the individual managers. Such a portfolio *will* underperform the index approach.

Beating the Market

On average, timing the market does not work. This is true for switching individual stocks, mutual funds, sectors, or the stock/nonstock mix. The average investor tries to time by buying when investments look good—when prices have risen. Then the investor sells when investments look bad—when prices have fallen. This is called "buying high and selling low." Such behavior leads to bubbles, with their severe consequences. Do not do this!

A firm called Dalbar measures not just the performance of investments but of investors themselves. Dalbar reports that investors routinely underperform their investments, substantially, because of their poor timing. Dalbar also reports that the performance of investors who work with an advisor who encourages them to keep invested and not do a lot of buying and selling is much better than the performance of the average investor (Dalbar 2006).

Many researchers believe that you will get the best overall return using an indexing approach with an asset allocation that includes big and small companies and domestic and international investments. Many researchers also believe that depressed companies (value-oriented companies) outperform growth companies, on average, over a long period of time.

Timing Buying and Selling

If you are moving money from one investment to another to diversify your account, you can do it at any time—you are selling high and buying high or you are selling low and buying low.

It may be different if you are switching from cash to stocks. Some recommend you do this over a period of time (a practice called dollar cost averaging). Others argue that since stocks increase on average two-thirds of the time, you should purchase stocks as soon as you have the money available to do so.

If you are using investment income for spending money, it is helpful to keep substantial cash on hand. If you have 6–12 months of spending in cash, you may be able to reduce the chances of needing to cash in investments after they have fallen substantially in price. Consider liquidating investments after the price rises.

Should You Invest More Conservatively As You Get Older?

Possibly, but not necessarily. If you have met your investment goals and are most concerned about preserving your principal, you might choose to move to a more conservative approach. But, remember, there are consequences to conservative investing. You may have less income for the rest of your life.

People used to apply the "rule of 100" (100 – your age = % of stock) to determine the percentage of stock in their portfolio. As you get older, the percentage of stock gradually decreases. Your portfolio becomes less risky and the total return decreases. As we are living longer and will need investment income for more years, many people believe instead in the "rule of 120": at 20 you are 100% invested in the stock market; at 50, 70%; and at 80, 40%.

At whatever age, if you need a high return to pay for your lifestyle, you will want to consider some stock in your portfolio. Over longer periods of time, stocks have produced a higher total return than cash or bonds. Even at age 70–75, your money may need to last another 20–30 years (Goetzmann and Ibbotson 2005).

Paying Your Mortgage Off Early

Many retirees consider paying off the mortgage early, but you should look at the trade-offs before you do this. From a strictly financial sense, you might get a higher return than your mortgage interest rate on other investments. More liquid investments (investments from which you can more easily withdraw money) would make the money more available for temporary emergencies than if you had it tied up in home equity. Maintaining the itemized deduction of mortgage interest from taxable income can be valuable and should also be worked into the equation.

Here is a calculation that will help you decide if it is financially worthwhile to pay off your mortgage:

R = rate of return on alternative investment

I = interest rate on mortgage

T = marginal income tax bracket
(This is the tax rate on your last dollar of income and depends on your income and filing status. It currently varies between 10% and 35%. Use last year's return to calculate your tax rate.)

B = balance of mortgage owed

The extra annual cost for paying off the mortgage is:

(I x (1 – T) – R) x B (if you itemize expenses and deduct mortgage interest)

(I – R) x B (if you do not itemize expenses)

For example, if an alternative investment pays 7%, your mortgage rate is 6%, your marginal tax bracket is 31% (federal plus state), and your remaining mortgage is $100,000, then the consequence of paying off your mortgage is:

(6% x (1 – 0.31) – 7%) x 100,000 = (4.14% - 7%) x 100,000 = -$2,860

In this example, it would cost you money to pay off your mortgage early—assuming you achieve the rate of return you estimated for the alternative investment. The tax break you get on mortgage interest combined with the return you would get investing the money in an alternative investment would result in $2,860 in net lost income per year.

There are psychological benefits to paying off your mortgage. Only you can decide how to weigh your options.

WORKSHEET

My Portfolio Diversification Plan

In chapter 13 you made a list of your investments. Now it's time to decide what you think is the ideal diversification plan for you.

First, consider what you'll need for your day-to-day living:

Cash-on-hand requirements (see page 211)

	Actual	Desired	Difference
Checking/savings			
Emergency funds			

Next, look at your current investment portfolio:

Percentage of stock in current portfolio __________ (see page 201)

Desired type of investment portfolio (see page 209)

	Very Conservative	Conservative	Balanced Growth	Growth	Aggressive
	☐	☐	☐	☐	☐
Stock	Up to 30%	55%	70%	85%	95%
Nonstock investments	At least 70%	45%	30%	15%	5%
U.S. large	90%	65%	54%	42%	36%
Foreign large	3%	14%	21%	26%	28%
U.S. small	7%	19%	21%	27%	30%
Foreign small	0%	2%	4%	5%	6%
Growth	35–50%	35–50%	35–50%	40–55%	40–60%
Value	50–65%	50–65%	50–65%	45–60%	40–60%

Management approach (see page 213)

	Actual	Desired	Difference
Percentage actively managed			

My Portfolio Diversification Plan *continued*

Use your numbers from the worksheet in chapter 13 to make a plan for diversifying your investments to match your diversification plan:

Type of Investment	Current Dollars	Current %	Desired %	% Difference	Dollar Difference
Cash					
Stocks					
Bonds					
Other					
New contribution					
Total		100%			

Stock Asset Class	Current Dollars	Current %	Desired %	% Difference	Dollar Difference
U.S. large					
Foreign large					
U.S. small					
Foreign small					
Other					
New contribution					
Total		100%			

Stock Investment Style	Current Dollars	Current %	Desired %	% Difference	Dollar Difference
Growth					
Blend					
Value					
New contribution					
Total		100%			

Calculate the current percentages by dividing the current money for each asset class by the current money total. You can calculate the money differences by multiplying the percentage difference for each asset class by the current money total. Use the information on pages 218 to 220 to help you make a plan for rebalancing your portfolio.

WORKSHEET

My Contribution Schedule

Record how much you plan to contribute this year in each of your accounts.

Amount of Contribution (include your employer match)	Account (401(k), SEP account, regular savings, etc.)

Rebalancing Your Portfolio

Even if you do not add money to your portfolio, gains and losses will shift the percentages in each asset class. Rebalancing your portfolio each year will help you maintain the right mix of asset classes.

The easiest way to design your new portfolio is to sell everything and start over. But that approach could have high transaction costs for buying and selling and could subject your portfolio to capital gains taxes (see chapter 15).

When you are moving money around, remember that each individual account does not need to be balanced—it is the portfolio as a whole that should be properly balanced.

Here is the order of planning to balance your portfolio:

1. First, if you are still adding to your investments, you may consider contributing in a way that will balance your portfolio. For instance, if you have one asset class that is lagging, you may focus your investments in that area. As a result, other investments will take on a smaller overall percentage of the total.
2. Next, go to accounts with limited choices, such as a 401(k) or other plans at work. Choose the most appropriate alternatives there first; then work on your other accounts.
3. If you are planning to use investments with account minimums, identify and plan those next.

Selecting New Investments

Whether you are buying new investments because you have new savings or because you are making a change to rebalance your portfolio, the following process will help you make decisions.

1. Does the new investment fit with your diversification guidelines?
2. What is the quality of the investment? Consider the following factors. Get information about a potential investment from its annual report, prospectus, or from an independent source such as Lipper (*www.lipperweb.com*), Morningstar (*www.morningstar.com*), or Value Line (*www.valueline.com*).

Passive Investments

For passively managed investments, evaluate how closely the investment matches the index or asset class it is trying to replicate and look at its costs.

Active Investments

There are four dimensions to evaluate:

- **Performance, compared to the relevant benchmark.** Be careful to identify the actual composition of the investment, or you will be comparing to the wrong benchmark.
- **People.** If the performance depends heavily on the skills and expertise of the money manager, it is important to know that the current money manager is the same person as the one responsible for past performance.
- **Process.** For performance to be repeated there must be a method for investment selection, management and sale, and the method must be used consistently. Look carefully at the prospectus to see if their process makes sense.
- **Costs.** Compare the costs to other investments of the same type.

WORKSHEET

Rebalancing My Portfolio

Use information from the "My Portfolio Diversification Plan" worksheet on page 216 to determine the changes you need to make to diversify your portfolio. Use the worksheet below to make your plan.

Change	Amount	Investment	Date Complete
Example: _____ Buy _____ Sell __✗__ Transfer	$24,000	From: Bank X - Money Market Account To: AAA Bond Fund	4/30
_____ Buy _____ Sell _____ Transfer		From: To:	
_____ Buy _____ Sell _____ Transfer		From: To:	
_____ Buy _____ Sell _____ Transfer		From: To:	
_____ Buy _____ Sell _____ Transfer		From:	
_____ Buy _____ Sell _____ Transfer		From: To:	

Do It Yourself or Get Help?

Now is a good time to think about whether you need help managing your finances. To do it successfully yourself, you need three important ingredients: time, interest, and skills. Think about what it means to be missing just one of these:

- If you have the skills but not the time or interest, you will probably not do a good job of managing the process.
- If you have the time and interest but not the skills, you have a different problem. A lack of skills can result in substantial mistakes. Even if you are working on a small scale, the repercussions of those mistakes may not be small.

Some of the challenges of doing it right are the rapidly expanding number of planning tools and investment products, unsubstantiated claims of some investment options, and even the tax code. You need enough time to be current with planning, products, and the tax code if you are to develop effective approaches. Keeping up can be a full-time job—which some people love and others hate.

Finding the Help You Need

You may want help with some aspects of your plan. What should you look for in a financial advisor? There are two major components: trustworthiness and effectiveness. The information below will help you know what to look for in a financial advisor. The Financial Planning Association offers an online search tool to help you find a Certified Financial Planner in your area (*www.fpanet.org*; click on "Find a Planner").

Can the Advisor Be Trusted?

- **Disclosure.** Planners are required to disclose written information to prospective clients, including:
  - What they do
  - With whom they are affiliated
  - How they are paid
  - Professional designations and memberships
  - Whether they've had regulatory problems

  Advisors are also required to have a written contract describing responsibilities, terms of the contract, and fees for the work done. If you request this information from a potential advisor and he or she does not provide it, be wary.

  Financial planners are required to be registered with an investment advisor firm. That firm is required to be registered with the state or the U.S. Securities and Exchange Commission (SEC). Registered investment advisors (IAs) may provide investment advice for a stated fee.
- **Professionalism.** Objectivity is a key component of professionalism. This means outlining the alternatives, with their advantages and disadvantages, and helping you understand their implications for you. Then you can make up your own mind about what is best for you.

Is the Advisor Effective?

- **Skills.** Look for both education and experience. A Certified Financial Planner designation is probably the most respected and widely accepted formal education for planning. It is independent, comprehensive in its approach, and is a good starting point for a planning professional. Two other industries train professionals in planning—the American Institute of CPAs gives the Personal Financial Specialist designation and the insurance industry promotes the Chartered Financial Consultant degree. Beware of other alternatives—there are many watered-down programs of little merit.

  There is no good substitute for experience. Look for breadth and depth. If the advisor has been doing his or her job for many years, he or she will have experienced a range of economic cycles and a variety of tax laws.
- **Defined process.** Whoever helps you should have a defined and comprehensive process for determining what is appropriate for you. In order to be personalized, it should take your family, health, and dreams into account. Ask potential advisors about the process they use.

- **Communication skills.** In order for your advisor to be effective, he or she must be a good listener. Your instincts will tell you if the chemistry is right—if you are being heard and understood.
- **Implementation.** You may hire someone to help you figure out what you should do. You may also want some help in implementing recommendations. Think first about what you need. Then find out about the potential advisor's capabilities in this area.
- **Accountability and progress.** Sometimes you may know what you need to do, yet you do not do it. For example, most people know that they need a will, yet as many as 70% of people die without one. Working with an advisor on an ongoing basis will help you be accountable to yourself and move you steadily toward your destination. It will help you adapt to changing circumstances—in your own situation and in the world at large.

Questions to Ask Financial Planners

When you meet with a prospective financial planner, bring a list of questions, take notes, and make sure you're comfortable with the answers he or she gives. Here are a few questions you'll want to consider asking.

- **What are your qualifications and experience?** Find someone who has many years of experience working with retirement planning and experience relevant to your needs. Look for a Certified Financial Planner. Be sure to ask about other certificates, degrees, and awards.
- **How do you approach financial planning?** There are many different ways to create a financial plan. Make sure your planner's approach fits your style and goals.
- **How are you paid?** A planner may be paid a salary, an hourly rate, a percentage of your assets, commissions based on products sold, or a combination of these methods. Understanding how a planner is paid may provide insight about what products and services he or she recommends. If he or she receives commissions on products sold, you'll want to get as much information as possible about the commission structure to ensure you're getting advice that's in your best interest, not the planner's.
- **Can you provide an estimate of costs based on the work you'll need to perform?**
- **Have you been disciplined for unlawful or unethical actions in your career?**
- **Will you provide client references?** Call other clients and find out if they're happy with the planner's service, accessibility, and performance. A planner is prohibited from using testimonials.
- **Can you put it all in writing?** A written agreement with details on the services that will be provided, estimates, and other information will be a handy reference.

In addition to the questions you have for the planner, note the questions he or she has for you. The planner should be at least as interested in your goals and the details of your life as you are in the planner's methods and goals. He or she should ask about your family members and potential financial issues related to them, as well as your goals and tolerance for risk.

What Financial Advisors Do I Need?

You may have more than one planner or advisor for different aspects of your financial life. For example, you might have an accountant, a financial planner, and an estate-planning attorney. You will want to make sure that you and your advisors are addressing your complete financial picture. This checklist can help you determine whether you're getting what you need—or if your advisors are focusing on the same things, and it is time to eliminate one.

Put an "*X*" next to each role to indicate who is addressing that aspect of your financial life.

Role		Advisor 1	Advisor 2	Advisor 3
Advisor:	**You**			
Goals, values				
Help determine				
Help accomplish				
Investment income management				
Review cash flow				
Organize current investments				
Help diversify investments				
Review investments ______ times per year				
Rebalance investments ______ times per year				
Reduce taxes on investment income				
Help identify and manage income risks				
Financial modeling				
Build a financial model				
Project if enough money for lifestyle				
Other				
Identify estate planning issues				
Other ________________________				
Other ________________________				

What changes do I need to make in my financial advisors?

Questions & Answers

Q. What investments should I avoid?

A. Avoid buying investments that do little to diversify your portfolio. Your fifth mutual fund containing primarily U.S. large companies will not add very much to your diversification. Choose your investments to develop a diversified portfolio.

Q. Should I use index funds?

A. Many people do. Index funds are a passive management approach. The fund owns assets that mirror a particular portion of the market, and they usually have low management costs. There are many different types of index funds that match different benchmarks. Owning one index fund doesn't make a diversified portfolio. For example, Standard & Poor's 500 Index funds own the same company stocks that make up the Standard & Poor's 500. The Standard & Poor's 500 Index funds are weighted by the size of the companies. This means that the 50 largest U.S. companies—the mega-companies—comprise most of the fund, and the other 450 companies have much less of an effect. You might consider using a collection of index funds that represent different asset classes to create a diversified portfolio.

Q. I am a do-it-yourselfer. I own stocks through an online brokerage account and I own mutual funds directly with the mutual fund company. Is there evidence that I would do better if I had professional investment help?

A. Research suggests that investors who invest on their own routinely underperform their investments. The performance of investors who work with an advisor who encourages them to keep invested and not do a lot of buying and selling is much better than the performance of average investors on their own (Dalbar 2006).

Q. Where can I learn about reverse mortgages?

A. If you are over 62, a reverse mortgage could give you access to equity in your home without having to sell it. There are pluses and minuses to doing this. Check with your financial advisors before signing an agreement. The Federal Trade Commission website is a good source of information (*www.ftc.gov* search for "reverse mortgages"). The AARP website is another resource (*www.aarp.org/revmort*).

IN THIS CHAPTER

Chapter 15

Managing Tax Obligations

Knowing the rules to keep money in your pocket

TAXES ARE THE PRICE WE PAY FOR CIVILIZATION.

—*Oliver Wendell Holmes Jr., U.S. Supreme Court Justice*

Many investments have tax benefits. Some are associated with the type of account in which the investment is held; others are associated with the investment itself. For example, if you own an investment in an account such as a 401(k) or a pretax IRA, you earn interest tax-free and only pay taxes when you take money out of the account. Other types of accounts and investments have other tax benefits.

Lowering the taxes you pay increases the spendable income an investment produces. Money that would have gone to pay taxes can remain in your account to generate future income. Over time, reducing or postponing taxes will be well rewarded.

Mark Fischer
Certified Financial Planner

Tax Management Strategies

Taxes are one of the major costs of an investment portfolio. It is important to have strategies in place to manage your tax obligations.

There are four main strategies:

- Own investments in a tax-advantaged account such as a 401(k) or IRA account
- Own investments that have tax breaks, such as stocks and municipal bonds
- Manage your investments for tax advantage
- Live in a state with lower income taxes

Some of these strategies eliminate taxes entirely; others postpone taxes. You need to consider the costs that go along with the tax benefit to determine whether it is worth it. Postponing taxes is usually an advantage. If you properly invest postponed taxes and let them compound, you will produce more income than you would if the taxes were paid right away.

Taxes raise revenue for the government and are the result of tax laws that are complicated and change frequently. If your situation is at all complex, you should consider working with a knowledgeable financial advisor and professional tax preparer to help you understand your options for minimizing tax payments.

Tax-Advantaged Accounts

There are several types of accounts with tax advantages; many are specifically designed for retirement savings.

Pretax Retirement Plans

Retirement plans are the most popular tax-advantaged accounts. All of them provide tax-deferred growth, and the contributions to many of these plans are also tax-deductible. Tax-deductible plans include 401(k)s, 403(b)s (similar to 401(k)s but for employees of religious institutions, schools, and other nonprofit organizations), 457 plans, traditional IRAs (if you have no other retirement plan or your income is not too high), many deferred compensation plans, Simplified Employee Pensions (SEPs), SIMPLE IRAs, and Keogh Plans, among others. Some of these are for employers to contribute to, others are for employees, some are for both, and some are for individuals. They are all variations on the same theme.

The IRS code has more than 10,000 pages describing retirement plans. Each retirement plan has its own rules for putting money in and taking it out. In general, there are penalties for:

- *Taking money out before age 59 ½.* The current penalty is 10% of the withdrawal. You can move money from one retirement plan to another retirement plan without penalty.
- *Taking too little money out too late.* You are required to make a withdrawal by April 1 of the year following the one in which you turn 70 ½ and each subsequent year. The Internal Revenue Service publishes the table of Required Minimum Distributions (*www.irs.gov*), which start at approximately 4% and increase each year. The penalty is 50% of the distribution.
- *Putting too much money in.* The penalty is 6% of the excess amount per year.

The strategy for using retirement plans is usually to put in as much money as possible (without going over the maximum) and to do so as soon as possible, unless you have a much better alternative available (such as a privately owned business). For distributions from retirement plans, the strategy is to take out as little money as possible by using other funds first.

If you have earned income, even from a part-time job, you can contribute to a traditional IRA. The contribution may or may not be deductible, depending upon your income tax filing status and your income level. Investment, Social Security, or pension income cannot be contributed to a retirement plan.

Type	Contributions	Growth	Withdrawals
Traditional IRA, 401(k), etc.	Uses pretax money (you do not pay taxes on the money you contribute)	Not taxed—tax deferred	Taxed at regular income tax rate
Roth IRA Roth 401(k)	Uses after-tax money (you invest money on which you have paid taxes)	Not taxed—tax deferred	Original investment not taxed Earnings not taxed after five years

Roth IRA and Roth 401(k)

If you have earned income and your income level is less than the maximum allowed, you can contribute to a Roth IRA or Roth 401(k). Roth IRAs and Roth 401(k)s are not tax deductible, and IRS rules limit the amount you can contribute each year. You do not pay taxes on the growth of the investment, or when you make qualified withdrawals from the account. Qualified withdrawals include those made after age 59 ½, if you become disabled, or, upon your death, made to your beneficiary or your estate. Check with your financial advisor or the IRS (*www.irs.gov*) for additional withdrawal information.

The table above shows how Roth IRAs and Roth 401(k)s compare with pretax retirement plans.

You are not required to withdraw money from a Roth IRA at any age, so the money in the Roth can grow indefinitely during your lifetime.

You can convert a traditional IRA to a Roth IRA under certain conditions (the law is changing). When you do so, you have to pay regular income taxes on the money converted. If you have money not already in a retirement plan that you can use to pay the taxes, there is a substantial benefit for doing the conversion. It is as if you have added the amount of the taxes to the Roth and the entire amount in the Roth will grow tax-free forever.

Annuities

Annuities are retirement contracts between you and an insurance company. You make payments into the annuity, either lump sum or in a series of payments, and in return the insurer makes periodic payments to you. Money inside the annuity contract grows tax-deferred but is taxed at your regular income tax rate upon withdrawal. You can also own annuities in other retirement plans.

Because internal fees inside annuities are generally higher than those in mutual funds, you should use alternatives to annuities unless the annuities have features that you particularly value, such as special guarantees or a higher return that is not otherwise available.

Life Insurance

Life insurance is a contract between you and an insurance company that has a death benefit. Cash-value life insurance has a savings component in addition to a death benefit.

You can take cash value from a policy without paying income taxes up to the total of all premiums paid. Depending on the type of policy, you can sometimes take additional income as loans against the cash value at little or no interest. This income also is not taxed.

Life insurance is particularly useful if you want to provide a bequest to a family member or your community, to replace assets being donated elsewhere, or even to replace some Social Security or annuity payments when one spouse dies.

General Partnership

Some investments, such as real estate or oil and gas ventures, are really ongoing businesses. If you own them as a general partner, you can deduct ordinary business expenses. For real estate, you can deduct depreciation of buildings against real estate income. For oil wells, you can deduct drilling costs against any income.

529 Plan

A state-managed 529 plan allows you to set money aside tax-deferred for postsecondary school tuition and fees. You can set up a separate account for each beneficiary (such as a child or grandchild). Contribution limits apply for each beneficiary separately and are governed by state law (each state law is different). Your contribution may qualify for the federal annual gift tax exclusion. The 2007 limit for the exclusion is $12,000 per year or a $60,000 gift once every five years. The money in a 529 plan grows tax-deferred; if used for tuition and fees at an approved post-secondary institution, then the growth is not taxed. You can change the beneficiary if needed.

Charitable Trusts

You can set up many types of trusts to contain some of your investments and pay you an income. One interesting type, called a Charitable Remainder UniTrust (CRUT), can provide income for your lifetime and even some years beyond that to your children. Whatever is left in the CRUT goes to the charity with which you've set up the trust.

If set up properly, you can decide on the fly whether you want to take income out of a CRUT in any given year. Money you do not take out in a given year can go into a makeup account to take out later.

CRUTs are tax-free, because charities ultimately benefit. Most assets (including cash and investments) you transfer into a CRUT will provide you with a partial deduction (with limits) against your taxable income. If you transfer assets with large capital gains into a CRUT, the trust can sell them without paying income taxes. You pay no taxes on the net return of the investments as long as they remain inside the CRUT. But you pay taxes on income you receive from the CRUT when you receive it.

Investments with Tax Breaks

Many investments have some type of tax advantage. In fact, the list of investments that do not provide tax benefits is shorter than those that do (they include savings accounts, money market accounts, certificates of deposit, and corporate bonds). Capital gains from stocks or other investments sold after being owned less than one year are also taxed at the regular income rate. These investments have tax benefits:

Stocks, Real Estate, or Mutual Funds Holding Stocks

Capital gains are the increase between the value of a stock or real estate when it was purchased and the current value (if the value went down it is a capital loss). You pay taxes on capital gains only when the stock or real estate is sold, which can be many years from the date of purchase. In the meantime, the taxes are deferred. Taxes on any gains on your stocks or real estate that you have not sold are forgiven entirely upon your death.

Long-term capital gains (stocks or real estate with a gain owned for one year or more before sale) and qualified dividends are taxed at the capital gains tax rate, which is lower than your regular tax rate.

Municipal Bonds

U.S. government bonds are free of state income tax. Most bonds issued by state or municipal governments are free of federal income tax.

Municipal bonds pay out less income than taxable bonds, and you need to compare the two. Choose municipals only if their return is greater than taxable bonds of comparable quality after you will have paid taxes on the income. Municipal bonds lose their tax advantage in a retirement plan—do not put them there.

Oil and Gas

Taxes on the sale of oil and gas are reduced by the oil-depletion allowance.

Affordable Housing

Each year Congress allocates a tax deduction to owners of affordable housing—of the entire investment, spread out over 15 years. This benefit is in addition to possible capital gains at the end of the investment.

Tax-Managed Investing

There are a number of ways you can manage investments to reduce taxes.

If you do *not* need income from your stock portfolio now, here are a few tools you can use to delay paying taxes:

- Construct a portfolio of stocks that pay few, if any, dividends.
- Wait to sell stocks with gains until a year or more after their purchase (so that they are taxed at the lower long-term capital gains rate).
- Sell stocks with losses to offset the gains from other sales.

Some mutual funds use this approach. But most frequently people use portfolios of individual stocks to accomplish this objective.

If you *do* need the income now, you can use the following techniques to manage the taxes on the bulk of your investments:

- Take money from cash accounts as your source of income. But be careful. If you do too much of this, you will change the balance of stocks to nonstocks, thereby increasing the risk and potential return of your investment portfolio.
- Cash in some stocks with little or no capital gains.
- Sell your losers so that you can deduct capital losses against capital gains and even deduct against regular income up to $3,000 per year.

Series E U.S. Savings Bonds are a tool to tax-manage bond income, because taxes are postponed until you cash in the bonds. There is no way to offset that income with other losses. Remember that many government bonds held too long eventually stop paying interest.

State of Residence

Some states (currently Alaska, Florida, Nevada, South Dakota, Texas, Washington, and Wyoming) do not have a state income tax. If you live there, you pay only federal income taxes. Two states (New Hampshire and Tennessee) tax only dividend and interest income. Some states with a state income tax do not tax most municipal bond interest issued by their or even other states. Make sure you understand the details of the tax laws in your state of residence.

If you move to another state to take advantage of this opportunity, make sure that you:

- Demonstrate unequivocally that you are a resident of the new state.
- Consider other fees and taxes, such as property and sales taxes, in your decision of whether or not to move.
- Consider all costs, including possible multiple residences and extra ongoing travel expenses if you live part of each year in each location.
- Consider nonmonetary costs, including the emotional toll of leaving your current community and residence.
- Verify that your wills, trusts, and other legal documents will work properly in your new state of residence.

Your Tax Management Plan

You have many opportunities to invest your money in tax-advantaged accounts. Taking advantage of these options will allow you to save on or postpone taxes, have more money to spend, and enjoy a richer, more meaningful lifestyle. Use the worksheet on page 231 to examine how you are managing your taxes.

WORKSHEET

My Tax Management Plan

Evaluate how you are managing the tax implications of your investments. List the amount of money you have in each type of account. If you have completed the "An Inventory of My Investments" worksheet on page 200, you may have already calculated many of these numbers.

Tax Approach	Amount
Tax-Advantaged Accounts	
Retirement plans	
Traditional IRAs, Roth IRAs	
Annuities	
Life insurance	
Business/partnership	
Charitable trust	
Investments with Tax Breaks	
Tax-benefited products	
Municipal bonds	
Oil/gas	
Affordable housing	
Individual stocks	
Individual real estate	
Not Sheltered	

What changes do I want to make to better manage my taxes?

Questions & Answers

Q. I have a choice between contributing to a traditional IRA or to a Roth IRA. Which should I choose?

A. If you believe your tax rates will increase after retirement or your deductions will be smaller (when there is no mortgage interest to deduct), then Roth IRAs may be more appropriate.

Q. I am still working and have a 401(k) plan at work. Should I contribute to it?

A. Yes, unless you will need the money very soon or before age 59 ½, when there is a penalty. Work retirement plans offer convenience, automatic saving, tax benefits, and sometimes an employer match.

Q. Do trusts provide income tax breaks?

A. Except for the charitable trust, generally not. They are expensive to set up and manage but can be extremely useful to manage assets owned by the trust and control and distribute payments from the trust.

Q. Both 401(k)s and IRAs offer up-front tax deductions and tax deferred growth. What are the differences?

A. A 401(k) may offer a loan provision and the ability to withdraw money at 55 instead of 59 ½ without penalty. IRAs offer more investment choices, the ability to split into multiple IRAs with different beneficiaries, or withdrawal strategies. Some employers permit employees to roll over 401(k) proceeds to IRAs, even when they are still working.

IN THIS CHAPTER

Chapter 16

Making Your Money Last a Lifetime

Determining how much you need and how much you can withdraw from your investments

A NICKEL AIN'T WORTH A DIME ANYMORE.

—Yogi Berra, Yankees catcher

Mark Fischer
Certified Financial Planner

Karen Hansen
Attorney

These are the most frequent ways people complete the sentence—"I need enough . . ."

- For the rest of my life.
- So that I don't have to worry about money.
- So that I'm not dependent on my children.
- So that I don't lose everything I've worked for.

You have probably heard the dramatic and newsworthy stories of retirees who have gotten into trouble. You may wonder how these things happened. People who ran into trouble did not plan to fail, but they may have failed to plan.

If you prepare well, you will probably do fine early in retirement. But beware. It is later on when money problems most often occur.

The more time you have to prepare for retirement, the easier it is to accomplish what you want. Because of compounding—the fact that your earnings generate their own earnings over time—one of the best ways to accumulate more money is to invest it for a longer time. The sooner you begin saving, the easier it will be for you to achieve your financial goals.

If you combine good investment strategies with a conservative approach to spending, you are more likely to have financial security as you age. This chapter will address ways to determine how much you need, how much you have, and strategies to address possible shortfalls.

Will You Have Enough?

There isn't an answer to the question of how much you need that is both quick and accurate. For an accurate answer, you need to take into account major lifetime challenges—longevity, inflation, health, and investment uncertainty.

There are, however, some rules of thumb that can help you find a ballpark answer quickly. There are more complex ways to get a more precise answer. The worksheets on the next few pages will help you do both.

W O R K S H E E T

Will I Have Enough? A Fast-Track Way to Get Thinking

If you want to get a quick sense of how much investment savings you will need for a financially secure retirement, this worksheet is for you. If you would rather do a little more work and get a more accurate number right from the start, you might want to skip this worksheet and go right to the one on page 237.

First Rule of Thumb

The sustainable rate of withdrawal from your investments each year is about 4% of the value of your investments (assuming that your return on those investments is at least 8%–10%).

This is the amount you can withdraw and still maintain a pool of money that will produce the future income you will need from the investments.

To maintain your principal with a 4% withdrawal rate, you will need an investment pool at least 25 times as large as the amount you withdraw each year. For example, if you will need $30,000 per year from your investment income (to supplement your Social Security payments and pension payment, if available), you will need investments worth $750,000 (the value at the time you want to make the withdrawal, not today).

Annual Dollars I Will Need*	x	25	=	Value of Investments I Will Need
______________	x	25	=	______________

* Use the amount of expenses you listed in the worksheet in Chapter 12 as a starting point and adjust as you see fit. Remember, this is just a ballpark estimate.

Will I Have Enough? A Fast-Track Way to Get Thinking *continued*

Second Rule of Thumb

Compound interest will likely make what you have today worth more in the future.

For example, $100,000 compounded at 8% for 10 years will be worth $215,000. How much will what you have saved be worth when you retire? There is no simple formula for calculating this number because of the effect of compound interest. (There are many calculators available on the Internet, such as at American Public Media's Marketplace Money website, *marketplacemoney.publicradio.org/toolbox*, that will help with the calculations.) For right now, it is probably enough to make a ballpark estimate. We will talk about how to make more detailed and accurate projections later on in this chapter.

Estimated Dollars I Will Need*	Current Value of My Investments**	Estimated Value of My Current Investments at Retirement***	Difference between What I Need and What I Have
______________	______________	______________	______________

* From previous equation (25 x annual amount needed).

** From the worksheet in Chapter 13.

*** The easiest way to get this number is to use an online calculator (*marketplacemoney.publicradio.org/toolbox/calculators/RetirementIncome.html*).

Third Rule of Thumb

The earlier you accumulate savings, the easier it will be to reach your goal.

For example, if the difference is $300,000, your investments grow at an 8% rate and you have 10 years to accumulate the money, you will need to put aside $20,000 per year into savings. If you had 20 years to accumulate the $300,000, then you would need to save $6,250 per year.

WORKSHEET

Will I Have Enough? A More Precise Calculation

To answer the question "Will I have enough?" more precisely, you need to estimate the return on your actual investments and take into account your expenses, longevity, inflation, and investment uncertainty. Here is a straightforward way to get started. Later in the chapter we will talk about financial models that will help you get an even more precise answer.

Step 1

Return on Investments

Once you know what investments you have, you can estimate future income from them. The table below shows the approximate historical returns—from the past 75 years—for various types of investments.

You can use the historical figures or your own estimates in your calculations. A pessimistic investor might choose to use an estimate that is a percentage point or two below historical returns, while an optimistic investor might choose to use an estimate that is a percentage point or two above historical returns. Remember, past performance does not guarantee future performance.

If you completed the "My Portfolio Diversification Plan" worksheet on page 216, use the figures to complete the "Value of My Investments" column below.

Asset Class	Historical Annual Returns*	My Estimated Return	x	Value of My Investments	=	Total Annual Income
Stocks						
U.S. large companies	10%					
Foreign large companies	11%					
U.S. small companies	12%					
Foreign small companies	13%					
Contracts						
Cash	4%					
Bonds	6%					
Other						
Real estate	8%					
Other						
Total Income on Investments						

* Past performance does not predict future performance.

Will I Have Enough? A More Precise Calculation *continued*

Remember that if you reallocate assets to include more money in the historically higher-paying asset classes, you might generate more income. But you will also increase your risk—which could result in losses to your portfolio.

This calculation assumes that you do not touch your principal. If you need more income than your portfolio can support and you dip into principal, then you start a downward spiral in your investment values. This is because you have used up some of the principal, yet you may need even more the following year. Your principal could be gone in 15 years or even less. Then there will be no investment income at all.

Just as you do not want to dip into principal, you may not want to use all of your return each year. Instead, you will want to reinvest some of this money to match increases in inflation.

Step 2

Sustainable Investment Income

In the ballpark estimate in the worksheet on page 235 we suggested a sustainable withdrawal rate of 4% of your investments. Here you can calculate a more accurate estimate that is based on your estimates for return, inflation, and a buffer for investment uncertainty. Remember, your sustainable investment income is the amount of income you can take from your investments without endangering the future potential for income. Calculate your sustainable investment income below.

Total annual income on investments			$ ______	(from page 237)
Total value of investments			$ ______	(from page 237)
Rate of return on total investments			______ %	(Return ÷ value x 100)
	Historical	Your Estimate		
Inflation rate	3–4%	____%		
Buffer for variable returns	1–2%	____%		
Total adjustment (inflation + buffer)			______ %	
Sustainable investment return (Rate of return – Adjustment)			______ %	
Sustainable investment income (Sustainable return x value of investments)			$ ______	

Is your sustainable investment income a negative number? If it is, you will not be able to withdraw from investments and still protect your principal. You might need to consider a more aggressive investment strategy to increase your average annual returns (see chapter 14).

Step 3

Estimate of My Retirement Income and Expenses

You will have retirement income sources in addition to your investment income. You will also have expenses, and they may be more or less than your current expenses. If you want to calculate income and expenses over the rest of your life, you will want help making the calculations (with an online calculator, for example). But it is relatively easy to estimate your income and expenses for the first year of your retirement (especially if it is close), and that may help you know how well you are doing.

If you have done earlier worksheets, you have collected most of this information already.

Retirement Income	Amount in First Year of Retirement
Sustainable investment income (From above, or use an online calculator to help estimate the value in your first year of retirement.)	
Pension	
Social Security	
Earned income	
Other	
Total Income	

Retirement Expenses	Amount in First Year of Retirement
Current expenses (From exercise in chapter 12, adjusted for inflation, on average 3–4% per year.)	
How much will you be able to reduce your expenses in this period of your life? (Many people estimate 10–30% less.)	
What additional expenses will you have to meet your retirement goals? (This depends on your goals. See the worksheet in chapter 11.)	
Total Expenses	
Difference between Income and Expenses	

Will I Have Enough? A More Precise Calculation *continued*

Is it enough?

What changes do I have to make so that it will be enough? Save more? Earn more? Spend less?

Building a Financial Model

An even more precise way to calculate how much you will need and how much you will have is to build a financial model. Here are some ways to do that:

- If you have a technical bent and are familiar with spreadsheets such as Excel, you can build your own. State your assumptions and show, year by year, what happens to the money.
- You might check out online financial calculators. American Public Media's Marketplace Money (*marketplacemoney.publicradio.org/toolbox*) has a number of calculators that might be helpful.
- You can purchase software packages on disc or over the Internet that will help you build a model.
- You can work with a professional planner who will already have the software you need and can work closely with you.

A model can give you insight, but remember that the calculations are only as good as the assumptions you use. Make sure the assumptions are stated explicitly and that they are reasonable and not too aggressive.

Here are some assumptions that you might try to get you started:

- **Projected rates of return:** 6–11%, depending on how aggressive your investments are
- **Longevity:** through your 90s
- **Inflation rates:** 2–5%
- **Investment uncertainty:** based on past history

You can also use a model to determine the effects of different choices, such as changing your spending levels, changing your investment return, or retiring at a different age. If you use a model over a period of years, you can see how the realities of passing years affect what is feasible.

It is possible to build complex and sophisticated models, taking into account your mortgage payoff, differing salaries, selling off property when needed, working part-time for a number of years, and even decreasing your expenses as you get older. Some models will even estimate the probabilities of various outcomes—for example, there is an 85% chance of having enough. Whatever you do, make sure your financial model is realistic for your situation.

Adapting Your Goals to Your Financial Situation

Harriet, a theater buff, dreamed of a retirement filled with trips to New York City to see Broadway shows. However, when she sat down to calculate her income, she realized that she couldn't afford the lavish hotels, five-star restaurants, and lengthy trips that she had once imagined. She was initially disappointed, but she was also resourceful. Living just a short drive away from Minneapolis, which has its own vibrant theater scene, she decided to see if she could get a part-time job as an usher at one of the major theaters in town. She was hired immediately. While she didn't make much money at the job, she got to see traveling Broadway shows for free—and the amount she earned in a year gave her enough money to travel to New York for several days and see all the productions she'd missed.

Problems with Estimating Future Income and Expenses

The poor elderly are generally 85 and older. They probably began to have small problems in their 70s that mushroomed as they continued to age.

Having enough during your lifetime means that your income is higher than your expenses, not necessarily every year, but overall. Retirees run into two main problems: lower income than expected and higher expenses than expected—over their lifetimes.

Lower Income

There are three primary reasons that your income may be lower than you expected:

- **Inaccurate estimates for returns.** If you are too optimistic in your estimates, you may not be able to withdraw as much money as you expected.
- **Excessive withdrawals or withdraws at the wrong time.** If you withdraw too much from your investments, you risk not having enough in future years because of inflation. Worse yet, you may be forced to dip into your principal. Even a well-diversified portfolio will have times when its value declines. If you take too much income out of your investments when the value has declined, you can seriously jeopardize the investment portfolio itself—the goose that lays the golden eggs. If you do not have enough money left after a large decline and withdrawals, even a substantial increase in the market will not help enough to recover.
- **Noninvestment income changes.** If you or your spouse dies, Social Security payments will decrease. (Your expenses will also likely decrease.) When you set up a pension or immediate annuity and select a payout, you may be able to choose between payout over one or both lives. If the payments are over one life and that person dies first, then the income for the survivor will be reduced.

The first two problems are related, and the best way to avoid these scenarios is not to spend all of your total return each year. You should reinvest some of your income to match inflation. And you should reinvest still more of your income to act as a buffer when investment returns are low or even negative.

The last problem can be addressed through a vehicle such as life insurance. How much life insurance is appropriate? If the survivor will have to replace $8,000 of lost Social Security for 10 years, then an $80,000 death benefit will be sufficient. Again, keep in mind that expenses will likely go down in the event of the death of a spouse. The need for coverage of this type decreases as you age.

Higher Expenses

Just as there are a few reasons behind lower income, there are a few basic issues behind higher expenses:

- **Inflation.** Some people describe inflation as an insidious hidden tax. Inflation appears to make little difference over a year or two. But over many years, inflation and increasing costs can catch up with you. Inflation has averaged 3–4% per year. This means that prices double, on average, every 18 to 24 years. During retirement your expenses can double or even triple. One way to address this issue is to reinvest some of your total return each year to allow for inflation costs.
- **Higher lifestyle costs.** Many people believe that their expenses will decrease upon retirement, and some experts say to budget for 20–40% lower lifestyle costs. While it's true that some of your expenses will decrease, others, like travel and entertainment, may increase if you have more time to play.
- **Higher health care costs.** Health care costs will probably increase as you age. The latest estimates are that the average health care costs for a couple from age 65 to death will be at least $200,000, even with Medicare. The calculation does not include experimental and other medical treatments, nor does it include the cost of long-term care—home or institutional care.

The most common approach people take is to use Medicare and Medigap coverage and pay for the rest of the expenses themselves. The biggest problem with this method is the possibility of one spouse using up a substantial portion of financial resources during his or her lifetime, and the other spouse being forced to live on what is left over.

Many people transfer the risk of long-term care (LTC) costs to an insurance company by purchasing an LTC policy. Such policies are much less expensive if you purchase them when you are young (and healthier). (For more discussion, see "Planning for Disability" on page 246.)

- **Longevity.** Your money has to be around long enough to support both you and your spouse, if you have one. How long is that? For two 65-year-olds, it is, on average, 27 years. This means that half the time they have both died before then, but for the other half at least one of them is still alive. These numbers are based on current longevity tables and do not include possible medical advances that could prolong life in coming years. Your money may need to last for decades.

Other Financial Factors to Consider

While the challenges of planning for a financially secure retirement may seem to be daunting, there are factors that may increase your income (or decrease your costs) during these years. You will receive cost-of-living increases from Social Security. And you may be able to take advantage of discounts on travel, entertainment, restaurants, and retail stores. Or, you may inherit money.

Strategies for Dealing with Insufficient Income

If you have gone through your calculations and there will not be enough income to support your meaningful lifestyle, you have a few alternatives. The choices are difficult.

Generate More Income

You need to evaluate your resources for their capacity to generate more income. You can potentially get more income from investments by including more higher-paying alternatives, such as stocks. If you take this approach, you have to have enough cash for living expenses to weather financial storms and enough psychological stamina to deal with substantial fluctuations in the value of investments.

If you are still working for pay, you can find ways to increase your income so that you can save more money, which you will be able to use later upon retirement. If you are retired, perhaps you can convert unpaid work to paid work. This strategy works particularly well if you convert your hobby or passion to paid work, even if the pay rate is lower than in previous jobs.

There are particular challenges to finding higher-paid work if you are 50 or older because of widespread (even if illegal) age discrimination, so this alternative may not be realistic for everyone. You may have more success if you are self-employed, use your highly developed skills, and work on a project basis. This approach can take substantial amounts of energy and carries risks of its own.

Scale Back Your Lifestyle

If you catalog your spending habits, you have an opportunity to see where your money goes. Perhaps you can redirect your spending from less important to more important activities.

Sometimes parents have unwittingly encouraged adult children to become dependent on them. Too much gifting can be bad for both children and parents. If your grown children always need money, it is unlikely that they will be able to help you out later if you have used up too much of your own money supporting them.

Wait to Retire

If you are still working and enjoying it, you can consider postponing retirement. Waiting provides three major advantages:

- Working longer gives you more opportunity to save money out of your income for the future. The power of compounding investments will depend on how much you have already accumulated. If you started late but have the ability to save substantial amounts of money now, new money can have a big effect.
- Working longer and not touching your investments or their income lets the investments grow larger. When investments are larger, they can provide more income later.
- Working longer means that your investments will not have to last as long because you will not be around as long to use them. This is important if you are dipping into your principal.

These factors can work together to have a large effect. Working longer is more feasible now that the average lifespan has increased.

Planning for Disability

You may be concerned about whether you have enough money if you or a close family member face a serious illness or disability. If you need home health care, assisted living, or a nursing home, do your research first. Costs will vary tremendously depending upon your medical situation, the ability of family and friends to help, the type of facility chosen, the length of stay at such a facility, and whether long-term care or other medical insurance will be available to you. The U.S. Department of Health and Human Services Medicare website offers a long-term care planning tool (*www.medicare.gov/LTCPlanning*) that you may find helpful.

See "Preparing an Advance Directive," page 155.

Once you have the range of costs for such care, examine your income, keeping in mind that many of your current expenses for things like entertainment and travel will be reduced in this situation. Even if you are not using all of your income to live on now, you should review what income would be available to you if you needed it for your support. If you won't be able to afford it, you might consider purchasing long-term care insurance. The federal government's Medicaid program may be an option as well. You might also consider creative solutions such as living with a family member, exchanging free rent for live-in assistance, or creating a community of friends who share living expenses and agree to provide care for each other.

There are many financial implications to your choices, whether you fund care by yourself or get assistance from government programs. Get advice from a financial planner and/or elder law attorney. You will want to seek advice before giving assets to children or others, or giving away a controlling interest in your finances. Federal regulations and state laws are complex and change frequently, and rules restrict what and how much you can give away without jeopardizing your financial situation. Additionally, you will want to make sure that you are very comfortable with the idea of having someone else in control of your finances. There are situations where you can end up much worse off by having given assets away before obtaining good advice.

Withdrawing from Investments

Methods of Withdrawing Income from Investments

The most common method of deciding how much money to withdraw from investments is to determine how much you need to pay your bills and expenses. If the costs increase from year to year, take out more money as needed. Recent research shows that this method works well, as long as you do not withdraw excessive amounts that jeopardize the longevity of your money. Here are some suggestions:

- Consider withdrawing increasing amounts from year to year based on increases in the Consumer Price Index (*www.bls.gov/cpi*). For example, if you withdrew $30,000 from your investments last year and inflation has been at the rate of 4%, consider withdrawing an additional 4%, or $1,200, this year.
- If inflation becomes very high (for example, greater than 6% in a year), consider using a cap on the annual increase.
- If there are substantial multiyear changes in the value of your assets, consider increasing or decreasing your withdrawals.

With tight regulation of your spending in this way, your sustainable withdrawal rate from investments may be 5–6% of your money instead of the 4% we spoke of earlier.

This approach—purchasing power adjustments to spending—may work better than drawing a fixed percentage of investments each year, an approach that has two dangers:

- That your income will vary widely from year to year if the stock market goes through turbulent times.
- That your purchasing power may not keep up if inflation picks up substantially.

Which Investments Should You Withdraw from First?

There are a variety of ways to draw an income from your retirement accounts. The conventional wisdom is for you to withdraw money from your retirement plans and IRAs only after you have used up your other money (Plan A). This approach will:

- **Postpone paying taxes during your lifetime.** This argument is the same as the one for using retirement plans to accumulate wealth for retirement—money that would have gone to the Internal Revenue Service will remain in your account and produce its own compounding income. Yes, you will eventually pay taxes, but your after-tax income will be greater then.
- **Postpone paying taxes until after your death.** If your retirement money is in IRAs and not other retirement plans, it will be possible for your children or grandchildren to stretch required distributions from IRAs even beyond your death.

There is a counterargument (Plan B). If your nonretirement account money is in tax-managed investments and you use up your retirement account money first, you will pay income taxes as you go along. But since taxes on capital gains are forgiven upon death, you can pass on your estate to the next generation without paying any income or capital gains tax at all.

Plan A is preferable if:

- You believe that income tax rates will remain the same or shrink in the future.
- You are collecting Social Security and your other taxable income is very low. In this approach you may be able to avoid paying tax on the Social Security payments for a few years.

Plan B is preferable if:

- You believe that income tax rates will increase.
- There will be a substantial inheritance for the next generation and that next generation is already in a high tax bracket.

Sometimes people use a mix of Plans A and B. They take just enough money from retirement plans and IRAs to remain in a low tax bracket and keep taxes on Social Security to a minimum (*www.socialsecurity.gov*). Remember that after age 70 ½ you are required to take some money from many retirement plans (and pay income taxes on withdrawals), whether you need the money or not. The IRS specifies the amount that you are required to withdraw each year. Check with your financial advisor or with IRS publications (*www.irs.gov*) to figure the amount.

WORKSHEET

My Withdrawal Plan

Based on what you have learned, determine how you will withdraw your investments to meet your goals. These numbers may change over time, so you will want to review them annually.

Schedule of distributions from investments

$ Amount to Withdraw per Year	From What Account?
$	
$	
$	
$	
Total	

Questions & Answers

Q. I am a single parent and have struggled to find enough money to invest for retirement. My youngest child is finishing college this year, and I will finally have $2,000 to put in a retirement account. How do I get started?

A. If your employer offers a 401(k) or 401(b) plan or a pension plan, start by investing there. Many employers will match your contributions, making your contributions even more valuable. If you don't have the option of a 401 plan, open a Roth IRA or a traditional IRA account. You can do that at a bank, credit union, online brokerage company, or directly with a mutual fund company. You can invest the money in your IRA account in a CD or money market fund (very safe investments) or in mutual funds, stocks, or bonds (riskier investments but with the potential for higher returns) or many other types of investments. See more in "Investing Basics" and "Making the Most of Your Investments" (chapters 13 and 14, respectively).

Q. I have questions about my Social Security payments. Where can I get answers?

A. Look at Social Security Online at *www.socialsecurity.gov* or call the Social Security Administration at 800-772-1213. Have your Social Security number handy when you call.

Q. How do you take uncertainty in investment returns into account in a financial model?

A. The most popular computer software tools available now use "Monte Carlo simulation." Instead of using a single figure for investment returns, the software uses a different value for each year—using the most likely returns more frequently than less likely returns. Then the software repeats the calculation, perhaps thousands of times, each with different combinations of investment returns, to determine the likelihood that the money will last long enough.

IN THIS CHAPTER

Chapter 17

Passing On What You Have

Leaving a meaningful legacy

DO SOMETHING WORTH REMEMBERING.

—*Elvis Presley, American pop icon*

Karen Hansen
Attorney

Your estate plan addresses what you will leave behind, how your affairs will be handled, and who will be in charge. You should take an active role in planning your estate. Doing so provides you the opportunity to reflect upon who and what has meaning and importance in your life, and how you wish to remember those you care about when you are no longer living.

Estate planning involves more than preparing a will or saving on taxes. It means having your legal affairs in order at the time of your death. It also means being prepared in case you become disabled or unable to manage your own financial, legal, and medical affairs. A good estate plan addresses the many potential scenarios that could affect you and your family. It is essential that you get the necessary legal documents in place to take care of the possible outcomes.

Your estate plan should:

- Provide a guide for your family to carry out your wishes
- Take care of the people and organizations that matter to you so that they inherit your possessions and assets after your death
- Minimize or eliminate the need for court involvement and reduce court costs
- Reduce or eliminate estate taxes

Every estate plan is different. Yours should reflect who you are and what is important to you. Decide on your goals first. Then you will be able to choose the best arrangements and appropriate documents to meet your objectives. Unless your situation is very straightforward, you will benefit from having a lawyer experienced in estate planning or elder law prepare your estate plan.

Periodically review your plan to make sure it is up to date with your changing personal and financial circumstances, as well as changes in the laws and the tax code. By taking this responsibility, you can minimize the involvement of the court system in your affairs and make the aging and dying process easier on you and your family.

Getting Started with an Estate Plan

Step 1: Make Key Decisions

- Decide who and what is important to you. Above all, you should make sure you are at the top of the list of important people.
- Decide whether there are special considerations you want to address, such as a special-needs child.
- Decide whom you trust to handle financial and medical decisions for you if you are incapacitated. Also decide whom you trust to carry out your wishes after your death.

These people and considerations may change in the future, which is fine. You can always adapt your estate plan as circumstances evolve.

Step 2: Prepare a Financial Summary

Determine the assets in your estate. This includes everything that you own or have a right to, including your investments, retirement accounts, death benefit of your life insurance, any pensions or trust benefits, fair market value of your real estate, and any business that you own. Use the "My Current Net Worth" worksheet in chapter 12, pages 189 and 190, to list your assets and liabilities.

Step 3: Find a Trustworthy, Knowledgeable Lawyer

Look for a lawyer who is experienced in estate planning and/or elder law—not simply a relative or friend who practices law. You can ask your financial planner, accountant, or other family members and friends for recommendations.

Plan to meet with several lawyers before choosing one with whom you can work well. It is not a matter of who is the most expensive and who is the least expensive, but rather who is the best fit for you.

Introductory meetings with prospective lawyers should be on a no-charge, no-obligation basis. Ask the lawyer about:

- Experience
- Number of estate plans written
- Experience with administering plans after the death of a client
- Cost

Finding the right lawyer is similar to finding the right doctor: The lawyer should listen to you, ask questions, and then offer recommendations appropriate for your situation. Doctors expect you to be able to identify your

WORKSHEET

What Do I Want to Include in My Estate Plan?

At my death, whom do I want to inherit my assets? Who needs your assets or will appreciate the inheritance? This list can be as long or as short as you wish.

How do I want to allocate what I leave? You may consider allocating by specific assets, specific dollar amounts, specific percentages of your estate, or a combination of the three.

Do I want to put restrictions on anyone's share? For example, perhaps you want your grandchildren to use the money only for college, or you want your second wife to use the money during her lifetime, but you want what's left to go to your children at her death.

Whom do I trust to carry out my wishes?

You may not have all of the answers to these questions before you go to see a lawyer to have your estate plan prepared. Your lawyer can offer suggestions or present alternatives if you are not sure what is best for your situation.

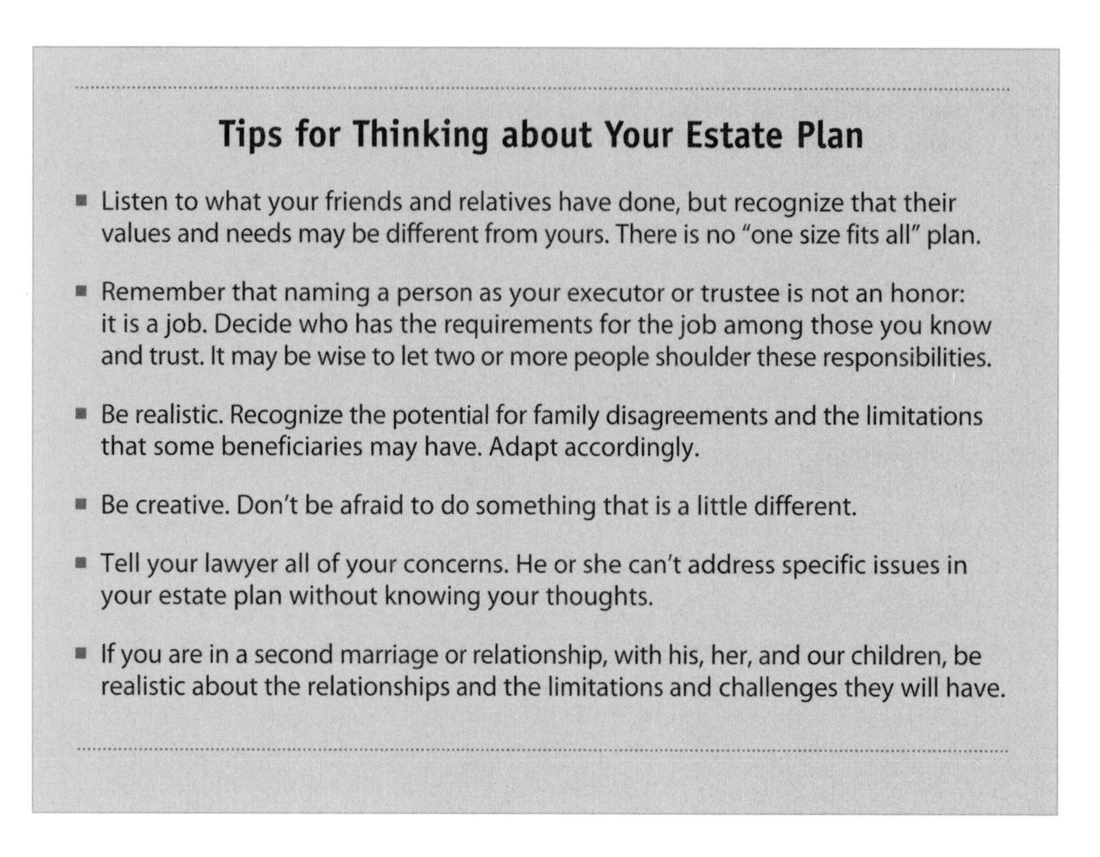

Tips for Thinking about Your Estate Plan

- Listen to what your friends and relatives have done, but recognize that their values and needs may be different from yours. There is no "one size fits all" plan.
- Remember that naming a person as your executor or trustee is not an honor: it is a job. Decide who has the requirements for the job among those you know and trust. It may be wise to let two or more people shoulder these responsibilities.
- Be realistic. Recognize the potential for family disagreements and the limitations that some beneficiaries may have. Adapt accordingly.
- Be creative. Don't be afraid to do something that is a little different.
- Tell your lawyer all of your concerns. He or she can't address specific issues in your estate plan without knowing your thoughts.
- If you are in a second marriage or relationship, with his, her, and our children, be realistic about the relationships and the limitations and challenges they will have.

symptoms, thoughts, and concerns, but they do not expect you to have already diagnosed yourself and have decided what prescription is best for you. Likewise, a lawyer will "prescribe" an estate plan that accomplishes your specific goals. You should keep interviewing lawyers until you find the one that fits for you.

If you have an uncomplicated situation, you may be able to write your estate plan with documents you've gotten from software programs or the Internet. It is difficult, however, to make sure the forms you can buy or find are specific enough to your situation, are aligned with your state's laws, and are up to date. If you do write your own plan, it is a good idea to have an estate planning lawyer review it. If the plan you write for yourself turns out not to fit your situation, it can be very costly, resulting in court proceedings, litigation, additional taxes, family controversy, and broken relationships.

A Primer of Legal Terms

Before you go to the lawyer, you may want to learn some of the legal jargon. Here are definitions of some of the useful terms as well as additional information you might need as you progress with your estate plan.

Will

A will spells out who inherits your assets, and whether there are any restrictions to that inheritance. A will also names the executor(s) or personal representative(s) who will administer your estate. Executors and personal representatives can be family members, friends, business advisors, business partners, or a trust company.

Probate

Probate is the court process of approving your will and appointing the executor(s). This process occurs after your death. Every state has a different procedure for probate—some states have a short, simple procedure, while other states require lengthier, more complex proceedings. Court fees, lawyers' fees, and accountants' fees can make this a very expensive procedure in some states. In a probate, the will is filed with the court and becomes public. Some states require filing an inventory of all of your assets. This becomes part of the public record. Other states only require a list of assets if your estate is controversial.

The majority of probates are quite simple. However, if you die without enough money to pay your bills, or if your family members are prone to disagreement, it can become more time-consuming and expensive. For some situations, having the court involved with the probate of your estate can be an advantage—there will be someone supervising the administration to make sure everything is handled properly and fairly. Many states also allow you to make a legally binding personal property list.

Power of Attorney

This document addresses who will take care of your finances if you are unable to do so. The reason may be temporary (an extended trip) or long term (you have a debilitating illness). This is a very powerful document, and you must completely trust the person(s) you have named. If you are married, you would generally name your spouse as the first choice, but not every spouse has the ability to handle this job, for health or other reasons.

continued on page 256

A Primer of Legal Terms *continued*

Revocable Trust (Living Trust)

A revocable trust is a legal arrangement that you create with a trust agreement. It is sometimes called a will substitute. The agreement designates who controls the assets of the trust while you are living. Generally, you are in charge as the trustee during your lifetime, as long as you are interested and capable. If you become incapacitated, the trust documents specify the successor trustee to take care of your finances. The agreement also indicates who will inherit the property owned by the trust after your death. A living trust is frequently designed to avoid probate. It is revocable, meaning that you can change the trust during your lifetime, just as you can change a will.

You transfer ownership of many of your assets while you are living to yourself as the trustee of your trust: your real estate, investments that are not tax deferred, and many of your cash investments (money market accounts, savings accounts, CDs). The trust generally does not own retirement accounts, life insurance, or annuities.

You will name a trustee to administer the revocable trust during your lifetime (usually yourself and possibly your spouse) and after your death. A trustee has two jobs: overseeing the investments and deciding when to hand out money to those who are supposed to receive it. The job is similar to that of an executor: the person you name needs to be trustworthy, responsible, and organized. You can choose from your family, friends, business advisors and partners, or a trust company.

See "Preparing an Advance Directive," page 155.

Living Will or Advance Directive

You may want to legally designate which family members or friends will make your health care decisions if you are incapacitated. This document is called a living will, health care directive, advance directive, or medical power of attorney.

In this document, you name who will make medical decisions for you if you cannot communicate. You may indicate your philosophy in terms of medical treatment and decisions if you are in a terminal condition or persistent vegetative state.

You can obtain a living will form from your lawyer, your physician or hospital, or your state's department of health. Aging with Dignity, a nonprofit organization, offers a living will document called "5 Wishes" on the Internet at *www.agingwithdignity.org*. But be careful. Every state has its own form. If you obtain a form from the Internet, a friend, or a national organization, make sure that the form is legally recognized and honored in your state.

Implementing Your Estate Plan

You will need to take care of other details after your estate plan has been written to ensure that your estate plan and other documents are aligned. If the details are not coordinated with your written documents, you can accidentally and permanently overrule your entire estate plan. Here is some information you should know.

Beneficiary Designations

Beneficiary designations are more powerful than your estate planning documents. Here are two examples:

- If you add a child's name to your bank account, the entire account belongs to that child at your death. He or she is not required to share it with siblings. A beneficiary named on any account will receive that account after your death, regardless of the terms of your will or trust.
- If your ex-wife is named as the beneficiary on the life insurance policy you took out 25 years ago, she will inherit that policy, even if your will leaves everything to your new spouse.

Asset Ownership

The ownership of assets may be more powerful than your estate planning documents.

For example, if you own something in joint tenancy, the other person inherits that property at your death. That may or may not work in coordination with the other provisions of your estate plan. Joint tenancy is sometimes referred to as a poor man's will—it is simple, but may not fit your situation.

If your estate is potentially subject to estate taxes, the ownership of assets will have a critical impact upon whether your estate plan works. Overusing joint tenancy can completely undermine the entire estate plan.

The lawyer writing your estate plan will recommend who should own each of your assets (just you, or you combined with other persons), how they should be titled (as joint tenants, in your revocable trust, or some other method of ownership), and who should be designated as the beneficiary of certain assets, such as life insurance, annuities, and retirement accounts. You will want to be careful before adding a name to an account, putting a transfer on death (TOD) or payable on death (POD) designation on any asset, without first making sure it is consistent with your estate plan.

It is a good idea to have both your financial planner and lawyer coordinate these details with you.

Discuss the Plan with Others

Discuss your plan with your family or beneficiaries. It is not important to discuss every detail with those who are close to you, or to share the contents of your estate plan with them. However, it is a good idea to tell your family where you keep important documents and how they would access them in an emergency. You will want to let executors and trustees know in advance that you have named them to help you carry out your wishes.

An Estate Plan Brings Peace of Mind

Bob and Betty are in their 60s. They have three children.

Carol (40 years old) lives in California, is married with two children, and is financially successful. She takes being the oldest child seriously and can be quite bossy with her siblings. Carol owns her own company, but it has recently been facing financial problems. Eddie (38 years old) is in his third marriage and has four children and two stepchildren with his current wife. Eddie spends every dime he earns. Nancy (34 years old) is single and has one child. Nancy has difficulty holding a job and managing money. She has been diagnosed with clinical depression. She and her daughter are currently living with Bob and Betty.

Bob and Betty's goals are to make sure Nancy and her child have a place to live, provide for their grandchildren's education, support charities that are important to them, and provide an inheritance for their children.

After their death, their estate will be distributed as follows:

- 15% will be put into a trust for their grandchildren's education, including Eddie's two stepchildren.
- 10% will go to charitable organizations.
- 75% will be divided into three separate shares for their children. Nancy's share will include the house so that she has a place to live.

Bob and Betty signed a power of attorney, which names each other first, and then the children to pay their bills if either Bob or Betty becomes incapacitated. If any of the three children use the power of attorney, they must account to each other for their actions.

They completed a living will, giving each other the authority to make medical decisions. If either cannot communicate, any two of their three children may serve as alternates.

They have accomplished all of their goals with this estate plan. They plan to review everything in three years to see if any changes are appropriate.

Review Your Plan Regularly

You should review your estate plan when:

- Your financial situation changes significantly or there is a change in your family (you get married or divorced, a child dies, grandchildren are born) or you move to a different state.
- You or a close family member is diagnosed with a life-threatening or degenerative disease.
- Every three to five years. The laws change, as do your own goals and important people in your life.

Know What to Do If Someone Becomes Ill or Dies

There are opportunities for last-minute estate planning when someone is diagnosed with a life-threatening or terminal illness. Here is a checklist:

- Make sure the power of attorney and the advance directives are up to date and accessible.
- Call your lawyer to determine whether any changes should be made to asset ownership or beneficiary designations. Ask your lawyer to coordinate this with your financial planner, stockbroker, and insurance agent.
- Be cautious of advice given to you by bankers and friends. Do not change the ownership of assets or beneficiary designations without checking with your lawyer.
- If a plan has not already been developed, determine how you will proceed if the caregiver becomes ill or dies before the terminally ill person.

This is often a time when significant income and estate taxes can be saved and probate can be eliminated. Every state has different laws, every situation is different, and the tax law is complex and changes frequently. Seek qualified advice.

At the death of a family member, you will want to call your lawyer. Do not make any changes in the ownership of the assets before consulting with the lawyer—once title is changed, retirement accounts are rolled over, life insurance is collected, or checks are cashed, it may be too late to take advantage of saving income or estate taxes. Again, well-meaning bankers and financial planners may give you advice on handling financial affairs, but you want to make sure your actions are in keeping with the person's estate plan.

Also seek the advice of your accountant at this time. If you have always prepared your own income taxes, consult with a CPA to make sure you know what is required in the year of the death. There are many special tax rules that are not covered in the software tax programs. A low-price tax preparation shop may not have experience in this area. If there is a probate involved or a trust, a fiduciary income tax return may need to be filed. Ask for a referral to a CPA, and then check to make sure he or she has experience with fiduciary tax returns, if one is required.

An estate tax return may need to be filed if the person who died had assets of more than the amount exempt from estate taxes. You should consult with your estate planning lawyer or CPA to see if one needs to be filed. The time limits for filing and paying estate taxes are generally nine months after the death, and the penalties can be large if this deadline is not met.

This is also the time to make any necessary changes to your own estate plan.

Estate Taxes

Do you need to be concerned with estate taxes? Most people wish to take advantage of legitimate legal opportunities to reduce estate taxes. Before you set this as one of your goals, you will need to find out whether your estate or family will pay taxes at your death. Less than 2% of Americans pay estate taxes at their death. If you are in that 2%, you'll need to make sure that estate planning options to reduce taxes fit your goals and personal situation.

Here is some basic information on the types of taxes your family may pay at your death:

- The IRS imposes federal estate taxes on estates that are over a certain size. These amounts change from year to year. You can find out what the current exemption is by checking the IRS website (*www.irs.gov*). Your estate pays this tax after your death.
- Each state has its own estate tax, which varies considerably from state to state. Some states have no estate tax, some have tax exemptions that are less than the federal exemption, and some have the same exemption as the federal government. You can check the Internet or with your professional advisor to find out what your state's estate current tax exemption is and whether it will affect you.
- A few states still have a state inheritance tax, which is a tax the beneficiaries of the estate pay.

Even if the size of your estate will require payment of estate taxes at your death, there are exemptions from these taxes, generally for amounts given to spouses and charities. There are also deductions available for your debts, liabilities, and expenses of administration.

Your estate planning lawyer should tell you if these taxes are a consideration. Many estate taxes can be reduced or eliminated with the right type of planning. It is critical, however, that you make sure reducing estate taxes does not become a more important goal than taking care of yourself during your lifetime and your beneficiaries at your death.

If your estate is large enough to pay a tax at your death, Congress has legislated many ways to reduce the estate tax:

- If you are married, revocable wills or trusts can be arranged to reduce estate taxes.
- You can give assets to charity during your lifetime or at your death.
- You can give assets to family and friends during your lifetime.
- You can create an irrevocable trust. This is a trust that is permanent and designed to reduce estate taxes.

Income Taxes

Your estate or your beneficiaries may be required to pay income taxes that you deferred while you were living, such as on your retirement accounts and annuities. If you do not withdraw everything from these accounts during your lifetime, your estate or beneficiaries will need to pay the income taxes after your death. The rules on when the taxes are due change frequently. The person you name as the beneficiary can affect when income taxes are due. Careful consultation with your estate planning lawyer, CPA, and/or financial advisor is strongly recommended.

Challenges You Might Face

Here are some special considerations many families face:

- **Family feuds.** Many families have members who do not see eye to eye. While you are living, you may be able to keep disagreements in check. However, these relationships may become more strained during a significant period of stress, which is natural when you are ill or after your death. Discuss the situation with your lawyer. Families cope much better when an estate plan is well thought out and everything is in writing. You may also want to have conversations with your family before your death, so that they all know what the plan is and who will be in charge.
- **Dividing up your personal effects.** This can become a battleground for settling long-standing disputes, especially between siblings. A clear list and a fair person presiding over the discussion can keep a battle from occurring.
- **Special-needs family member.** If you have a family member with a physical or mental disability, you will want to make additional plans. Congress and most states now encourage people to set up a supplemental needs trust for that family member. This type of trust will allow for assistance to be given to the person without jeopardizing his or her government benefits and programs. Make sure that your estate planning lawyer is familiar with this area of the law, because it is quite specific.
- **Marriage.** You may wish to consider having a premarital or antenuptual agreement before you get married. This document determines who will receive your assets if the marriage ends in divorce, and/or who inherits your assets after your death. You may want to make sure your children inherit the assets that you owned prior to this marriage. Or you may wish assets to go into a trust for your surviving spouse, but have what is left distributed to your family, and not to your spouse's family.
- **Nontraditional family relationships.** More people are living in relationships that were not common 20 years ago: same-sex partnerships, cohabitation without marriage, living arrangements with grandchildren, and others. Your definition of family may not match what the law traditionally considers to be your next of kin. This affects not only who will inherit your assets but also who has the legal right to make decisions for you and the others in your family. These considerations should be reflected in your estate planning documents.
- **Family member who is not financially capable.** If you have a spouse, child, or grandchild who is not financially mature or capable, your will or trust should address this situation. You may want to place the person's inheritance in a trust. You can determine who will serve as the trustee to manage the investments and make distributions to the person as he or she has need.
- **Marriage to a non-U.S. citizen.** Special tax laws apply if a non-U.S. citizen is receiving an inheritance. You will want to consult with your estate planning lawyer in this situation.
- **Leaving money to a charity.** There are many options available if you would like to give to a charity or leave some other kind of legacy. You may give the gift during your lifetime or after your death, and you may designate it to be used for specific purposes.
- **Property transfers.** You may wish to set up a structure to eventually transfer ownership and control of a vacation home, business, or farmland. You can set up a program whereby you begin now to make the transfer or gift of the asset. You may wish to sell the person the asset, or it could be that he or she ultimately inherits it. This will take a combination of advice from your lawyer and your CPA to find out what is best for you. Leaving it up to your family to figure out may not be the best plan of action to take.

See "Challenges in Relationships," page 41.

Questions & Answers

Q. I've already got a will. What now?

A. If you already have a will, review it in light of the information you've gained from this chapter. Your life, family, financial situation, and the laws may have changed since you last prepared this document.

Q. I'm trying to choose between a revocable trust and a will. What do I need to take into consideration?

A. A revocable trust may be preferable to a will if:

- You own real estate in more than one state. This includes most time shares. Without a trust, there will need to be a probate in every state in which you own real estate, meaning that your executor will need to hire a lawyer in each of those states. And in some states, lawyers and/or the courts charge a percentage of the value of the assets that are in probate.
- You want the provisions of your estate plan to be private. A trust is not filed with the court after your death.

IN THIS CHAPTER

Chapter 18

Pulling Together Your Financial Plan

A guide for your financial life

REDUCE YOUR PLAN TO WRITING. THE MOMENT YOU COMPLETE THIS, YOU WILL HAVE DEFINITELY GIVEN CONCRETE FORM TO THE INTANGIBLE DESIRE.

—*Napoleon Hill, author of* Think and Grow Rich

Mark Fischer
Certified Financial Planner

You can take a professional approach to money management by constructing a comprehensive financial plan to guide your money decisions.

A financial plan brings all parts of your financial situation together into one document. If you are working with a financial advisor, he or she will likely help you create a financial plan. If you have done the worksheets in the previous chapters, you are well on your way to having a financial plan. In this chapter we will help you complete it.

Your Financial Plan

Writing the plan helps provide clarity and focus. You can show it to others, get feedback, and use it to provide continuity from year to year, and as circumstances change.

Start with the end in mind. When you are done planning, you should have a summary document that will help you manage your money on a day-to-day basis.

WORKSHEET

My Financial Plan

Date Reviewed ______________________

Retirement/Life Goals (from chapter 11)

____

____

____

My Current Annual Income and Expenses (from chapter 12)

Income ______________________

Expenses ______________________

Net cash flow ______________________

Current Net Worth (from chapter 12)

Assets ______________________

Liabilities ______________________

Net worth ______________________

Cash on Hand (from chapter 14)

Checking/savings ______________________

Emergency funds ______________________

My Financial Plan *continued*

Investments (from chapter 14)

Current retirement savings ______________________________

Retirement savings goal ______________________________

Contribution schedule

What amounts will you contribute this year to what accounts? ______________________________

Current Diversification (from chapter 14)
(If your current diversification is not your *ideal* diversification, use the worksheet in chapter 14 to help you reallocate your investments.)

Type of investor (very conservative, conservative, balanced growth, growth, aggressive) ______________________________

	Percentage	Amount
Stocks	________	________
Large U.S.	________	________
Small U.S.	________	________
Large foreign	________	________
Small foreign	________	________
Growth	________	________
Value	________	________
Nonstock investments	________	________
Actively managed	________	________
Passively managed	________	________

My Financial Plan *continued*

Tax Management Plan (from chapter 15)

Percentage in tax-advantaged accounts ____________________

Percentage in tax-benefited investments ____________________

Percentage not sheltered ____________________

Expected Annual Return on Investments This Year (from chapter 16)

____

Withdrawal Schedule (from chapter 16)
What amounts will you withdraw over the next five years and from what accounts?

Year 1 ____________________ from ____________________

Year 2 ____________________ from ____________________

Year 3 ____________________ from ____________________

Year 4 ____________________ from ____________________

Year 5 ____________________ from ____________________

My Financial Plan *continued*

Disability Plan (from chapter 16)

I have considered long-tern care insurance and have it in place if I need it ☐ yes ☐ no

Estate Plan (from chapter 17)

My will is up to date ☐ yes ☐ no

My living will/advance directive is up to date ☐ yes ☐ no

I have a power of attorney ☐ yes ☐ no

Advisors (from chapter 14)

Who will help me with:

Planning ______________________________

Investment ______________________________

Insurance ______________________________

Legal ______________________________

Tax preparation/management ______________________________

How will I hold myself accountable for sticking to my financial plan?

____

____

____

____

Next review date ______________________________

Resources

Finding a Financial Planner

Financial Planning Association
www.fpanet.org
(Click "Find a Planner")

General Investment Information

American Public Media's Marketplace Money
marketplacemoney.publicradio.org/toolbox
Information about investing, including online calculators, links to other websites, and a list of books on investing.

America Saves
www.americasaves.org
Information to help individuals build wealth.

Board of Governors of Federal Reserve System
www.federalreserve.gov
Topics include consumer information and personal finance.

NASD
www.nasd.com
A private sector regulator of the securities industry.

U.S. Securities and Exchange Commission
www.sec.gov
Investment information; includes a link to the Ballpark Estimate Retirement Calculator.

U.S. Financial Literacy and Education Commission
www.mymoney.gov
Topics include responding to life events, financial planning and retirement planning

Information on Particular Investments

Lipper
www.lipperweb.com
Independent information, analysis, and benchmarks for mutual funds.

Morningstar
www.morningstar.com
Independent information and analysis of stocks, mutual funds, and other investments.

Value Line
www.valueline.com
Investment information on stocks, mutual funds, and other securities. Value Line University provides free online investment education on investment basics, investment strategy, building a portfolio, and studying a stock.

Standard & Poor's
www.standardandpoors.com

Taxes and Social Security

Internal Revenue Service
www.irs.gov

U.S. Social Security Administration
www.socialsecurity.gov

Long-Term Care

Medicare
www.medicare.gov
(Click "Long-Term Care")

Estate Planning and Living Wills

Aging with Dignity
www.agingwithdignity.org
Information about living wills and sample forms.

Grandma's Yellow Pie Plate
www.yellowpieplate.umn.edu
Addresses how to divide your personal property at your death.

WORKSHEET

Action Plan for Managing Your Money

Are you moving in the right direction to achieve your goals? To help you think about the changes you might want to make, mark (**X**) the following on the scale between *No Change Needed* to *Needs Immediate Attention.*

MANAGING YOUR MONEY	No Change Needed		Needs Immediate Attention
Chapter 11 – Knowing How You Want to Live			
Knowing my life goals	●	·········	●
Chapter 12 – Taking Inventory of Your Resources			
Calculating my current income and expenses	●	·········	●
Estimating my future income and expenses	●	·········	●
Increasing my savings contributions	●	·········	●
Understanding my nonfinancial resources	●	·········	●
Chapter 13 – Investing Basics			
Understanding investment options	●	·········	●
Chapter 14 – Making the Most of Your Investments			
Developing my investment strategy	●	·········	●
Rebalancing my investment portfolio	●	·········	●
Finding a financial planner	●	·········	●
Chapter 15 – Managing Tax Obligations			
Developing a tax management strategy	●	·········	●
Chapter 16 – Making Your Money Last a Lifetime			
Determining if I will have enough	●	·········	●
Chapter 17 – Passing On What You Have			
Creating an estate plan	●	·········	●
Preparing a living will/advance directive	●	·········	●
Chapter 18 – Pulling Together Your Financial Plan			
Creating a comprehensive financial plan	●	·········	●

Action Plan for Managing Your Money *continued*

What are my retirement goals for managing my money? Write your goals here and on "My Retirement Map" on pages 10 and 11.

What barriers do I need to overcome to achieve my goals?

What am I going to do to achieve my goals? Use the action steps worksheet on the next page to write down the steps and track your progress.

W O R K S H E E T

Action Steps Worksheet – Goal #1

Steps I Am Going to Take	Target Completion Date	My Progress	Notes
		started complete!	
		started complete!	
		started complete!	
		started complete!	
		started complete!	
		started complete!	
		started complete!	

WORKSHEET

Action Steps Worksheet – Goal #2

Steps I Am Going to Take	Target Completion Date	My Progress	Notes
		started complete!	
		started complete!	
		started complete!	
		started complete!	
		started complete!	
		started complete!	
		started complete!	

Conclusion

On with Your Journey!

TWENTY YEARS FROM NOW YOU WILL BE MORE DISAPPOINTED BY THE THINGS YOU DIDN'T DO THAN BY THE ONES YOU DID. SO THROW OFF THE BOWLINES. SAIL AWAY FROM THE SAFE HARBOR. CATCH THE TRADE WINDS IN YOUR SAILS. EXPLORE. DREAM. DISCOVER.

—*Mark Twain, American writer*

Whether you are in the middle of your retirement journey or just in the planning stage, we hope you find the navigational tools in *Mapping Your Retirement* helpful.

Explore the options, challenge yourself, and discover the things that give *your* life meaning. Active planning will make it easier for you to recognize opportunities and to adjust to unexpected turns in the path.

Studies show that the choices we make—more than heredity—determine how well we age (Rowe and Kahn 1998). What better reason to set goals and take action?

We wish you a healthy, productive, and financially secure retirement. Enjoy the trip!

References

Introduction - **Retirement for the 21st Century**

National Cancer Institute. 2006. How to evaluate health information on the Internet: Questions and answers. www.cancer.gov/cancertopics/factsheet/Information/internet.

Chapter 2 - **Building Strong Relationships**

Antonucci, T. C., and H. Akiyama. 1995. "Convoy of social relationships: Family and friendships within a life span context." In *Handbook of aging and the family*, edited by R. Blieszner and V. H. Bedford, 355–71. Westport, CT: Greenwood Press.

Antonucci, T. C., and H. Akiyama. 1987. Social networks in adult life and a preliminary examination of the convoy model. *Journal of Gerontology* 42(5): 519–27.

Barnes, M. L., and R. J. Sternberg. 1997. "A hierarchical model of love and its prediction of satisfaction in close relationships." In *Satisfaction in close relationships*, edited by R. J. Stenberg and M. Hojjat, 79–101. New York: Guilford Press.

Blieszner, R., and K. A. Roberto. 2004. "Friendship across the life span: Reciprocity in individual and relationship development." In *Growing together: Personal relationships across the lifespan*, edited by F. R. Lang and K. L. Fingerman, 159–82. Cambridge: Cambridge University Press.

Brown, P. L. 2006, 27 February. Growing old together, in a new kind of commune. *New York Times*. Retrieved www.nytimes.com 3/4/06.

Carmichael, A. 2006, 13 February. Idealizing your spouse good for you. eathalalguy.blogspot.com. Retrieved 5/6/06.

Connidis, I. A. 2005. "Sibling ties across time: The middle and later years." In *The Cambridge handbook of age and ageing*, edited by M. L. Johnson, V. L. Bengtson, P. G. Coleman, and T. B. L. Kirkwood, 429–436. Cambridge: Cambridge University Press.

Holmes, T. H., and R. H. Rahe. 1967. The social readjustment rating scale. *Journal of Psychosomatic Research* 11: 213–18.

Kahn, R. L., and T. C. Antonucci. 1980. "Convoys over the life course: Attachments, roles, and social support." In *Life-span development and behavior*, vol. 3, edited by P. B. Baltes and O. G. Brim Jr., 253–86. New York: Academic Press.

Lang, F. R. 2001. Regulation of social relationships in later adulthood. *Journal of Gerontology B: Psychological Sciences* 56: 321-36.

Putnam, R. D. 2000. *Bowling alone: The collapse and revival of American community.* New York: Simon & Schuster.

Taylor, S. E., L. C. Klein, B. P. Lewis, T. L. Gruenwald, R. A. R. Gurung, and J. A. Updegraff. 2000. Female responses to stress: Tend and befriend, not fight or flight. *Psychological Review* 107(3): 411–29.

Uehara, E. S. 1995. Reciprocity reconsidered: Gouldner's "moral norm of reciprocity" and social support. *Journal of Social and Personal Relationships* 12: 483–502.

Chapter 3 - **Using Your Time**

AARP. 2006. Industry leaders announce new alliance on boomer workforce. www.aarp.org/research/press-center/presscurrentnews/boomer_workforce.html.

Alzheimer's Association. Stay mentally active. www.alz.org/we_can_help_stay_mentally_ active.asp.

Bowen, K., and J. Schuck. Don't be surprised if . . . Women reflect on the retirement transition. Unpublished.

Candland, C. 2003, 11 August. Preparing for the looming talent shortage. Issues@Work; U.S. Bureau of Labor Statistics and Employment Policy Foundation. *Westchester County Business Journal* (online).

Civic Ventures. 2007. MetLife Foundation/Civic Ventures new face of work survey. www.civicventures.org/publications/surveys/new-face-of-work.cfm.

Cohen, G. 2005. *The mature mind: The positive power of the aging brain.* Cambridge, MA: Basic Books.

Deloitte Consulting, LLP. 2005. Skills gap report: A survey of the American manufacturing workforce. www.deloitte.com/dtt/research/0,1015,sid%253D2222%2526cid% 253D100752,00.html.

Dychtwald, K., T. Erickson, and R. Morison. 2006. *Workforce crisis: How to beat the coming shortage of skills and talent.* Boston, MA: Harvard Business School Press.

Goldman, C. 2004. *The ageless spirit*. 2d ed. Minneapolis, MN: Fairview Press.

Luks, A., and P. Payne. 2001. *The healing power of doing good: The healing and spiritual benefits of helping others.* Lincoln, NE: iUniverse, Inc.

Mathews, G. 1996. *What makes life worth living? How Japanese and Americans make sense of their worlds.* Berkeley and Los Angeles: University of California Press.

Novelli, W. 2001. Aging issues: The end of retirement. www.aarp.org/about_aarp/aarp_leadership/on_issues/aging_issues/a2002-12-31-novelliretirement.html. Retrieved 6/26/07.

Serendip. 2007. Physiological benefits of stress reduction. serendip.brynmawr.edu/local/suminst/bbi00/projects/VladHomep2.HTML.

U.S. Census Bureau. 2002. U. S. economic census 2002. www.census.gov/econ/census02.

Chapter 4 - **Making a Difference**

Corporation for National & Community Service. Volunteering in America: State trends and rankings. www.nationalservice.gov/about/volunteering/ind.

Eisner, D. 2005, 18 May. Engaging baby boomers in meeting the challenges of the 21st century. Remarks made at the Policy Committee for the 2005 White House Conference on Aging.

Lear, N. 2006. Interview by David Brancaccio on the PBS program *NOW*.

Michels, P., and J. Roles. 2004. Civic organizing 101: A curriculum guide for MACI lead organizers. Unpublished.

Skoll Foundation. What is a social entrepreneur? www.skollfoundation.org/aboutsocialentrepreneurship/whatis.asp.

Vital Aging Network. Vital communities toolkit. www.van.umn.edu/advocate/index.asp.

Chapter 5 - **Staying Healthy**

Claflin, E. 1998. *Age protectors: Your guide to perpetual youth*. Emmaus, PA: Rodale Press.

Cohen, H. 2000. *Taking care after 50: A self-care guide for seniors*. New York: Three Rivers Press.

Creagan, E., ed. 2001. *Mayo Clinic on healthy aging*. Rochester, MN: Mayo Clinic Foundation for Medical Education and Research.

Creagan, E. (with S. Wendel). 2003. *How not to be my patient: A physician's secrets for staying healthy and surviving any diagnosis*. Deerfield Beach, FL: Health Communications.

Fries, J. 1999. *Living well: Taking care of your health in the middle and later years.* Reading, MA: Perseus Books.

Komaroff, A., ed. 2005. *Harvard Medical School family health guide.* New York: Free Press.

Margolis, S., ed. 2002. *The Johns Hopkins medical guide to health after 50.* New York: Medletter Associates.

Mayo Clinic. 2007. Weight loss: Obesity. www.mayoclinic.com/health/obesity/ DS00314/DSECTION=1.

Mosby Consumer Health and Institute for Research and Education. 1997. *Well advised for people over 50.* Boston: Mosby Consumer Health.

National Institute on Aging. 2005. U. S. Department of Health and Human Services. AgePage: skin care and aging. www.niapublications.org/agepages/skin.asp.

Reader's Digest. 2001. *Looking after your body.* Pleasantville, NY: Reader's Digest Association.

Schneider, E. L., and E. Miles. 2003. *Ageless: Take control of your age and stay youthful for life.* Emmaus, PA: Rodale Press.

Upton, A., and E. Graber, eds. 1993. *Staying healthy in a risky environment: The New York University Medical Center family guide*. New York: Simon and Schuster.

Chapter 6 - **Eating for Life**

Institute of Medicine of the National Academies. 2004. Dietary reference intakes: Water, potassium, sodium, chloride, and sulfate. www.iom.edu/CMS/3788/3969/18495.aspx.

Partnership for Healthy Weight Management. www.consumer.gov/weightloss. Retrieved 4/16/06.

United States Department of Agriculture (USDA). www.mypyramid.gov. Retrieved 3/20/06.

United States Department of Agriculture (USDA). 2006. National nutrient database for standard reference. www.ars.usda.gov/Services/docs.htm?docid=8964.

Chapter 7 - **Keeping Strong, Fit, and Active**

Carpinelli, R., and R. Otto. 1998. Strength training: Single versus multiple sets. *Sports Medicine* 26(2): 73–84.

Exercise and physical activity for older adults. 1998. *Medicine & Science in Sports & Exercise* (30)6: 992–1008.

High, D. M., E. T. Howley, and B. D. Franks. 1989. The effects of static stretching and warm-up on prevention of delayed-onset muscle soreness. *Research Quarterly for Exercise and Sport* 60(4): 357–61.

Nied, R., and B. Franklin. 2002. Promoting and prescribing exercise for the elderly. *American Family Physician* 65(3): 419–26.

Shrier, I. 1999. Stretching before exercise does not reduce the risk of local muscle injury: A critical review of the clinical and basic science literature. *Clinical Journal of Sports Medicine* 9(4): 221–27.

Westcott, W., and S. Ramsden. 2001. *Specialized strength training*. Monterey, CA: Exercise Science Publishers.

Whaley, M., P. Brubaker, R. Otto, and L. Armstrong for the American College of Sports Medicine. 2006. *ACSM's guidelines for exercise testing and prescription*. Baltimore: Lippincott Williams & Wilkins.

Wolf, S., H. Barnhart, N. Kutner, E. McNeely, C. Coogler, and T. Xu. 2003. Reducing frailty and falls in older persons: An investigation of tai chi and computerized balance training. *Journal of the American Geriatric Society* 51: 1794–1803.

Chapter 8 - **Maintaining Mental Fitness**

Albert, M., and G. McKhann, 2006. *Progress report on brain research*. New York: Dana Press.

Alzheimer's Association. 2006. 10 warning signs of Alzheimer's disease. www.alz.org/AboutAD/Warning.asp.

Bourne, E. 2000. *The anxiety and phobia workbook*. 3d ed. Oakland, CA: New Harbinger Publications.

Chopra, D. 1994. *The seven spiritual laws of success*. San Rafael, CA: Amber-Allan Publishing.

Costa, P., and R. McCrae. 1989. "Personality continuity and the changes of adult life." In *The adult years: Continuity and change*, edited by M. Storandt and G. VandenBos, 45–77. Washington, DC: American Press.

Linehan, M. 1993. *Skills training manual for treating borderline personality disorder.* New York: Guilford Press.

Nussbaum, P. 2003. *Brain health and wellness.* Tarentum, PA: Word Association Press.

President's Council on Bioethics. 2005. *Taking care: Ethical caregiving in our aging society.* Washington, DC: Author.

Rowe, J., and R. Kahn. 1998. *Successful aging.* New York: Dell Publishing.

Ryff, C. 1995. Psychological well-being in adult life. *American Psychological Society* 4:99–104.

Sharma, R. 1997. *The monk who sold his Ferrari.* New York: HarperCollins.

Sperry, L., and C. McNeil. 1996. "Normal human aging today and tomorrow: Insights from the Baltimore Longitudinal Study of Aging." *In Aging in the twenty-first century: A developmental perspective*, edited by L. Sperry and H. Prosen, 59–72. New York: Garland Publishing.

Sperry, L., and H. Prosen, eds. 1996. *Aging in the twenty-first century: A developmental perspective*. New York: Garland Publishing.

Chapter 9 - **Creating Your Health Care Team**

Center for Spirituality and Healing, University of Minnesota. 2006. Navigating the healthcare system. www.csh.umn.edu/health.

Creagan, E. (with S. Wendel). 2003. *How not to be my patient: A physician's secrets for staying healthy and surviving any diagnosis*. Deerfield Beach, FL: Health Communications.

Joint Commission on Accreditation of Healthcare Organizations. 2002. Speak up: Help prevent errors in your care. www.jointcommission.org/GeneralPublic/Speak+Up.

Kohn, L., J. Corrigan, and M. Donaldson, eds. 1999. *To err is human: Building a safer health system*. Committee on Quality of Health Care in America, Institute of Medicine.

Minnesota Citizens Forum on Health Care Costs. 2004. *Listening to Minnesotans: Transforming Minnesota's health care system*. Final Report. www.mncitizensforum.org/Meeting %20materials/CFHC%20Final %20Report.pdf.

Seigal, B., and A. Yosaif. 2003. *Help me to heal: A practical guidebook for patients, visitors and caregivers*. Carlsbad, CA: Hay House.

Chapter 10 - **Finding Nontraditional Paths to Health**

Ananth, S. 2002. *Health Forum/AHA 2000–2001 complementary and alternative medicine survey*. Chicago: Health Forum LLC.

Astin, J. 1998. Why patients use alternative medicine: Results of a national study. *Journal of the American Medical Association* 279: 1548–53.

Astin, J., K. Pelletier, M. Ariane, and W. Haskell. 2000. Complementary and alternative medicine use among elderly persons. *Journal of Gerontology* 55A: M4–M9.

Barnes R., E. Powell-Griner, K. McFann, and R. Nahin. 2004, 27 May. Complementary and alternative medicine use among adults: United States, 2002. *Advance Data from Vital and Health Statistics 343*. U.S. Department of Health and Human Services, Centers for Disease Control and Prevention, National Center for Health Statistics.

Benson, H. 1975. *The relaxation response*. New York: Avon.

Berman, B., L. Lao, P. Langenberg, W. Lee, A. Gilpin, and M. Hochberg. 2004. Effectiveness of acupuncture as adjunctive therapy in osteoarthritis of the knee: A randomized, controlled trial. *Annals of Internal Medicine* 141: 901–10.

Cameron, M. 2006. "Yoga." In *Complementary/alternative therapies in nursing*, edited by M. Snyder and R. Lindquist. New York: Springer Publishing Company.

D'Eramo, A. 2001. A program on complementary therapies for long-term care nursing assistants. *Geriatric Nursing* 201–7.

Keating, T. 1995. *Open mind, open heart*. New York: Continuum.

Kreitzer, M. 2002. "Meditation." In *Complementary/alternative therapies in nursing*, 4th ed., edited by M. Snyder and R. Lindquist. New York: Springer Publishing Company.

Wolf, S., H. Barnhart, N. Kutner, E. McNeely, C. Coogler, and T. Xu. 2003. Reducing frailty and falls in older persons: An investigation of tai chi and computerized balance training. *Journal of the American Geriatric Society* 51: 1794–1803.

Chapter 14 - **Making the Most of Your Investments**

Bogle, J. 2003. *The mutual fund industry in 2003: Back to the future.* Bogle Financial Markets Research Center. www.vanguard.com/bogle_site/sp20030114.html.

Bowen, J., and D. Goldie. 1998. *The prudent investor's guide to beating Wall Street at its own game.* New York: McGraw-Hill Trade.

Carhart, M. 1997. On persistence in mutual fund performance. *Journal of Finance* 52: 1.

Dalbar. 2006. Quantitative analysis of investor behavior. www.dalbarinc.com/pages/QAIB2006Highlights.pdf.

Goetzmann, W. N., and R. G. Ibbotson. 2005, 6 April. History and the equity risk premium. Yale ICF Working Paper No. 05-04. ssrn.com/abstract=702341.

Seeking Alpha. 2006. Is your fund manager a "closet indexer"? You better hope not. seekingalpha.com/article/15772.

Conclusion - **On with Your Journey!**

Rowe, J., and R. Kahn. 1998. *Successful aging.* New York: Dell Publishing.

Index